Embracing Democracy

Embracing Democracy

HERMANN BROCH, POLITICS AND EXILE, 1918 TO 1951

Donald L. Wallace

PETER LANG

Oxford · Bern · Berlin · Bruxelles · Frankfurt am Main · New York · Wien

Bibliographic information published by Die Deutsche Nationalbibliothek
Die Deutsche Nationalbibliothek lists this publication in the Deutsche
Nationalbibliografie; detailed bibliographic data is available on the Inter-
net at http://dnb.d-nb.de.

A catalogue record for this book is available from the British Library.

Library of Congress Cataloging-in-Publication Data:

Wallace, Donald L., 1968-
 Embracing democracy : Hermann Broch, politics and exile, 1918 to 1951 /
Donald L Wallace.
    pages cm
 Includes bibliographical references and index.
 ISBN 978-3-0343-0770-3 (alk. paper)
 1. Broch, Hermann, 1886-1951--Criticism and interpretation. 2. Broch,
Hermann, 1886-1951--Political and social views. I. Title.
 PT2603.R657Z955 2014
 838'.91209--dc23

                        2014007230

Cover picture: Hermann Broch's grave, Union Cemetery, Killingworth, CT,
USA. Photo by the author.

ISBN 978-3-0343-0770-3 (print)
ISBN 978-3-0353-0648-4 (eBook)

© Peter Lang AG, International Academic Publishers, Bern 2014
Hochfeldstrasse 32, CH-3012 Bern, Switzerland
info@peterlang.com, www.peterlang.com, www.peterlang.net

This publication has been peer reviewed.

Printed in Germany

For Sarah and Nathan

Contents

Acknowledgements

Like Broch, I believe that 'humans need other humans', and I am grateful for all of the help generously given me in the writing of this book. I thank the Naval Academy Research Committee and Reza Malak-Madani and Rae Jean Goodman for their funding and support; the Beinecke Library staff, especially Crista Sammons; and all my colleagues at the Naval Academy who read and commented on chapters at the department Works in Progress, especially Lee Pennington. There are also many people whose professional/ intellectual contributions to this book were enormous and are deeply appreciated, but whose personal contribution to the betterment of my life were much greater and are much more significant to me: Mark Thompson, Aaron O'Connell and Sharika Crawford; Richard Ruth, who comes close to being the person Broch wanted to be; David Luft, who remains a primary intellectual and spiritual influence in my life; Hamilton Stapell, who continually reminds me that thoughtfulness and vitality are synonyms, not antonyms; and Laurel Plapp, editor, scholar and friend. Lastly, I thank my partner, Sarah Malena, whose contributions are too numerous to list – so I will simply say thank you, Sarah, for being here.

Introduction

> Great is the anguish of the man who becomes aware of his isolation and
> seeks to escape from his own memory; he is obsessed and outcast [...]
> there awakens within him a doubly strong yearning for a Leader to take
> him tenderly and lightly by the hand, to set things in order and show him
> the way. [...] Yet even if the Leader were to come the hoped-for miracle
> would not happen [...] it is the breath of the Absolute that sweeps across
> the world, and from our dim inklings and gropings for truth there will
> spring up the high-day and holiday assurance with which we shall know
> that every man has the divine spark in his soul and that our oneness cannot
> be forfeited; unforfeitable the brotherhood of humble human creatures.
> [...] 'Do thyself no harm! For we are all here!'[1]

If Hermann Broch has a legacy in the twenty-first century, it is still almost
fully dependent on his literary work. Yet, the letters and essays found in his
Nachlass clearly show that politics held the central position in his intellectual activity during the last two decades of his life. Throughout the 1930s
and 1940s, Broch worked continually on defining the problems of Western
mass political culture, such as the failures of democracy and the dangers
of fascism, and theorizing on the possible solutions to the dangers of mass
culture, such as international cooperation and legal protection of human
life.[2] He also fought for the psychological protection of the individual
from the pressures of mass culture and what he described as mass culture's

---

1   Hermann Broch, *The Sleepwalkers*, Willa and Edwin Muir, trs. (New York: Vintage
     Books, 1996), 647–648.
2   Throughout the book, I refer to Broch's theories on the development of international
     institutions for diplomatic conflict resolution, international criminal courts and laws,
     an international declaration for the sanctity of human life, and global educational
     institutions through the generic term of 'internationalism'.

We need not only human rights, but spiritual ones?

neurotic flight from death, that is, mass culture's inability to understand death as a source for value creation.

In the final lines of his novel *The Sleepwalkers* (quoted above), Broch displayed all the contradictions of his political thought – optimism pessimistically proclaimed, the individual and the absolute, the death of God and the permanence of God, humanism for an inhumane time. And, most central to the thesis of this book, he highlighted the epistemological danger to the individual mind from the mass politics of the modern world. In tracing Broch's life from its roots in *fin-de-siècle* Vienna to his exile from National Socialist terror in the United States, this book charts the development of his ethical and aesthetic thought into an active political program for post-fascist democracy. It is the story of how he became conscious of the importance of politics as an intellectual undertaking. He did not manifest this new awareness through a simple shift from literature to political theory nor did he reject his pre-exilic intellectual worldview for a new post-exilic one. The model for ethical creativity that he developed in turn-of-the-century Vienna, in fact, contained the liberalism, humanism and ego-based psychology central to his political turn. This is the story of how Broch merged his central European *Bildung* with the political demands of exile.

The book surveys, in terms of political engagement, his experiences from the founding of the Austrian First Republic to his exile in the United States (1918 to 1951). The book posits two seemingly contradictory narratives in terms of Broch's political consciousness – uniformity and change. On the one hand, Broch held an intellectual position in his post-exilic political theory that was consistent with the philosophy of history, psychology and epistemology of his Viennese milieu. On the other hand, he significantly reconceived the utility of politics to his theory of value construction, while also moving from disengagement to engagement in terms of political activism. The two narratives show that Broch's cultural criticism in his Viennese environment was idealistic and that such a position allowed him to relegate politics to a mundane and avoidable level. In particular, he lacked a political understanding of the enduring force of mass political action and nationalism. If one were to identify a political stance in his pre-exilic period, it would only appear as a vague democratic impulse, which really only referred to the centrality of the individual to ethical and aesthetic social activity. This stance developed out of the context of nineteenth-century liberalism and the Enlightenment. In the Austrian First Republic Broch merged his democratic impulse with Social Democracy as he recognized that the economic collapse of the post-war period necessitated a broader interaction between workers and producers.

Additionally, his ethical and aesthetic theory, developed in the late imperial and post-First World War period, heightened for him a sense of empty bourgeois materialism. These ideas formed the basis for his theme of aestheticism and his image of Vienna as a metropolis of kitsch. Such anti-materialism, however, did not push him into an active Marxist position. In fact, I argue in my second chapter that Broch's anti-bourgeois stance expressed itself through a greater commitment to intellectual elitism and a traditional liberal attraction to aristocratic and cosmopolitan values. The result was that Broch found no political platform that could respond to the changing nature of politics in post-Empire Austria. Political action had in that context coalesced in the masses and centred on the imagery of the nation. Socialism's political goal of a post-nationalist world order also explains his intellectual affinities to Austro-Marxism in the First Republic. Such internationalism, however, existed only in terms of an aggressive Soviet program for international revolution and, thus, Broch maintained strict boundaries between his activities and those of Social Democracy throughout the First Republic.

Broch did not develop his theory on internationalism during his pre-exilic period. Instead, he sustained a cosmopolitan view on cultural unity that corresponded more directly to the cultural idea of Central Europe, what David Luft refers to as a Cisleithanian cultural identity found in writers like Musil, Broch, Hofmannsthal and Kafka.[3] Broch's cultural identity was, I would argue, even larger than this German-speaking culture of Cisleithania; he demonstrated strong links to Magyar, Polish and German cultural production as well, especially neo-Kantianism. His attraction to

3   David S. Luft, 'Keynote Address', MALCA National Conference, Austin, TX, February 2014.

Kant and to neo-Kantianism, however, showed the ultimate difference between his and German cultural identity, that is, Broch's lack of nationalism. One sees this most readily in the difference between his philosophy of history and that of German idealist novelists and historians.

Fascism challenged Broch's idealism and his cosmopolitanism. And in exile, he refashioned his cultural criticism into a theory of mass delusion. He promoted his mass psychology as an explanation of mass political aberrations and as an *Arbeitsprogramm* for establishing a new form of humane democracy. This new political theorizing and activism maintained its antinational characteristics, as he turned his central European cosmopolitan impulses into a more rigorous platform for international cooperation and the protection of human rights. His political theory of mass delusion placed Broch in line with the extra-national theories of human rights and the protection of human dignity found in the program of the United Nations and organizations like Amnesty International.[4] But, as Hannah Arendt argued, the basis for his internationalism as well as his reforms to democratic structures relied on the theoretical acceptance of fundamental and shared human cognition. Such universalism left his ideas on 'total democracy' and internationalism too locked into the individual cognitive experience and the closing of value systems. It was completely blind to the real dangers of the violent closing of the public sphere.

Pre-exile, Broch saw pragmatic politics as valueless, an expression of kitsch, because he believed that historical development progressed through individual creative and epistemological change. Such a belief allowed him to reject political ideology and activism in favour of aesthetic creativity. Post-exile, Broch saw pragmatic politics as a duty, a necessity for the maintenance of human freedom and progress. He repackaged his philosophy of history and his theory on ethical free will into a political program of citizen rights and responsibilities. The result, however, was an integration of his cognitive model of ethical creativity (value construction), which continued to operate in a non-political environment, with a public idiom

4   See also Paul Michael Lützeler, *Die Entropie des Menschen: Studien zum Werk Hermann Brochs* (Würzburg: Königshausen & Neumann, 2000), 11–12.

for citizen duties and state activism. The question Broch failed to answer was how a cognitive basis for humane activity could challenge the development of state power and the forces of nationalism. In the following chapters, I explore the foundation of his intellectual understanding of modernity, his political mentality during the Austrian First Republic, his post-exilic development of political theory and his position in the 1940s American dialogue on democracy and freedom.

For Broch, the challenge for democracy in the context of fascism and world war was to construct democratic institutions that protected and nurtured the source of ethics, the individual. Thus, he challenged European and American limitations to their own democratic principles. He extended his political theory from defining the relationship among democracy, values and the individual to the creation of human rights and the protection of human dignity. Ultimately, he packaged his democratic theory and his commitment to human rights in a program for the protection of life through economic reform, cultural vitality and internationalism. In my discussion, I summarize his views on democracy as a force to combat totalitarianism, the structure of citizenship and the ethical efficiency of the individual in the maintenance of democratic freedom. I outline how Broch's political theory responded to his intellectual and cultural education in early twentieth-century Vienna and the United States during the 1930s and 1940s.

In particular, I examine how Broch's value theory reflected the context of a contested view of humanism in the modern world. Positivism and an optimistic view of human progress heralded modern Europe as the culmination of mankind's cultural and technological ability. With European potential appearing unlimited, bourgeois values and a capitalistic worldview assumed either the burden of spreading civilization or the battle of social Darwinism and its cultural interpretation of the survival of the fittest. Both views supported European expansion throughout the world through militarization and imperialism. By the mid-twentieth century the combination of European self-admiration and self-justified domination of the globe had produced multiple attempts at genocide and two world wars. The ultimate combination of human technological advancement and unchecked visions of superiority was realized in Germany in the early

1940s. The mechanized murder of European Jewry was blatant evidence of the power of human ingenuity and the emptiness and savagery of the human spirit. It proved to many that the Enlightenment project and its cult of rationality had a dangerous, instrumental side. It was what Theodor Adorno and Max Horkheimer called the dialectic of the Enlightenment.[5]

For Broch, the problem of instrumental reason and the dangers of unmediated rationality had been clear since his youth. As a modernist thinker, he challenged the meaning of 'real' and 'objective'. He felt these terms had been misappropriated by relative value systems whose only claim to 'objectivity' or 'truth' relied on forcible suppression of other truth claims. In a state of competing relative values, one ends up with a disintegration of values. Nevertheless, he did not abandon the Enlightenment and his belief in the human mind's capacity to construct an open democratic society. He did not call for the abandonment of liberalism or free markets. Broch, like Nietzsche, Wittgenstein and others, paved the road for post-modernism's attack on truth and realism through his linguistic arguments about meaning and correspondence in language, but he did not take the post-modern turn.

He argued instead for a recommitment to the understanding of the irrational through science and epistemology. The Enlightenment's goal of individual autonomy became his solution to the collapse of liberal democracies in Europe. In both Vienna and the United States, he allied himself to a critical humanist stance as he attempted to alleviate the negative aspects of modernity without abandoning the hope for progress and development. The key separation between him and the post-modernists was his sustained optimism versus the post-modernists' idea of despair. Broch's modernism and his humanism allowed him to retain the notion of autonomy and thus to retain the possibility of individual action and change.

From a post-modernist point of view, the theories of Broch were a half-hearted journey towards truth. He saw the relativism of modernity. Instead of embracing it and discovering the truths it could reveal about the political structure of power, he chose instead to hide from modernity's

---

5   Max Horkheimer and Theodor W. Adorno, *Dialectic of Enlightenment: Philosophical Fragments*, Edmund Jephcott, tr. (Stanford, CA: Stanford University Press, 2002).

relativism and to employ its own attributes – reason and human autonomy – to correct and end it. Because of his humanism, contemporary scholarship has often misinterpreted the political aims of his theory or failed to see the ways in which he still has relevance. As seen in the affirmative/critical debate below, Broch's focus on totality and empowerment has been read as proto-fascist and authoritarian. Since the rise of post-modernism, the humanist stance itself has been relegated to the conservative spectrum.[6] Broch's political theory has for this reason been conceived either as utopian or reactionary. I hope that my book opens a dialogue expressly with post-modernism and challenges the perceptions of naïveté in Broch's critique of democracy. His thought was not as simple as utopian or conservative when seen from a historical point of view. His thought was leftist and progressive in the context of 1930s (yet not Marxist). From a twenty-first-century point of view, one can argue he supported an epistemology that propagated a power structure designed to oppress and marginalize, because his fundamental idea was a universal law for human knowledge and society. His optimism, however, can also be a source for continued dialogue and individual growth, especially his belief in internationalism and his struggles for protecting human dignity. A historical reconstruction of his intellectual/political maturation also suggests that his ideas have relevance to a modern audience that goes beyond scholars and antiquarians. Broch criticized capitalistic materialism and its empty (anti-humanist) values while he simultaneously highlighted the dangers of a revolutionary challenge to the market system. Such changes opened mass politics to the psychological manipulation of the individual and his/her fears. His work promoted a creative outlet for ethical action without overturning the instruments for stability and the rule of law.

Broch was born in Vienna, Austria on 1 November 1886 and died in New Haven, Connecticut, USA on 30 May 1951. He was a Viennese Jewish exile who in his youth participated in the intellectual world of *fin-de-siècle* Vienna and in his final years engaged in the intellectual world of New York

---

6   See Martin Halliwell and Andy Mousley, *Critical Humanisms: Humanist, anti-Humanist Dialogues* (Edinburgh: Edinburgh University Press, 2003).

and New England. I tie together, through an examination of his political theory, these two distinct experiences. Both of these milieus provide insight into the disparate strands of intellectualism that offered themselves up to Broch as a means for understanding and correcting what he saw as the deficits of modernity. These deficits included the unchecked outbreak of mass hysterical events: fascism, militarism and genocide.

Broch devoted the last decade of his life to developing theoretical bulwarks against totalitarian forms of government. It is hardly surprising that an Austrian Jewish intellectual writing during the 1940s in American exile would devote his abilities to questions of fascism and human rights. What was surprising about his intellectual approach to the problems of modernity, however, was that his solutions represented nineteenth-century ethical formulations. There was no significant shift in the foundations of his ethical value system and ideas on social justice between his Austrian and American periods. Broch remained wedded to the Enlightenment's notion of individual autonomy, nineteenth-century conceptions of the irrational, a critical approach to positivistic science, as well as the hope for cosmopolitanism as an antidote to national and ethnic identity.

This is not to say that the Holocaust did not affect Broch in a profound way; the personal and social tragedy of the war and National Socialism served, in fact, to heighten his already elevated sense of duty. Intellectually, however, Europe's bid at self-destruction during the first half of the twentieth century did little to shake Broch's confidence in the very concepts that seemed unable to prevent and, in some cases, appeared to aid, the actual destructive impulse. By examining more closely his model for an ethical value system, we gain a broader understanding of the possible reactions to these catastrophic events within the European, Jewish intellectual community. Specifically we see the paradoxical connections among totalitarian ideologies and enlightened Western society.

Broch's 'Political' Theory of the 1920s

While politics did not play a principal role in Broch's Viennese writings, his intellectual maturation within Vienna established an ethical commitment that would underlie his exilic political writings. His political theory reflected an active engagement with various major intellectual movements, even if it was a refashioning of disparate elements of the movements: movements such as liberalism, the Enlightenment, *Lebensphilosophie*, positivism and psychoanalysis. The refashioning makes Broch's thought difficult to categorize. When viewed in isolation, his thought can appear vacillating. The eclectic nature of his mind corresponded to the eclectic nature of his education and the family dynamics of his youth. A crisis of identity, which developed out of his Jewish assimilation and his relationship to an oppressive father, produced a duality in his thought, a neurotic tension between productivity and impotence. Alongside the historical influence of assimilation and liberalism, his personal development was crucial for the direction of his political thought. His lack of professional, academic training prevented a strict specialization and fostered a dilettantism, which reflected Broch's early engagement with journalistic philosophy and *Kulturkritik*. His neurotic personality fuelled his growing intellectual critique of a European value vacuum throughout the first decades of the twentieth century. In the 1930s, however, the political reality of fascism refocused Broch's psychological battles onto the field of politics. The result was a psychologically based theory for the development of total democracy, that is, a democratic system in which the vitality and agency of freedom is balanced by responsibility imposed by force of law.

Broch's political theory and activism strove to accomplish two main goals: to create a stable, open democracy in which the individual's human rights and dignities were protected and to guide the individual towards an ethical value system. I describe this political approach as critical humanism in that he demanded that individuals take a rational and critical stance vis-à-vis the social institutions and the cultural values of the world in which they live. I borrow the term 'critical' from Steven Beller and Allan Janik, who use the term to characterize the intellectual world of Vienna, the world in which Broch lived for the first 52 years of his life.[7] In their work, they argue that the key characteristic of the Viennese intellectual milieu during the first decades of the twentieth century was a politically and ethically engaged public. They attribute this engagement to the creation of an isolated group of Jewish intellectuals, who paradoxically in the process of assimilation carved out their own independent cultural identity. This parallel Jewish culture then set out to understand the paradox of its own formation, that is, how an attempt to formulate a universal identity resulted in the formation of an alternative identity. As the role of anti-Semitism grew in Austrian politics, their inquiries took on more urgency, and they by necessity focused their energies on the modern world, the ultimate source of their intellectual freedom and their cultural exclusion.

Broch's humanism fits this paradigm in terms of both time and theme. He was an Austrian Jew who, born in 1886, came to intellectual maturity over the last years of the Habsburg Empire and the initial years of the Austrian First Republic. He, like many of his contemporaries, feared the growing imbalance between rationality and irrationality. He saw the growing rationalism of science and its increasing specialization as disconnected from the spiritual needs of the individual. Such a position stands in many ways in opposition to the Viennese traditions of logical positivism and scientific materialism. Rudolf Haller points out that Viennese philosophy was marked by an emphasis on scientific materialism over German Idealism.[8] David Luft also stresses the influence of scientific materialism over German Idealism among a wide spectrum of intellectuals; Luft, however, stresses that Vienna was distinguishable by its integration of scientific materialism and philosophical irrationalism.[9] In recent years, scholars such as Malachi Hacohen have effectively argued for the existence of a more varied and

7   See Allan Janik, 'Vienna 1900 Revisited: Paradigms and Problems', in *Rethinking Vienna 1900*, Steven Beller, ed. (New York: Berghahn Books, 2001), 27–56.

8   Rudolf Haller, *Questions on Wittgenstein* (London: Routledge, 1988), 1–26.

9   David S. Luft, *Robert Musil and the Crisis of European Culture* (Berkeley: University of California Press, 1980).

humanistic intellectual milieu within post-war and interwar Vienna.[10]
Broch's philosophical development, his attraction to Kant and his rejection
of scientific philosophy support Hacohen's view.

Broch's ethical and humanistic approach to politics, however, did
not match the progressive politics, which Hacohen sketches through the
figure of Karl Popper. In the end, Broch occupied a place between the
progressive, late Enlightenment world Hacohen discusses and the world
of philosophical irrationalism described by Luft. It was a political culture
of critical humanism, where political engagement equalled the construction of value systems based on the universal experience of being human
– ironically exemplified by death. Critical humanism was a blending of progressive notions of liberalism with a philosophical irrationalist's approach
to human nature, sexuality and the ethical impulse. In both cases, scientific
materialism underlies the basic epistemological assumptions of Broch.
Although his experience does not form a general pattern for all Viennese
Jewish intellectuals, I show that the Jewish intellectual in Vienna in the first
decades of the twentieth century had a diverse set of intellectual identities
from which to choose. Furthermore, Hermann Broch, like Karl Popper in
the case of liberal progressivism, was the vehicle for the migration of critical
humanism after the 1938 annexation of Austria to Germany.

The First World War confirmed for Broch the destructive force of
modernity – unlimited technological capability unchecked by ethical
forces and mass irrationality as a tool for *Realpolitik*. In this atmosphere
of dissolution, his humanism was a search for a new democratic totality.
He did not envision the fulfilment of totality in political terms (Marxist,
Hegelian, nationalist, *et al.*). Indeed, his search for totality started with
ethics and value theory. In this sense, he fit well Janik and Toulmin's characterization of Wittgenstein's Vienna.[11] Broch sought during the period

10 Malachi Hacohen, *Karl Popper – the Formative Years* (New York: Cambridge
University Press, 2000).

11 Janik and Toulmin set Wittgenstein's positivism in the context of an Austrian cultural
crisis and the intellectual reactions to such a crisis by a variety of 'young Viennese'
thinkers such as Kraus, Hofmannsthal, Musil and even Broch. The awareness of crisis
thus resulted in a reimagining of the ethical through linguistic game playing. Allan

1908 to 1935 to provide German-speaking Europe with a linguistic model for pursing an absolute truth.

His epistemological search for truth centred on the aesthetic realm and promoted two basic ideas: 1) Following on Kant, he saw the ego as the source for ethical value construction; 2) following on the liberal tradition of the nineteenth century, he saw the freedom of the individual as the primary element for ensuring a Kantian development of value construction. By and large, he took the second notion for granted as a stable and accepted historical development of his epoch. For this reason, he remained apolitical for most of his pre-exilic life. Broch saw being pragmatically political as a relativistic social activity connected to crass materialism or anarchical nihilism. More importantly, he understood the ethical collapse of turn-of-the-century Europe not only as a cognitive problem, but also as a historically determined process. In his philosophy of history, value systems were not eternal and history was not linear; it was cyclical. Value systems developed as a means of organizing human action and guiding the individual in his or her ego development. A central value was of particular importance for individuals in aiding them in their conflicts with the non-ego (the external world, ultimately defined as an emptiness or death). Individuals formed communities secondarily to their own existence, which for Broch was a priori – thus, the ego could never know itself fully. What an individual ego can know are the sources of panic and conflict with which the fear of total aloneness (mythically defined as death) confronts the ego. By pulling aspects of the non-ego into the consciousness of the ego, through rational and irrational means, as well as through thinking and living, individuals could build patterns for their lives.[12]

Janik and Stephen Toulmin, *Wittgenstein's Vienna* (New York: Simon and Schuster, 1973).

12   Broch, undated draft manuscript, Hermann Broch Archive, Yale Collection of German Literature, Beinecke Rare Book and Manuscript Library (BMLY). See also Hermann Broch, *Massenwahntheorie*, in *Hermann Broch Kommentierte Werkausgabe*, 12, Paul Michael Lützeler, ed. (Frankfurt am Main: Suhrkamp Verlag, 1979), 43–66 and 101–230. My discussion of Broch's political and mass psychological works, as well as his autobiographical works, come from my reading of both the unedited and

These patterns include community building and then rule making (value system construction). The final step in the construction of an initial value system is the mythical and artistic symbolization of these values. This is the role for the artist and the scientist. It is the reason that '*logos*' and the understanding of how to express values played such an important part in Broch's work. This was not a surprising position for a central European intellectual in the late nineteenth and early twentieth century, especially a Viennese thinker. Almost all of Viennese intellectual history during this period can be explained as conversation over how one 'talks' about existence.

In Broch's system, aesthetics played handmaiden to ethics; those who labour in cognition provided a visible expression of the 'style of the age'. In a sense, just as Vergil guided Dante through the underworld of death, the artist guided members of a value system toward its centripetal value. His choice of a dying Vergil for the central character of his novel *The Death of Virgil* was a timely symbol for art's failure in the interwar period to serve as a guide to humane social action. The book also marked the birth of his political consciousness and his shift to pragmatic politics. The aesthetic failure he acknowledged in the 1930s was a logical outcome of the historical philosophy mentioned above. For, value systems develop, establish a central value, and then build through mythology the rules for maintaining the life affirming security of that system. But, these systems develop within a cyclical history of birth, openness, closure, disintegration, rebirth (or more accurately renovation – the creation of a novel paradigm for confronting the dangers of the non-ego). The historical characteristics of any epoch are a reflection of the epoch's relationship to this cyclical process of value construction. Broch saw the European culture of late nineteenth and early twentieth century (reaching a seeming extreme with the First World War) as a 'no longer, not yet' moment in the cycle of value construction.

---

unpublished manuscripts in the Beinecke Library, as well as the edited and published versions found in Paul Michael Lützeler's *Kommentierte Werkausgabe* in 13 volumes (*KW*). When quoting or working from the archival sources, I reference when possible the corresponding and redacted sections from Lützeler's editions. When working from Broch's *KW*, I cite the specific volumes and pages. All translations from German are mine, though some quotations are in English in the original archival source.

By the nineteenth century, the Christian worldview could no longer accommodate advances in knowledge; the recognition of what Nietzsche called the 'murder' of God by science thus left individuals and communities without any agreed upon rules of engagement. The result was that individuals felt more and more the encroachment of the non-ego. This set off a panic in the individual and the result was the individual's search for 'conviction', a truth one could use to hold off death. Individual identities and value systems atomized and in an atmosphere of relativism, individuals set relative, yet absolute, systems off against each other – driving modern European culture into a permanent war footing (metaphorically and literally). The danger of this disintegration of values was that it took place at the same time as the historical development of industrialization and urbanization. In this modern context, cultural combat gained access to the tools of mass society and opened up the process of disintegration to the occurrence of mass aberration.

With his theory of a value vacuum, Broch connected his contemporary world to the historical problem of modernity. He described modernity as a hypertrophy (an overabundance) of identity; in the modern age, group and individual identities centred on an exclusive character trait, and they set themselves off from other traits and identities. Thus, modernity isolated and excluded the individual and the group from experiencing universal, common human traits, such as rationality, irrationality, human rights and, most importantly, death. For Broch, modern identity was overly exclusive – even in religion, modern humans chose between strict interpretation of scripture and the sensual contact of mysticism. Modernity broke down universal human experience through the increased possibility of experiences. Rationality served as the catalyst to this walling off of identities into competing, autonomous value systems: 'Like strangers they exist side by side, an economic value system of "good business" next to an aesthetic one of *l'art pour l'art*, a military code of values side by side with a technical or an athletic one, each autonomous, each "in and for itself", each "unfettered" in its autonomy'.[13] Broch described the creation of modern autonomous

13   Broch, *The Sleepwalkers*, 448.

value systems as a 'gigantic Machiavellianism', that is, an unfolding of a radical, instrumental rationality.

In his eleven-part discursive 'The Disintegration of Values', from the third book of the *The Sleepwalkers*, he summarized the extension of radical rationality into the construction of European values:

> The logic of the army demands [...] that all military resources be exploited [...] resulting, if necessary, in the extermination of peoples, the demolition of cathedrals, the bombardment of hospitals. [...] The logic of the business man demands that all commercial resources be exploited. [...] The logic of the painter demands the principles of painting shall be followed to their conclusions. [...] The logic of the bourgeois climber demands that the watchword 'enrichissez-vous' shall be followed. [...] In this fashion, in this absolute devotion to logical rigour, the Western world has won its achievements [...] this is the style that characterizes our age.[14]

He went on to explore how Europe failed to offset this hypertrophic commitment to rationality. He clarified how the opposing commitment to a valueless irrationality[15] proved unable to satisfy the spiritual needs of man, who was now face to face with the infinite.

The crisis of Machiavellian rationality was an inescapable characteristic of modernity.

> But man, who was once the image of God, the mirror of a universal value created by himself, has fallen from his former estate: he may still ask himself what is this superimposed logic that has perverted his life; yet he is driven out into the horror of the infinite, and, no matter how he may yearn to return to the fold of faith, he is helplessly caught in the mechanism of the autonomous value systems, and can do nothing but submit himself to the particular value that has become his profession, he can do nothing but become a function of that value – a specialist.[16]

Broch saw the difference between the historical epoch of the Middle Ages and the Modern Age as the difference between an open value system (one that maintains an absolute source for individual and group value

---

14   Ibid, 445–446.
15   Seen in both Romanticism's and conservativism's turn to an idealized past.
16   Broch, *The Sleepwalkers*, 448.

construction) and a hypertrophied system (one that elevates multiple, competing sources for value construction). Of course, his overly simplistic understanding of the Middle Ages revealed a weakness of nineteenth-century historical thought; but it helped to define his view of the modern age as psychically conflicted and embattled.

Broch's Political Theory of the 1940s

What becomes clear in his writings from the 1940s is that Broch's humanist politics were not liberal in the classical liberal tradition. His political theory, while focused on the individual, conceived of citizenship not simply in terms of freedom, but also in terms of responsibility. His idea of total democracy emphasized, on the one hand, the responsibility of states to not oppress their citizens, or stated differently, the freedom of citizens to prevent state intrusion into their lives (liberalism equalling freedoms 'from'). On the other hand, citizens must be legally compelled, through reference to the force of equality implied in natural law, to respect the freedom and humanity of fellow citizens. His position demanded an active legal structure for the maintenance of such citizen responsibility. While technically not Rousseauean and not part of the positive (freedom to) versus negative (freedom from) rights debate, which reached its height during his exile with the implementation of President Roosevelt's New Deal, Broch's thought nonetheless found American democracy's purely constitutional foundation as untenable and even dangerous.

Throughout the 1940s, Broch questioned whether the democratic tradition of the United States could survive the growing irrational forces of modernity with appeals only to the Bill of Rights. While governmental structures and citizen freedoms could be sustained or safeguarded in this fashion, constitutional democracy provided no protections for human on human violence once it became sanctioned by appeals to irrational fears of invasion, internal contamination and the like. At the same time, he saw the increasing importance of the masses in modern politics. He did not see mass politics as an expansion of democracy and did not see the masses as a mere collection of individuals. Individuals retain the ability to reason; the masses, however, are formed out of the express desire to slip out of reason and into a 'twilight consciousness'.

From his adolescence in the nineteenth century through two world wars, Broch engaged with the questions of modernity. During the 1920s and 1930s, his theory of the disintegration of values and his theory of kitsch demanded a new form of art, which could express the historical moment of disintegration and suggest a path forward towards a new centripetal value. In both theories, he argued for a cultural crisis defined by a civilization-wide disconnect between the producers of ethics (artists) and the consumers (public culture). With the annexation of Austria by Hitler, however, his approach to cultural crisis shifted from art to politics and his ethical theory became more proscriptive and pragmatic. The ethical duty of modern humans, citizens and their states was 'Thou shalt not kill'. It was the protection of human life and dignity, what he termed the 'earthly absolute'.

Structure of the Narrative

My book addresses more directly an American audience and highlights Broch's position in American intellectual history. This book accesses an English reading audience, whose understanding of Broch as a political theorist is extremely limited. The majority of new work on his political theory has been written by German-language scholars and published with German-language publishers. Broch's intellectual legacy is more and more being defined as European and being read only in Europe or by specialists in the United States.[17] Throughout the book, I reference English translations, when good, widely available ones exist. Beyond his literature, however, most of his work is not translated. I open up Broch's political thought through the analysis, summary and translation of its key works.

My study is an intellectual biography in the sense that I intertwine the historical context of Broch's life with the historical development of his thought. For this reason, I provide a good deal of biographical information alongside analysis of his work. My analysis, however, is not limited to the biographical or purely textual value of the material. I also construct a historical narrative of how this material relates to the political and intellectual developments of the specific milieus in which they were conceived and operated. In particular, I want to provide readers less familiar with Hermann Broch, central Europe and the intellectual migration of the interwar years enough context to evaluate changes in Broch's ideas and to understand the relevancy of his thought to its historical moment and to contemporary debates on freedom and democracy.

There are two good sources available to an English audience when it comes to Broch's biography and his intellectual importance: the translation of Paul Michael Lützeler's biography and Ernestine Schlant's broad

---

17   See Thomas Eichler, Paul Michael Lützeler and Hartmut Steinecke, eds, *Hermann Broch: Politik, Menschenrecht – und Literatur?* (Oberhausen: Athena Verlag, 2005); Monika Klinger, *Hermann Broch und die Demokratie* (Berlin: Duncker und Humblot, 1994); *Hermann Broch, ein Engagierter zwischen Literatur und Politik*, edited by *Österreichische Liga für Mensche* (Innsbruck: Studien, 2004); Patrick Eiden, *Das Reich der Demokratie:Hermann Brochs Der Tod des Vergil* (Munich: Wilhelm Fink, 2011); Hartmut Jäckel, 'Hermann Broch and Politics' and Joseph Strelka, 'Politics and the Human Condition: Broch's Model of a Mass Psychology', in Stephen D. Dowden, ed., *Hermann Broch: Literature, Philosophy, Politics* (Columbia, SC: Camden House, 1988); Almund Greiter and Anton Pelinka, 'Hermann Broch als Demokratietheoretiker', in Richard Thieberger, ed., *Hermann Broch und Seine Zeit* (Bern: Peter Lang, 1980), 24–36; Christian Borch, 'Modern mass aberration: Hermann Broch and the problem of irrationality', *History of the Human Sciences*, 21/2 (2008), 63–83; Daniel Wiedner, 'Hermann Broch and the Ethics of Exile', in Eckart Goebel and Sigrid Weigel, eds, 'Escape to Life', *German Intellectuals in New York: A Compendium on Exile after 1933* (Berlin: De Gruyter, 2012), 162–181.

exploration of Broch's intellectual theories. Schlant's book, last reprinted in 1986, is an excellent resource for an English reader to get to know the breadth of his intellectual development and activity. The work is, however, primarily literary (chronologically structured around his main literary works). She bases her examination of the texts, however, on a wide-ranging survey of his philosophical, epistemological and political essays. The first and last chapters provide the most detailed non-literary discussion, clarifying Broch's early influences from *fin-de-siècle* Viennese culture and Kantianism. Her last chapter examines his exile period from the point of view of political engagement. Overall, the book provides an excellent summary of his intellectual development.

My goal is not to overturn the ideas of Schlant or to replace her work, but to shift the focus from primarily literary to primarily political. I show Broch as an American intellectual and not just a European thinker in exile. Some of Schlant's conclusions on his political theory will be challenged in my text, but primarily I provide more direct and in depth discussion of his political engagement from interwar Vienna to his American period. In addition to examining the primary texts and personal writings of Broch, my book will incorporate the contemporary literature on his politics – the majority of which has been done by European scholars working in German, French, Italian, Dutch and Polish.

Throughout the book, I examine and analyse Broch's political theory in order to clarify its relationship to his biographical context and the intellectual context of its composition. I do not provide an in-depth analysis of its theoretical value viz contemporary political theory or ideologically based critical theories. The usefulness of such an undertaking is clear, and comparisons between Broch and thinkers such as Arendt, Benjamin, Sartre and Lukács would demonstrate both similar recognition of the problems of modernity and different solutions to those problems. My book, however, is an intellectual biography of his ideas and actions as they relate to experience of world war, the rise of fascism, exile and the growth of American power. I would like to introduce Broch to an English-speaking audience in terms of his engagement with the issues of modern mass politics, democratic reform and internationalism.

My narrative positions Broch within the socio-economic, cultural and political worlds of interwar Vienna/central Europe, America during the Second World War and post-war America. I demonstrate that his position as artist and intellectual opened the world of political engagement to him, and then I examine how and why he embraced or rejected his opportunities. I argue that his historiographical legacy needs reconsideration in order to justify a continued relevance to studying not only his published literature, but also his unfinished work on political psychology and democratic reform.

The key contention in my book is that Broch changed his relationship to politics owing to his experience of fascist authoritarianism and terror. Such a contention may sound on its surface to be obvious and expected. My study, however, provides a historical narrative of his actions and ideas during this transition and shows that the changes were not purely reactive. Broch thought through his redefinition of politics, and he did so by synthesizing his earlier European cultural criticism with a new appreciation for direct political action. My argument takes seriously the difference between engagé politics and active politics. The former conception (engagé) defines political engagement in a very board manner: cultural criticism, aesthetic activity, scientific investigation and spiritual guidance. It is a definition that in its Marxist genealogy (superstructure vs substructure) provides for a form of praxis and not simply theory. Yet, Marxist praxis is a problematic model for analysing Broch. He rejected the fundamental claims of Marxist action, its historical determinism and its material, class-based revolution. Broch's philosophy of history, which informed his relationship to praxis, rejected a materialist and linear unfolding of history. His strong belief in the historical value of cognition mirrors much of the aesthetic based political programs of Italian Marxism. He, however, shows little connection to such developments in Marxism, as he took a Platonic/Kantian route to social criticism. Furthermore, he distanced himself from more practical Marxists like Kautsky and was too distance from the realism and materialism of Lukács. His relationship to Austro-Marxism is much closer, but as I show that relationship was determined by both historical necessity (the vacuum of Empire) and limited to a purely theoretical agreement. Broch played no practical role in the fate of Social Democracy in the interwar period.

What Broch wanted was revolutionary change without revolution. In Vienna of the 1920s, this fostered both conservativism and bourgeois liberalism in him. Through Kantianism, modernism (of Joyce and Kafka) and liberalism, he manufactured a subjective pragmatism that from either an Aristotelian or Marxism point of view severed him from real political engagement. In exile, he questioned the efficiency of subjective and purely cognitive social reform. He re-examined his claims about the moral vacuity of politics and public debate. He fashioned new roles for the scientist and educator; no longer would they focus their energies on stylization or myth creation. They would now apply their ideas to the protection of the individual – mainly on a psychological and cognitive level, but now with a greater recognition that the material world posed real and immediate dangers. These dangers required real choices and actions in order to direct and mitigate their destabilizing influences. Faced with such dangers, he argued for a new commitment to ethical creativity. He demanded of artists, philosophers, scientists – that is, intellectuals – direct and immediate actions. Intellectuals had to choose sides and help construct democratic defences against the spread of fascism. Throughout this change in political awareness, however, his intellectual persona remained consistent. He was what I would call a natural philosopher or scientist in its most philosophical definition. The change was that he transitioned from the scientist qua artist to the scientist qua politician.

Broch's shift in political awareness parallels Jean-Paul Sartre's definition of engagement from the same period. Sartre also came to stress the necessity of the writer to acknowledge agency and take action. For Sartre, there were two key ideas in play in terms of political engagement: individual agency and material security.[18] These ideas fall directly in line with much of Broch's writings from his exile, as he acknowledged that a purely 'esoteric' intellectual position is untenable in the context of fascism. Hannah Arendt's ideas on praxis and *logos* are also a useful definition for

---

18   See Jean-Paul Sartre, *What is Literature?*, Bernard Frechtman, tr. (New York: The Philosophical Library, 1949).

my reconstruction of Broch's developing political awareness in US exile.[19] However, he did not incorporate a theory of praxis or the active life into his cognitive and psychological work on mass hysteria; from a historical point of view, his action demonstrate a new consciousness of the its importance. Nonetheless, Arendt, who worked closely with Broch during his exile and read and influenced his political theory, still criticized him for his utopian and naive relationship to the 'active life'. Her criticism of Broch relates to his cognitive and psychological theory within his *Theory of Mass Delusion*, the ideas that represent his continuity of philosophy from Vienna. In comparison to her theory on political action, he may appear theoretically too naive, but my argument is that from a historiographical point of view, one can argue that Broch's relationship to political praxis shifted a great deal over the period from 1918 to 1951. During this time, he moved much closer to the pragmatic, Aristotelian/Arendtian position in his exile than he ever could have in his central European context. Though, his Platonic/Kantian focus on the idealism and individual cognition obscured the magnitude of that shift.

In Chapter 1, I examine Broch as a historical subject – his importance as a subject of study and his relevancy to his own milieu and the contemporary world. In the chapter, I connect him to the larger historical process of modernism and demonstrate his importance to the central questions of modernity. In Chapter 2, I examine his life and political thought during the interwar period in Vienna. In the chapter, I argue that Vienna influenced the humanistic aspects of his thought, but that the cultural milieu in which he lived led to a disengaged relationship to politics. In the third chapter, I continue my examination of his Viennese upbringing with specific reference to his first novel *The Sleepwalkers*, which shows more fully the disengaged nature of his thought, as well as his epistemological and aesthetic approach to modernism. Chapter 4 examines Broch's transition to engaged politics in the context of his geographical transition from Austria to America. In the chapter, I show how his thought shifted away from

19   Hannah Arendt, *The Human Condition* (Chicago: University of Chicago Press, 1958).

an epistemological discussion of aesthetics to politics. My examination focuses on his concern for human rights, his growing internationalism and his efforts to educate the world about democracy. The fifth chapter looks directly at how politics became more central to his intellectual activities. I examine his statements on democracy and how they reflected his experience of exile and the growing danger of fascism. I define for the reader his criticism of American democracy and his ideas for reforming its limitations. In my conclusion, I re-evaluate the historiographical narrative of Broch's exile experience and, based on the awareness of Broch's growth in political engagement, argue that the sense of tragedy often connected to this narrative needs reconsideration.

Throughout the book, I draw the reader's attention to the complex networks of influences that guided the development of his theories. From the individual personal influences of his family and psyche, to the larger cultural influences of education and assimilation, to the historical shifts and political developments of war and fascism, Broch's life and thought expose a complex and contested European understanding of the modern world.

Broch's Modern Relevance

The question of Broch's position in the United States is complicated by the incomplete nature of his *Mass Delusion Theory* (*Massenwahntheorie*). The result has been to limit his influence on American thought. Nevertheless, his political perspective, which was pro-American and pro-democratic, allows for an interpretative approach to liberal democracy that is devoid of nationalism and free from the debates over positive and negative rights. He left behind hundreds of pages of material on his impressions of democracy and freedom in the United States. By examining what he had to say about American democracy, we gain a new angle from which to understand that democratic tradition. His political ideas demanded that in promoting a liberal democratic world order the West must engage in an internal debate and not simply in external contestation. Is the West really democratic? Can it be in the modern world? The case study of Broch allows us to see that the foundations of Western democratic values were ambiguous. After 1945, the debate was sidelined by the clarity of good and evil in the Cold War, and especially with the challenge to Marxist ideology within the Western intellectual world of the late twentieth century. The issues raised by Broch and the intellectual milieu that brought forth these issues expose an active contestation about the meaning of freedom and democracy in the Western tradition and demonstrate some doubts about the current value system underlining the democratic West.

In an age when the threat of neo-fascism and extremism has steadily increased, an exploration of the history of the West's internal debate over these issues is informative and necessary. In 2001, the United States and Europe were quick to identify and stress the mutual legacy of democratic values and an ethical commitment to liberty. Within a year, however, the confessed similarity in outlook in terms of geo-politics was rejected by both sides. The reasons for these shifts are complicated and multiple, but the underlying issue of how Western democracy and freedom can be conceived of in two separate and somewhat hostile ways was made manifest in the growing gap between 'Old Europe' and the United States.

The foreign policy direction of the United States in the first decade and half of the twenty-first century provides an interesting introduction to the political issues that Hermann Broch confronted in his American exile. Do freedom and democracy require an aggressive policy of enforcement? Does the spread of democracy proceed on a policy of internationalism or nationalism? Is there a universal political value whose propagation throughout the world will establish the necessary universal value system for the protection of human dignity and world peace? The similarities and differences in the way that Broch answered these questions and the way in which the current policy direction in the United States has addressed them demonstrate an ambiguity in the relationship between freedom and force, between universal values and cultural norms. In many ways the current rationale of US foreign policy and Broch's efforts to promote an aggressive, forcefully engaged democracy are very similar. In other ways, his fears of the fascist and totalitarian tendencies in the way the United States perceived of freedom in strictly material terms resonate in the current debates of US pre-emptive and unilateral war.

My book will not attempt to answer the questions of twenty-first-century US foreign policy, but to demonstrate the fact that even today the issues that Broch engaged in the 1930s are still central to the internal debate concerning the meaning of democracy. Broch, as an intellectual émigré, allows us a bird's-eye view of the initiation of this debate at the time when the United States entered into its role as superpower. His work pointed out both the advantages and the dangers for democracy in this new position. He questioned the relationship of the United States to fascism. He suggested ways of conceiving of freedom and liberty in terms of human dignity and religion that foreshadow later American debates on civil rights and the generational conflict of the counter-culture movements of the 1950s and 1960s.

For the majority of Broch's writing career, he worked to diagnose the source of this lack of value impulse. He studied mathematics and philosophy as a way of investigating language and its degeneration. He began an epistemological theory of cognition and creativity, which he tied to his pursuit of literature as an aesthetic answer to the ethically empty language of the time. In the end, however, he rejected all of these as effective ways to address the issue. He rejected aesthetics in the most direct way in the mid-1930s with his *Death of Virgil*. Late in his life, he returned to literature as medium for understanding the post-Second World War global situation. Overall, however, Broch's fearful recognition that European and later Western culture had burned through its own means of expressing the ethical was never solved.

This book helps to answer the question of why Broch failed to solve that ethical dilemma, and in so doing shows him not to be tragic or decadent, but to be pragmatic. There were two reasons he never solved the dilemma. The first was that he believed that the dilemma could not be solved by a single ethical or creative act – only time would allow for the creation of an ethically suitable language of expression, a new style of the age. The second reason was that he made a pragmatic choice in the 1930s to deprioritize his search for universal creativity and ethical expression in order to pursue political stabilization. His goal was to aid democracy and economic individualism so that there would be enough time and history available to European/Western culture to develop a new form of ethical expression.

CHAPTER I

Metropolis of Kitsch: The Viennese Sources of Broch's Politics

> The ultimate meaning of poverty masked by wealth became clearer in Vienna, in Vienna's spirited swan song, than in any other place or time. A minimum of ethical values was to be masked by a maximum of aesthetic values, which themselves no longer existed. They could no longer exist, because an aesthetic value that does not spring from an ethical foundation is its own opposite – kitsch. And as the metropolis of kitsch, Vienna also became the metropolis of the value vacuum of the epoch.[1]

For Hermann Broch modernity was the over-abundance of valueless ideologies produced from a 'disintegration of values' into ethical relativism. Much of his early work defined the embodiment of such a vacuum in modern culture – from aesthetics to science. In particular, Broch saw Jewish assimilation in the modern world as the quintessential example of such a hypertrophy of particular values over universal ones. My study of Broch examines how he ultimately employed politics to address the problem of modernity; in particular, how he brought a humanistic vision of ethical creativity to bear on the political dangers of the twentieth century. His early writing recognized the weaknesses of modern political ideologies that ignored the importance of humanism, but these ideas were not translated into the active political theorizing until his exile in 1938.

It was not until after the First World War and the collapse of the Habsburg Empire that Broch made cultural criticism his primary mission.

---

1   Hermann Broch, *Hugo von Hofmannsthal and his Time*, Michael P. Steinberg, ed. and tr. (Chicago: University of Chicago Press, 1984), 81.

By the late 1920s, he took up the challenges of modernity as a novelist. Throughout the interwar period, his work addressed the dangers of mass society and bourgeois culture to the process of individual cognition. He viewed modernity as *impotent* in its ethical and artistic creativity.[2] He traced the impotence to a fear of death that was heightened by the destructive nature of technological society and world war. Moreover, he questioned whether scientific advancement could lead the way to a new, absolute source of cognition. Science, physics in particular, seemed to suggest that the universe was 'playing dice'.[3] The individual was left floundering between tradition and the relativity of knowledge. For many, the breakdown of any restriction on human knowledge and the unbound potential of human questioning and scientific experiment were positive steps toward freedom. Such a trust in positivism contained a paradigmatic belief in progress. History in this progressive model operated on a linear and upward trajectory. Broch, however, questioned progressivism's unabashed commitment to rationality and the Hegelian and Marxist historical models of unidirectional history. He especially condemned the bourgeois culture of valueless materialism, which attempted to ignore the moral implications of modern change.

Concern over the dangers of modernity was not new. The First World War, however, punctuated and intensified the longstanding intellectual debate on European decadence and cultural decline. Broch entered this debate as early as 1908, and following the war, he focused on both defining and curing the source of European degeneration. While he followed Nietzsche in terms of seeing the death of God as the centrepiece to value disintegration, he did not believe the cure lay in the abandonment of the universalist value that God represented. The cure would have to be the reinvention of a universal value system, that is, a value system that directed in a centripetal fashion human energy and creativity around the expression

2   Broch's autobiographical of concern for sexual impotence was a key source for his understanding of modernity's ethical and creative impotence.

3   William Hermanns, *Einstein and the Poet: In Search of the Cosmic Man* (Brookline, MA: Branden Press, 1983), 58. Einstein, whom Broch corresponded with during his exile, could not believe that nature was at its core random. Broch's concern about relativity links directly to his own encounter with Einstein's theory.

of vitality. He mostly discussed this idea in terms of overcoming its opposition, death.

It was history that justified his theory of value destruction by showing that history had a logical pattern (opening and closing). The logic of history proved that humanity could return (what he described as conversion) to an ethical plane, where knowledge and art facilitated expansionary and revelatory moments of human individual cognition. The individual thus retained his/her central role in the creation of universal values and the unfolding of history. The most significant prerequisite was the creative ethical potential of the individual and protecting the individual from delusional hysteria (hypertrophy) that accompanies the closing of a value system (the dying of God). History, again, was the key. It allowed communities to contextualize the pattern of closure and identify the false universality of absolute relativity in terms of valuation creation.

Though religious in language and spiritual in purpose, his theory concentrated more directly on the idea of human will and human psychology and relied heavily on mathematics and epistemology as proofs for demonstrating the historical possibility of change. In the 1920s, Broch attempted to build a meta-theory for explaining intricate interconnections of history, epistemology, aesthetics, science and psychology. He argued that no single elements in these activities could be viewed as prior or quintessential. In fact, he spent a great amount of his intellectual energy on showing how each of these activities could be universalized to the point of closing down humanity's will to value. If one could argue for a simple duality in his theory, it would appear in the contrast between the mental (*geistliche*) and the corporeal, cognition and materialism. This is not an absolute duality in Broch, but the Platonic and Kantian influences were primary in his theory of value construction.

The theory just outlined represented the major tenets of Broch's intellectual agenda from 1910s to the early 1930s. It was a theory that represented the eclectic blending of a wide-ranging, dilettante mind operating in an eclectic intellectual milieu, which was undergoing massive cultural and political change. It was also a theory characterized by its critical humanist goals and overwhelming apolitical expression. It was only outside the context of his Viennese milieu or perhaps more appropriately after the destruction of the European world of his youth that Broch's humanist idealism turned openly political. Nonetheless, the experiences of Catholic conversion and marriage, his Oedipal understanding of his sexual development and his exclusion from a classical education help to contextualize the foundation for his later commitment to humanist politics.

The foundation for his conceptual work is strongly autobiographical. Like much of the intellectual history of the second half of the nineteenth century, both Broch's personal letters and his artistic and theoretical work indicated a shift towards the questions of irrationality and desire. In this new intellectual terrain, the tendency to chart or explain the non-rational world through a merging of philosophical tradition and personal experience was widespread: Arthur Schopenhauer and his father's suicide as one of the sources for his rejection of the will; Freud's train ride to Vienna as a source for his Oedipus Complex; Nietzsche's and Kierkegaard's relationships to their Protestant, patriarchal upbringing as a source for their rejection of contemporary Christianity. From an examination of Broch's life it is evident that ethics and the notion of an unanchored modern 'self' developed out of his family history, as did the impulse for such deep immersion into the German intellectual tradition. He acknowledged the connections between his personal biography and his theoretical work in his autobiographical writings of the early 1940s. In these works, he narrated his struggle with the fear of impotence and his neurotic commitment to duty. He described himself as the quintessence of modern man, oscillating between a duty to his fellow citizen and a paralysing sense of impotence. In this chapter, I explore the connection between Broch's assimilation into the culture of the Viennese high *Burgertum* and the foundation for his politico-ethical engagement with European modernity.

Broch and Vienna

Hermann Broch grew up in a paradoxical social situation. On the hand, there was an increasing opportunity (social and economic) for Jewish citizens of the Habsburg Empire. On the other hand, there was an expansion of political anti-Semitism in Austrian politics, which ultimately brought about the almost complete elimination of Jews from Austrian society. While material wealth and social mobility marked Broch's youth and adolescence, his intellectual and cultural mentality reflected not only his upper middle class values, but also the eclecticism and neurosis of the outsider attempting to penetrate the inner circle of the German-Austrian aristocracy. His intellectual work, from his earliest notebooks in 1908 until his separation from his family and the world of business in 1927, diagnosed and criticized the ethical relativism of modern society. His historical and personal context, however (especially the process of assimilation and a generally conservative outlook), prevented him from openly challenging or rejecting the very society he found so diseased.

The paths to social integration and success in nineteenth-century Vienna had solidified into two key cultural beliefs: 1) *Bildung und Besitz*, trust in professionalism, wealth and *Gymnasium* as means to political and economic influence and 2) the enlightened belief in cosmopolitan secularism. Both of these cultural values connected directly to the liberal tradition of the mid-nineteenth century and to German *Kultur* and nationalism as the vehicle for their expression. Many culturally and politically active Jews of the nineteenth century had seen nationalism as the shining new path to social acceptance or at least tolerance.[4] The growing importance of anti-Semitism in the German nationalistic politics, however, closed down a political path for Jewish assimilation. The abandonment of ideas of tolerance and equality by the Liberal Party, under the influence of nationalism and anti-Semitism, left the legacy of rationality, individualism, cosmopolitanism, democracy

---

4   See William McGarth, *Dionysian Art and Populist Politics in Austria* (New Haven, CT: Yale University Press, 1974).

and even Empire to be carried on by a variety of early twentieth-century political and cultural groups.[5] By and large, however, such groups remained isolated and marginalized.

Following the First World War, the Jewish community, especially the leadership of the *Kultusgemeinschaft*, maintained strong support for rationality, cosmopolitanism and Empire, while social democracy remained the only deeply committed democratic and parliamentarian ideology.[6] Broch, tangentially aligned with both groups, also carried this liberal, enlightened legacy into the twentieth century. He, however, applied this legacy to aesthetic and epistemological theory as a means of building an ethically active value system. It was not surprising than that he exhibited deep influences and affinities to Austro-Marxism and upper middle class Jewish intellectualism in his ethical theories.

I examine Broch's life in Vienna as a means to understanding more clearly the politico-ethical system that he carried to the United States and adapted into a theory of democracy. His intellectual biography in his Austrian context introduces many of the fundamental emotional and intellectual positions that remained central to the formation of his exilic political thought. It also creates a better awareness of the complexity of the Vienna 1900 and the Austrian First Republic. His writings, especially those from 1919 to 1934, much like Carl Schorske's later thesis, emphasized a 'crisis of liberalism', which was isolating thinkers and artists from their own society. He acknowledged a crisis on both the individual and mass cultural level, and he saw both of them as expressions of a psychological process of panic, which he later defined as a twilight consciousness. As discussed later, the Viennese intellectual milieu and its experimentation with ego psychology and psychoanalysis, its scientific materialism and

5   See John W. Boyer, *Culture and political crisis in Vienna: Christian socialism in power, 1897–1918* (Chicago: University of Chicago Press, 1995) and Pieter M. Judson, *Exclusive Revolutionaries: Liberal Politics, Social Experience, and National Identity in the Austrian Empire 1848–1914* (Ann Arbor, MI: University of Michigan Press, 1996).

6   Harriet Pass Freidenreich, *Jewish Politics in Vienna, 1918–1938* (Bloomington, IN: Indiana University Press, 1991), see especially ch 2.

positivism, and its philosophical irrationalism contributed heavily to this psychological model for a 'new type of democratic man'.[7]

In Broch's early aesthetic theory, personal letters and literature there was a definite focus on ideas of loneliness and abandonment. This focus, however, did not signal an intellectual withdrawal into the garden of the aesthete; rather, it expressed an awareness of a growing crisis in the European value system. It was an ethical crisis that reflected the disintegration of any centralizing belief. Without a centralizing absolute truth, 'conviction' in limited truths directed individuals into communities of opposition and created more and more isolation and conflict. Like other artists and writers of the First Republic, Broch did not embrace empty or decadent pleasures to mask the isolating tendencies of modernity. Instead, he attempted to define these tendencies and later to overcome them.

This was an intellectual development pattern found throughout turn-of-the-century Austria and expressed in the historiography as 'critical modernism'. Critical modernist theory argues that Viennese modernism is at its root an ethical response to the combination of permanent cultural crisis with the diminishing efficacy of traditional patterns of thought. In Broch, we can paradoxically affirm and then question one of the key conclusions of the critical modernist trend – Jewish exclusivity. Certainly, one cannot deny the importance of Jewish identity to his experience or to the experience of a large percentage of Viennese thinkers of his generation. The claim that *fin-de-siècle* modernist thought was at its basis an 'internal Jewish debate' may, however, set too strict a framework on the process of intellectual development at the turn of the century.[8] From a presentist view, Jewish culture was so ubiquitous within the milieu that the historian can easily conceive of it as the fundamental element of modernist thought. Such clarity, however, produces too neat a conception of the actual historical process. By observing Broch's development, we see that Jewish identity

---

7   Broch, undated draft manuscript, Beinecke Rare Book and Manuscript Library MSS. For a discussion of the idea of scientific materialism and philosophical irrationalism, see David S. Luft, *Robert Musil and the Crisis of European Culture*, as well as Janik and Toulmin, *Wittgenstein's Vienna*.

8   Allan Janik, 'Vienna 1900 Revisited, Paradigms and Problems', 45.

interacted with various influences at various times. His intellectual production also suggests a worldview significantly defined by German *Bildung*
and the Austrian Baroque, as well as Kant and universal Christian ethics.

Like much of Viennese intellectual and cultural development in the
late imperial and republican periods, Broch's critical modernism reflected
a blending of liberal, German and Jewish culture. He himself provided the
most nuanced claim about the relationship of modernity and Judaism,
when he identified the Jew as the exemplar of modernist dislocation. It
was only with his arrest by the Nazis in 1938 that he came to realize that
in a pragmatic political sense it was his Jewish identity that was the sine
qua non of his social existence. Nevertheless, he never came to understand
his own Judaism in terms of exclusivity, even in regard to oppression. He
argued that Jews were simply the most exceptional in terms of their historical position at the forefront of modernity and its murderous capabilities.

Broch and Viennese Modernism

In the following section, I examine Broch's life in roughly chronological
order, but my focus is on several specific aspects of his Viennese life: 1) his
social and economic status, 2) his assimilation pattern, 3) his education, 4)
his familial relationships, especially from the 1910s to the late 1920s and 5)
his relationship to the liberal tradition within Vienna.

His father, Josef Broch, had a very different vision for his son's future
than becoming a novelist. It was the life of an engineer and textile manufacturer – an approach to life that found value in the support of the Empire
and collection of money. Josef (1852–1933) immigrated to Vienna as a teen-
ager and worked his way up from an office assistant to a successful textile
speculator. He tied his business speculations to the ever present need for
military uniforms within the Habsburg Army and quickly amassed capital

– a fact that deepened the political and ideological links between Josef and the monarchy.[9]

On 25 October 1885, Josef expanded his economic and social standing in Vienna through his marriage to Johanna Schnabel, the daughter of another émigré Jewish merchant. Her father, Hermann Schnabel, had immigrated to Vienna a generation before Josef. The Schnabel family was already financially established and well integrated into the Viennese merchant class. Hermann Broch's son describes the Schnabel family's social status as one of "'making eyes" at the gentry, keeping trotting and racing horses and cultivating a special kind of anti-Semitism peculiar to Austria, best exemplified by old Moritz Rothschild's statement: "There are Jews and there are Yids"'.[10] The marriage to Johanna Schnabel not only furthered Josef's social connections to the upper middle class, but it also expanded his economic fortune through new business relations with his in-laws.[11]

Josef Broch did not choose the path of assimilation common to most upper middle class Jews at the time: *Besitz und Bildung* (possessions and education, i.e. *Gymnasium*). Instead, he trusted in a social position defined exclusively by *Besitz*. Assimilation meant acquisition of money and business interest. The way to become a citizen was to earn money and support the monarchy. The education of his son in *Realschule* and technical universities underscored this attitude, as well as the purchasing of a textile mill in order to insure industrial careers for both his sons. Hermann Broch's assimilation, however, was complicated by his own choices and by the tension between his father's expectations and his own desires. Hermann's

9　　After little more than a decade in Vienna, Josef Broch was considered the 'most successful textile speculator in the Habsburg Empire'. Wolfgang Rothe, 'Der junge Broch', in *Neue Deutsche Hefte* 7 (1960), 780.

10　　H. F. Broch de Rothermann, *Liebe Frau Strigl: A Memoir of Hermann Broch by his Son*, John Hargraves, tr. (New Haven, CT: The Beinecke Rare Book and Manuscript Library, 2001), 4.

11　　Paul Michael Lützeler, *Hermann Broch: A Biography*, Janice Furness, tr. (London: Quartet Books, 1987), 6. By the mid-1920s the Broad of the Teesdorf Spinning Factory (operated by the Brochs) was almost exclusively held by the Broch and Schnabel families.

assimilation into Austrian society was, in fact, an exceptional case. He
intermarried with a Catholic aristocrat. He converted from Judaism. He
did not attend *Gymnasium*. All of this marked Broch as statistically exceptional – less than 1 per cent of Jews per annum converted in the first decade
of the twentieth century and the intermarriage rate was below 10 per cent
for pre-war Vienna.[12]

The depth of Broch's assimilation into Austrian aristocratic culture,
both in terms of the upper middle class emulation of aristocracy and the
Catholic imperial world of his in-laws, only seemed to heighten in him
a sense of class distinction and to promote the Jewish cultural anti-Semitism described above by his son. Yet, his assimilation was incomplete
and ultimately a failure. The reasons for the failure were contradictions
in the competing notions of materialism and intellectualism represented
by the various paradigms structuring his assimilation. His father's strictly
business-centred notion of social integration conflicted with Broch's own
intellectual tendencies, as well as with the intellectual and cultural influence of Judaism and the *Haskalah*. Broch would come to see his business
activity and his life at the Teesdorf factory as a burden and an impediment
to his epistemological and artistic efforts. Thus, it produced in Broch an
anti-materialistic worldview in terms of the rejection of the bourgeois
values of his father.

On the other hand, Broch embraced the materialism of his class and
wealth in terms of lifestyle and a sense of elitism. His main home was on
Gonzagagasse in the first district, though he also lived in other homes in
the first and ninth districts. These districts held the centres for shopping
and business and were the location of the University and the *Börse*. It was
a world of status and materialism that contrasted greatly with the lower
class districts such as Leopoldstadt or Florisdorf. Even though Broch's status
as a Jew continued to exclude him from complete integration in upper
class Viennese society, his youth still reflected a degree of affluence that,

---

12   Marsha L. Rozenbilt, *The Jews of Vienna, 1867–1914: Assimilation and Identity* (Albany,
      NY: SUNY Press, 1983), 128–132.

as Brigitte Hamann points out, made a strong impact on the unemployed and impoverished members of the city such as Adolf Hitler.[13]

Broch's upper middle class status allowed Broch to indulge materially in the world of *haute bourgeoisie*:

> [H]e had discovered the pleasures of wealth's externals, and in accord with his strongly developed aesthetic sense he had become quite the dandy. His tastes were always conservative – his whole life he wore only grey and black suits in winter, white and yellow linen suits in summer, and never anything but white shirts with black knit ties [...] at least fifty suits and coats and the same number of shoes were carefully hung and stored in the wardrobe which was specially built for them in Teesdorf [...] In his courtship days he was not just very fashionable, but also an extremely impressive figure, and it would not have required his collection of canes and tobacco-tins to lend him a truly aristocratic appearance.[14]

Pictures from the time also attest to Broch's fashionable appearance and his elegant style. It is clear from pictures of his home and apartments that Broch lived in the manner of the upper middle class bourgeois (which meant aristocratic) culture of late nineteenth-century Vienna.[15] It was an identity that infused Broch's manner of dress and his social sensibility with an inherent conservativism, which also tempered his political engagement. Yet, Broch's hold on this world was tangential and fragile. His wealth did not gain him a comfortable position as insider, and the conservativism associated with its materialist appeal only generated more conflict as it

---

13   Brigitte Hamann, *Hitler's Vienna: A dictator's apprenticeship*, translated by Thomas Thornton (New York : Oxford University Press, 1999), 325–359.

14   Broch de Rothermann, 15–16. The description of the Franziska von Rothermann and her family, which the following pages provide, comes from the memoir of Broch's son Hermann F. M. Broch de Rothermann.

15   See *Spiegelungen: Denkbilder zur Biographie Brochs*, Karin Mack and Wolfgang Hofer, eds (Vienna: Sonderzahl, 1984) for pictorial biography of Broch, including photographs of letters, furniture and personal positions, as well as family and friends. Original photographs can be seen at the Hermann Broch Archives, Yale Collection of German Literature, Beinecke Rare Book and Manuscript Library and the Hermann Broch Museum in Teesdorf, Austria.

contrasted with the intellectual and emotional attachments to the progressive ideals of social democracy.

Broch's marriage came to define another major process of assimilation that once again failed and in many ways reinforced the contradiction
between his materialist conservativism and his position as outsider to the
very communities that fostered his wealth and sense of class. In 1908, Broch
began to court Franziska von Rothermann.[16] The relationship led to marriage in 1909 and to the birth of a son, Hermann Friedrich, in 1910. Franziska
von Rothermann was aristocratic and Catholic. Although intermarriage
between Jews and Catholics was not unheard of in Vienna at this period, it
was not the path of assimilation that Josef Broch had desired.[17] It was not
a decision with which the von Rothermanns agreed either. In the end, it
was not a decision that pleased anyone, Hermann and Franziska included.[18]

The marriage to Franziska von Rothermann reflected a youthful
romanticism more than a desire for simple social elevation or assimilation. It was, however, a testament to Broch's well-developed sensibilities in
both dress and conversation that the union ever moved beyond the stage of
courtship. As Lützeler describes, 'All members of the Rothermann family
soon succumbed to his diplomacy, his elegant appearance, his sensitivity,
charm and modesty'.[19] The union indicated Broch's familiarity with the
cultural and social world of the Habsburg gentry.

With his conversion to Catholicism,[20] the last barrier to marriage
was overcome. Broch's aristocratic appearance and his new faith, however,
could not nullify the reality of the two families' divergent social and economic worldviews. On the one hand, Josef Broch, who may have dressed
and played the part of a bourgeois gentleman, had neither the money nor
social flexibility to imitate the world in which the von Rothermanns lived.

---

16   See Lützeler, *A Biography*, 24–27.
17   See Rozenbilt, Chapter 6.
18   The correspondence between Hermann and Franziska in the Broch Archive demon-
      strate that the attraction and emotional connection between the two was real and
      deep.
19   Lützeler, *A Biography*, 26.
20   On 16 July 1909, Broch was baptized into the Catholic faith.

'The Rothermanns were an old "Aryan" family from Northern Germany, having emigrated there from the Netherlands in the 16th century,'[21] and they were established members of the Hungarian aristocracy. Even though their patent of nobility was very recent (1884) and connected to business activities, the marriage was not a simple assimilation into Austrian *haute bourgeoisie*, but a vertical shift between classes. Josef's marriage to Johanna Schnabel had also represented upward mobility, but of a very different type. He moved up within the Jewish middle class, while Hermann married into higher social rank as well as wealth. In the end, it appears that both families were correct: the difference in social expectations, especially in role and use of money, eventually proved too much for the marriage.

The marriage to Franziska von Rothermann multiplied the identity crisis of Broch that assimilation had begun. Into the world of the liberal burgher, created for him by his father, he brought the world of the landed aristocracy, as seen in his son's description of his maternal family:

> In shooting season the family moved from castle to castle, in the winter they took a private train to Italy or the Riviera, and from time to time repaired to various spas and watering-holes [...] The big country house at Hirm, where my mother spent her childhood, and Castle Surány near Ödenburg, where she was born, were always teeming with family, and guests from the neighbouring estates [...] [the banquets] seldom numbered fewer than twenty and often fifty guests, and every holiday, whether religious or personal, was an only-too-welcome occasion for extravagant, tradition-laden celebrations.[22]

Neither Hermann nor Franziska foresaw the implications of the deep differences in their understanding of money and life.[23] Hermann had valued the practicality of money in terms of his lifestyle, and he understood the meaning of money in terms of the financial world. He, nevertheless, saw no role for money in terms of fulfilling life goals. Franziska had no less of an ambiguous relationship to money; its existence, however, held a central

---

21 Broch de Rothermann, 11.
22 Broch de Rothermann, 12–13.
23 Their attraction was based on deep affection, but tinged by a youthful romanticism (Beinecke). See also Broch de Rothermann, 12, for a brief profile of his Franziska.

position in her life. Leisure, supported by money, had been the focus of her childhood. Even though she did not emphasize the role of money in her life, its availability was never questioned. Furthermore, she had no practical conception of finances. This accounted for the paradoxical description of her by her son, which he ascribed to the entire von Rothermann family:

> But for all the love of grand gesture ... [the von Rothermanns] retained a certain petit-bourgeois side, even a peasant-like rudeness by no means unusual among the Hungarian landed aristocracy. As one often sees with the very rich (who have no real sense of the value of money except when dealing with very small sums), the family revealed, along with princely generosity, an appalling niggardliness where tips or other charities not prescribed by tradition were concerned.[24]

Hermann and Franziska both rejected the world of business and capital, but they did so from opposing points of view in terms the cultural importance of money.

Money and intellectual pursuits for Franziska Broch were pastimes, not ethical responsibilities as they were for Hermann's father vis-à-vis the former and for himself vis-à-vis the latter. If anything united Broch and his wife in terms of Teesdorf, it was the disappointing and restrictive nature of their existence in the mundane Teesdorf world. The shared disappointment of Teesdorf did not, however, transfer into a shared attempt to move beyond it. Hermann focused his energies on his intellectual pursuits and his social life in the Viennese café scene. Franziska focused her energy on a more material existence and felt more and more isolated within the Broch family home. They divorced on 13 April 1923.[25]

A further factor guiding Broch's assimilation was education and intellectualism. Education was for the most part out of his control for the first 30 years of this life. Josef Broch had been a dominating and controlling father: '[Josef] held firmly to Jewish tradition in this respect only: in the family, he was the *paterfamilias*, the supreme authority and the god of wrath, and he tolerated no rebelliousness or wilfulness except his own.'[26] Throughout

24   Broch de Rothermann, 13–14.
25   See Lützeler, *A Biography*, 22–30.
26   Broch de Rothermann, 5.

his education and his early adulthood, Hermann could only battle his father's control 'with difficulty and without outward expression'.[27] For decades, this battle was almost entirely internal; he was not openly rebellious. Questions about love, death, ethical value and moral duty seemed to Josef unimportant and impractical; and thus, they found no place in Hermann's education, which was almost entirely technical.[28]

Josef's plans for Hermann included vocational training followed by a career in the family textile factory – the life of an upper-class industrial burgher.[29] In an outline for a proposed novel, Broch projected his relationship with his father onto the hero of the work: 'There was never a doubt about that he should succeed his father in the leadership of this business. His college years in Harvard were directed to this purpose; he was studying engineering (as ordered by his father) and economics (tolerated by his father). All the other departments and especially the humanities had the sign of "No"; they were "forbidden".[30] Instead of a classical *Gymnasium* education,

---

27　Wolfgang Rothe, 'Der junge Broch', 780. See also Hermann Broch, *Das Teesdorfer Tagebuch für Ea von Allesch*, edited by Paul Michael Lützeler (Frankfurt: Suhrkamp Verlag, 1995). From July 1920 until February 1921, Hermann Broch kept a diary, written for Ea von Allesch. These letters capture better than any other document the internal/external split that Broch had created between his life within the family/ family business and his life within Viennese salon scene.

28　Broch's education was from the beginning vocational. He began school in 1897 at the *k. k. Realschule* in Vienna's first district. After he received his *Matura* from *Realschule* in 1904, he began the study of textile weaving at the Upper School and Research Institute for the Textile Industry (*Höhere Lehr- und Versuchanstalt für Textilindustrie*). Broch studied at the weaving school until 1906 and following his primary education in Vienna he entered Mülhausener technical school for spinning and weaving in Alsace. In the summer of 1907 he received his diploma in textile engineering, as well as a patent for a cotton-mixing machine, which he had developed with Heinrich Brüggemann, director of the Mülhausener school. To view a sketch of the mixing machine see Manfred Durzak, *Hermann Broch in Selbstzeugnissen und Bilddokumenten* (Hamburg: Reinbek, 1966), 29.

29　Josef Broch, in fact, bought the Teesdorf textile factor specifically for his sons; he himself was by inclination and training a trader not an industrialist.

30　Broch, undated draft manuscript, Beinecke Rare Book and Manuscript Library MSS.

which would have better prepared him for a career in the university or laid a foundation for his literary impulses, Broch became a textile engineer.[31]

The relationship among *Gymnasium*, the university and the artistic *avant garde* was not absolute, but as Steven Beller points out it was the general rule for Jews of Broch's class to enter *Gymnasium* and to proceed to university with the aims of pursuing a professional career. As Beller argues, 'Broch's case ... is the exception which proves the rule. Throughout his life he held a grudge against his father for refusing to send him to the *Gymnasium*, precisely because going to the *Realschule* effectively barred his way to the university, and hence to the world of the intellect. His subsequent life story reads very much like an attempt to overcome this setback'.[32] Josef's decision clearly stood in contrast to the majority of his class and forced the younger Broch to find extraordinary means of entering the cadres of intellectuals within the Viennese café scene and the university.

While we cannot understand Broch's marginal relationship to mainstream Jewish intellectualism as an unassailable barrier to engaged intellectualism, it did complicate his assimilation and directed his modernist outlook to influences outside of the exclusive Jewish modernism model outlined by Beller. Beller has argued that the incomplete nature of assimilation created the intellectual world of *fin-de-siècle* Viennese modernism. The culture of Vienna 1900 was an expression of Jewish exclusivity paradoxically formed from the integrative process of assimilation. The modernist culture was an outsider's culture created as an arena for tolerance and inclusion, but populated only by those denied access to German cultural identity owing to ethnic and racial nationalism of leaders such as Schonerer and Lueger.

Beller describes this modernist culture as critical, that is, marked by an ethical and intellectual engagement with society through its 'emphasis

31   Even in the highly negative portraits of the *Gymnasium* education, which Stefan Zweig described as 'monotonous, heartless, and lifeless', the benefits of the gymnasium education in terms of preparing one for philosophical and cultural engagement are clear. See Stefan Zweig, *The World of Yesterday* (Lincoln, NE: University of Nebraska Press, 1964), 29.

32   Beller, *Revisting Vienna 1900*, 49.

on education, on the ethical side of life, and on individual responsibility'.[33]
Clearly Broch represented the key characteristics suggested by Beller here:
Jewish, outsider, ethically focused. Yet, his pursuit of the ethical was not
strictly structured by a Jewish experience. His position as a Jewish outsider
to this Jewish milieu suggests that the ethical and progressive sources of
his value system and political theory cannot be linked exclusively to the
outsider mentality of Jewish critical modernism. His experience forces
us to consider an expanded source for the creation of the ethically based
critical modernist culture – including his auto-didactic relationship to
Platonic and Kantian universalism, his religious temperament connected
to the Austrian Baroque, his troubled familial relationships and his experience of world war.

Broch's exclusion from *Gymnasium* may have, in fact, fostered his
conservativism, for not only did it ensure his position as an outsider to
Jewish modernism, it distanced him from radical political reactions to the
problems of Imperial collapse, growing nationalism and anti-Semitism.
As Marsha Rozenbilt argues, the *Gymnasium* did as much to foster an
anti-assimilationist view as an assimilationist one: 'It was the graduates
of *Gymnasium* and university who created the political and intellectual
movements which rejected the dominant assimilationist mentality of the
Viennese Jewish community in the early twentieth century. Students, mostly
at the university, first formulated Zionism and diaspora Jewish nationalism
which challenged the nineteenth-century Jewish quest for assimilation'.[34]

---

33   Steven Beller, 'What is Austrian about Austrian Culture?' in *Weltanschauungen
      des Wiener Fin de Siècle 1900/2000: Festgabe für Kurt Rudolf Fischer zum achtzigen
      Geburtstag*, Gertraud Diem-Wille, Ludwig Nagl and Friedrich Stadler, eds (Frankfurt
      am Main: Peter Lang, 2002), 35. On the idea of critical modernism also see Allan
      Janik, *Wittgenstein's Vienna Revisited* (New Brunswick, NJ: Transaction Publishers,
      2001), especially Chapter 2 on Otto Weininger.
34   Rozenbilt, 125. Rozenbilt further argues that the city of Vienna itself, while serv-
      ing as the locus for assimilation did as much to promote Jewish exclusion: 'The
      urban environment facilitated their rapid transformation, and for the most part they
      became typical Viennese burghers, but by no means did the urban setting lead to
      total assimilation and the end of Jewish group identity. On the contrary, in Vienna,
      Jews created patterns of economic and social behaviour that continued to mark them

Because Broch entered the Viennese intellectual scene from the side door with his exclusion from *Gymnasium*, his sense of being an outsider grew in respect to both the assimilationist modernism described by Beller and the anti-assimilationist political reform movements (from social democracy to Zionism).

For Rozenbilt and Beller, the social history of Viennese Jews meant a dogged commitment to the tools of assimilations and a simultaneous creation of an exclusively Jewish culture. Jewish integration, even among wealthy, liberal, secular Jews, never overcame a visible sense of exclusion. Assimilated Jewish settlement patterns, burial practices and educational paths could reflect a modern, even Christian, worldview. But, Jews pursued these activities in the community of other Jews. As Rozenbilt posits, 'Jews institutionalized their separateness and created forums for publicizing Jewish identity in Vienna'.[35] She demonstrates through her examination of birth, marriage and tax records that the Jews of Vienna certainly assimilated into the bourgeois, urban mores of nineteenth-century Vienna, but that such acculturation did not mean total assimilation or disappearance of their Jewish group identity.

Broch never assumed that his assimilation to the German *Bildung* or conversion to Catholicism equated to a full rejection of his Jewish heritage or a full integration into Imperial, aristocratic culture. Family legend held that Broch's great grandfather 'was a kind of wonder rabbi with extraordinary mathematical powers'.[36] The esteem for learning, philology and ethics was visibly present in Broch's family.[37] It can be seen in familial letters that even Broch's father, who openly rejected an education or lifestyle centred

---

as Jews both to themselves and to the outside world. Jews experienced assimilation in the company of other Jews. By living in predominantly Jewish neighbourhoods, for example, and associating mostly with each other, Jews in Vienna prevented the kind of assimilation which might have led to the dissolution of the Jewish group' (Rozenbilt, 2–3).

35   Rozenbilt, 9.
36   Lützeler, *A Biography*, 4.
37   Lützeler points out in his biography of Broch that he may have been, as Broch himself claimed to be, 'distantly related' to the philosopher Edmund Husserl, see pages 4–5.

on these concepts, was deeply imbued with a wit and intellectual depth reflective of thoughtful cultivation. Since Josef Broch left home in his early teens and immediately entered textile trading on his arrival in Vienna, it seems that his penchant for intellectual activity was spread through cultural osmosis within the Jewish community. In Broch's letters and notebooks there is repeated use of both Yiddish and Hebrew terminology, as well as cultural idioms that indicate the presence and power of the Jewish intellectual culture even in the businessman atmosphere of Josef Broch's home.[38]

Sigurd Paul Scheichl claims that Broch's ancestry played an important role in his stylization, especially in terms of his use of humour and irony. In his personal correspondence, as with his editor Daniel Brody, his use of both Yiddish and Hebrew was 'a means of intensifying his communication with a man, with whom Broch shared a common socialization and ancestry'.[39] Clearly, Broch's Judaism provided much of the cultural idiom that informed his own language, his family relationships and the general intellectual milieu of Vienna 1900.

Furthermore, Broch's letters and literary work reflected an awareness of the fractured life of the modern, assimilated Jew. The image of the Jew became for him the exemplar of the cultural degeneration of the modern age. The Jew was not the sole locus of this phenomenon but its most visible expression. In terms of *anomie* or the fracturing of community, Broch stated, 'The most important Jewish characteristic has become his "unconditionality (*Unbedingtheit*)"', which in an age of value destruction is clearly no longer justified through religion, but on the level of individual values. Broch's Jewish identity and the abstract idea of the Jew as the exemplar of

38 See Sigurd Paul Scheichl '"Nebbich noch immer Princeton Hospital", Jüdische Selbststilisierung in Brochs Briefen an Daniel Brody', and Hartmut Steinecke '"Unpersönlich bin ich ein Opfer", Jüdische Spuren im Spätwerk Hermann Brochs', in *Hermann Broch, Neue Studien: Festschrift für Paul Michael Lützeler zum 60. Geburtstag*, Michael Kessler, ed. (Stauffenburg Verlag, 2003), 362–378 and 379–394.

39 Sigurd Paul Scheichl, 378. Scheichl examines Broch's 'Jewish Stylization' in terms of his letter exchange with Daniel Brody, who was like Broch a citizen and Jew of the Austrian Empire.

modernity coloured his intellectual work from his adolescence to his exile.[40] Broch understood, in spite of his own tendency to distinguish between 'Jews and Yids',[41] that the depth of the Jewish community's historical self-awareness, even to the individual level, was so great that modernity's requirement to break with tradition meant the Jew experienced modernity in a more destructive way than most,[42] making the Jew the 'strange prototype of modern life'.[43] He goes on to state:

> And so it stands that the Jew, having lived through many centuries in a kind of stunted tradition, finds himself through emancipation transferred into a completely different stream of tradition, i.e., he is suddenly requested to reorder himself in this new world, which had been his father's and his father's father's fiercest enemy, and which with its latent hostility, as he clearly perceives, invariably maintains its opposition to him – either he recoils in fear, therefore, before this task and builds for himself a kind of freely chosen Ghetto community, a strange hermaphroditic cross between modernity and a persistently atrophying tradition, in which everyone of the so-called Jewish characteristics awkwardly hypertrophies ever rampantly; or he plunges himself with all intensity into the foreign stream of tradition, in order to make himself, through a sort of Über-assimilation, unrecognizable to himself and his neighbours.[44]

Broch suggests two paths for the modern Jewish community, both of which make the Jew exclusive in Beller's sense; yet, for all this, Broch's choices in assimilation, his commitment to European culture and his intellectual

---

40   Even if this were not the case, anti-Semitic politics under Lueger would have forced his Jewish identity back on him.

41   See Chapter 2, this volume.

42   Jacques Le Rider, *Modernity and Crises of Identity: Culture and Society in fin-de-siècle Vienna*, Rosemary Morris, tr. (Continuum Books, 1993), 6. Jacques Le Rider's work on identity in *fin-de-siècle* Vienna shows that Jews, as Broch suggests in his own work, felt the dislocation of modernity sooner and with more force than other groups. For Le Rider, this was due to the duality of identity that assimilation brings: 'The case of the assimilated Jew is more complex, for here a single individual combines, on the one hand, the non-Jew with his identity pathology and, on the other, the Jew with his forgotten Judaism and the Jewishness of his actual experience, in short, the "imaginary Jew".'

43   Broch, *KW* 12, 399.

44   Ibid, 394.

goals remained defined by the choice of the universal over the particular. Where exclusion was most self-evident in him was in his sense of exclusion from the intellectual debate over the modernist dilemma. It was an exclusion that generated a sense of failure and impotence, not community or creativity. Broch's emphasis on the universal over the particular can be seen in the third volume of *The Sleepwalkers* where the collapse of community is not highlighted by the exclusive community of Jews discussed in the 'Salvation Army Girl' flashback, but in the sense of community found in the novel's final lines. This is a sense of community that is absolute in form and clearly Christian and Platonic.

Broch sought in his early attraction to Catholicism a connection to the beauty and tradition of the Baroque. It was a universal, artistic justification for a socially consistent and stable world, something lacking in his interpersonal relationships in his own household and in the perpetual mobility of his family's social positioning. Catholicism provided a harmony of existence between duty and the individual experience of love. Philosophically, Platonism played this same role for Broch, ordering the earthly life through eternal beauty. In an outline for a proposed novel (written in 1947), *The Victorious Defeat*, Broch sketched the familial background of the novel's hero.[45] The outline suggests an autobiographical insight to Broch's own relationship to his family and to conversion – such autobiographical allusions are visible in much of Broch's work. In this case, we must read 'Jew' for 'Protestant' in the last sentence:

> The cult of the Virgin in Catholicism touches him suddenly, and for a moment he thinks that this sensation is the grace (about which he never had the slightest real idea). He begins to attend Catholic services, and these secret church visits are a repetition of his secret readings in the library of his parents. He doesn't know that it is a repetition, but he feels himself in the same mood, and there is also the mood of opposition against his father in it. However, it is just this parallelism which is one of the causes for the failure of his catholic experiment: he couldn't become the poet, he

45 Broch presented the outline to the American novelist Francis Colby as a possible project for her. The outline is in the Broch Archive at the Beinecke Library, Yale and can be found in a footnote to Broch's letter to Erich von Kahler, Broch, *KW* 13/3, 173.

wished to be during his boyhood, and now he can't become the Catholic believer; instead of being a poet he is preparing himself for entering in the family business, and instead of changing religion he remains a Protestant [a Jew][46] like his ancestors.[47]

The passage suggests that Broch's conversion was an honest but failed attempt to define his intellectual and spiritual world based on emotional responses to the context around him.[48] In his 'Disintegration of Values',[49] Broch separated both Judaism and Protestantism from Catholicism. He separated 'the Catholic harmony of values' from 'absolute Protestantism which involves abasement before an abstract God'. And it is the Jew who exemplifies this separation most:

> The Jew, by virtue of the abstract rigour of his conception of infinity, is the really modern, the most 'advanced' man *kat' exochen*: he it is who surrenders himself with absolute radicality to whatever system of values, whatever career he has chosen; he it is who raises his profession, even though it be a means of livelihood taken up by chance, to a hitherto unknown absolute pitch; he it is who, unconditionally and ruthlessly following up his actions without reference to any other system of values, attains the highest summit of spiritual enlightenment or sinks to the most brutal absorption in material things: in good as in evil a creature of extremes – it looks as though the current of the absolute Abstract which for two thousand years has flowed through the ghettoes like an almost imperceptible trickle beside the great river of life should now become the main stream; it is as if the radicality of Protestant thought had inflamed to virulence all the dread ruthlessness of abstraction which for two thousand years had been sheltered by insignificance and reduced it to its minimum, as if it had released that absolute power of indefinite extension which inheres potentially in the pure Abstract alone, released it explosively to shatter our age and transform the hitherto unregarded warden of abstract thought into the paradigmatic incarnation of our disintegrating epoch.[50]

---

46   My addition.
47   *KW* 13/3, 173.
48   For a discussion of Catholicism in Broch's writing see Richard Brinkmann, 'On Broch's Concept of Symbol', in Stephen D. Dowden, ed., *Hermann Broch: Literature, Philosophy, Politics* (Columbia, SC: Camden Books, 1988), 193–206.
49   Broch, *The Sleepwalkers*, 525–529.
50   Ibid, 526.

Broch's critical stance toward the 'neutralization of the religious experience' suggested that his early, albeit failed, attraction to Catholicism reflected an intellectual conservativism and an intellectual commitment to Austrian tradition – Catholic and Baroque.

His characterization of the psychic split caused by Judaism also reflected two extreme views of the Jew in nineteenth-century Vienna, one clearly reminiscent of his father (materialistic businessman) and the other reminiscent of himself (a Christian mystic). Broch came to understand his conversion as a playing out of the Oedipal battle of father and son, which he believed characterized his entire relationship to his father. David Luft observes a similar spiritual impulse towards Christianity and away from Judaism in the conflicted personality of Otto Weininger.[51] Catholicism never produced the ultimate source of value for Broch, but it exposed an essential conservatism in his thought. The problem, in the end, was that Catholicism's access to a universalizing power came only through obedience to a Church structure that had lost its claims to value creation through the social hypertrophy of late Middle Ages – the Inquisition and the Counter-Reformation.

After the failure of Catholicism, Broch's solution would have to emerge from the region of the individual. It was here that his Christian Platonism met Kant's moral philosophy. Broch located the space for the modern 'conversion process' in the individual ego.[52] This time conversion would not be religious, but secular and humanistic. Kant was not his only guide to the ego; psychology (both in terms of Freud and Alder) also played a part. It was also in his developing Kantian thought that the basis for the individual as the source of value production came. As seen from his limited political writing from the period of the First World War, Kant played a significant role in the formation of Broch's human centred political theory.

---

51   David S. Luft, *Eros and Inwardness* (Chicago: University of Chicago Press, 2003), see especially Chapter 2.
52   See *KW* 12, 331–455.

Sexuality and the Irrational in Broch

Broch understood his ethical creation as a merger of various human attributes, both rational and irrational. He examined his own sexual maturity
from the point of view of ethical creation and used his experiences to
conceptualize the conflicting demands of rationality and irrationality on
ethics. The themes of individual psychic development, confrontation with
death and the establishment of an ethical humanitarianism became not
only features of Broch's intellectual worldview, they were also expressions
of the constraints and the demands of his life. In his autobiographical
works he transferred his ideas on cultural criticism to the personal realm:
the importance of totality – but a mystical notion of soul mates in place
of a Platonic good, the disruptive force of irrationality – but the fear of
humiliation in place of the fear of death, the tendency for hypertrophy –
but excessive philandering in place of mass hysterical actions (in both cases
the rational ego slipped into a 'twilight consciousness'), and responsibility
– but defined by the duty to provide emotional or sexual satisfaction in
place of the civic duty to protect fellow citizens.

His search for a Platonic, eternal truth pushed him psychically towards
the role of saint (though physically he acted more in accord with a young
Augustine than an older one):

> As a little boy – and that was one of the roots of my neurosis – I saw the grotesque
> day-dream, in which all adults were living, needless to say my parents too, and decided
> never to be the prey of a day-dream. What people call love, friendship, etc. is the
> partaking in a common day-dream, and since I didn't permit a day-dream to myself,
> I couldn't share it with others. (And nobody could impose his day-dreams on me.)
> Well, the result was that I couldn't 'love', and that for all those who are unable to go
> under the first surface of things and are operating in their easy way with 'love' etc –
> and also 'tragic' is an easy way – I seem to be 'cynical'; I can take it, for cynicism of
> that kind is the first step to truth and, therefore, to holiness.[53]

53   Broch, undated draft manuscript, Hermann Broch Archive. Yale Collection of
     German Literature, Beinecke Rare Book and Manuscript Library. The influence of
     Otto Weininger is most evident here. Through both Schopenhauer and Weininger,

Concepts such as the ego, duty, alienation, impotence, stability and dignity played an integral part in Broch's political theory. What we find here is a foundation for these ideas in his relationship to his family. He defined his relationship with his father and brother in terms of masculinity and power, and with his mother through sexuality and guilt. These relationships mirrored the conflicts of his assimilation and maturation described above by way of a defined and prolonged feeling of failure and disappointment in regards to his family.

From 1941 to 1943 Hermann Broch composed three autobiographical sketches: 'Autobiography as a Program of Work' (*Autobiographie als Arbeitsprogramm*), 'Self-psychoanalysis' (*Psychische Selbstbiographie*) and 'An Addendum to my Self-psychoanalysis' (*Nachtrag zu meiner psychischen Selbstbiographie*).[54] The consideration of the three works side by side shows the underlying unity of sexuality and epistemology in Broch's political and ethical theory. The three texts offer tangible proof that Broch's faith in the power of individual self-regulation was not simply a theoretical notion; furthermore, they demonstrate the degree to which his early psychic development informed, in a visceral way, his theoretical work.

The connection between his exploration of psychic sexual development and the growth of an intellectual *Weltanschauung* is an important step towards understanding the intellectual development of both Broch and of his milieu. Simply the decision to write autobiographical works that integrated intellectual goals and sex demonstrates this link. The works show

---

Broch carved out from his sexual neurosis a value system in which the role of spirituality and asceticism were central. In his book *Sex and Character*, Weininger focused his criticism on the two elements of modern society that were most responsible for its present state of degeneration: the woman and the Jew. In Broch's earliest work from the 1910s, Weininger's influence was limited to Broch's cultural criticism: the notions of degeneration (often expressed with sexualized vocabulary) and the role of the individual in creating value. Broch did not acknowledge or employ Weininger's critique of the Jew in either his early or his later writing.

54   The three self-reflective texts, which remained unpublished until 1999, were, as editor Paul Michael Lützeler points out, never conceived of as autobiographical in the general sense of the term. Paul Michael Lützeler, ed., *Psychische Selbstbiographie* (Frankfurt am Main: Suhrkamp Verlag, 1999), 145–146.

that Broch's intellectual metaphors, his literary and political goals, and his corporeal and mental touchstones were developed early in his life. And that the key historical experiences of his epoch – modernity, genocide and world war – serve as intellectual fulcrums for the bending and repackaging of a deeply felt and unbreakable connection to the individual's notions of duty and responsibility.

'Autobiography as a Program of Work' (1941) was the longest of the three autobiographical works, twice as long as the other two works combined. In published form it is just over sixty-five pages. The text was an outline of Broch's intellectual efforts to come to terms with the problem of ethical relativism in European society during the late nineteenth and early twentieth centuries. It was an explanation of the loss of ethical value in Europe, and the resulting world war. As he states at the opening of the work:

> This is not so much an autobiography, as it is an attempt to explain the history of a problem, which by pure chance is similar to my own problem, since I – like anyone from my generation who was willing to recognize it, have always held this problem before my eyes: it is, straightforwardly speaking, the problem of the destruction of the absolute, the problem of relativity, wherein there is no absolute truth, no absolute value and therein also no absolute ethic, presently, it is the problem and phenomenon of a gigantic Machiavellianism, which has been, in a spiritual sense, developing for some fifty years and whose apocalyptical legacy we are experiencing today in reality.[55]

The biography developed chronologically, starting with his essays on epistemology and ethics in the 1920s and moving to his literary work of the 1930s, especially *The Death of Virgil*, then his political theories of the forties, and finally his work on mass hysteria, which he was working on simultaneously to the autobiography. In many ways, the autobiography was a means for clarifying the problem he was attempting to solve in his work on mass hysteria.[56]

---

55   *Psychische Selbstbiographie*, 83.
56   As Christine Mondon states, 'Although the theory of mass hysteria has its roots in the Second World War, it does not refer simply to this limited and specific historical experience, rather it investigates the psychological and sociological development of history, which is characterized by the eruption of the Mass. The Masses, which

Broch's 'Self-psychoanalysis' (1942) was written as a letter to two women. The thirty-two single-spaced typed pages with a nine-page addendum added the following year can be found in the correspondence of both women: Ruth Norden and Annemarie Meier-Graefe, his second wife. The letter was an explanation of Broch's sexual relationships. It explored the psychic foundations for his relationship to women, to his work and to the world. The letter was written just before Broch restarted analysis with Paul Federn, and he hoped to prepare himself for the process by discussing a key metaphor found in all his writing, the notion of isolation. While isolation and the 'Loneliness of I' were important and necessary components of value production, they were on an individual level the source of Broch's neurosis: 'My fear of becoming isolated is a most painful feeling of loneliness that always accompanies me'.[57] He saw the tension between a sense of duty to others (here set in the realm of sexuality) and a feeling of impotence as the source of his neurosis, and he showed very little faith in being able to resolve the tension. Ultimately, he never did.[58]

Certainly, one cannot investigate Broch's account of his sexual development without considering the role of Viennese psychological theory. The influence of Adler and Freud in Broch's later political theory was evident in his language of duty and ego expansion/diminution and the Oedipal discussion of impotence and guilt. His awareness of psychoanalysis is clear from his letters and his philosophical work of the 1930s. Broch living in Vienna knew Freud's theory well. He began his own psychoanalysis in 1927 and

---

are the passive agents of history, represent the depletion of rationalism by pseudo-rational concepts of instinctual and impulse driven attitudes. Broch's proposal is to describe in an objectively perfect way these irrational and pathological features' (519). 'Hermann Broch und die Psychoananlyse', in *Hermann Broch, Neue Studien: Festschrift für Paul Michael Lützeler zum 60. Geburtstag* (Tübingen: Stauffenburg Verlag, 2003), 510–523.

57   *Psychische Selbstbiographie* , 17.

58   Broch makes it clear in his letters from exile that his experience of psychoanalysis in Vienna was an intellectual education (*bloss ein theoretisches Wissen*), but not one that offered him a sense of healing or overcoming of his neuroses. Letter to Ernst Polak, March 26, 1946 quoted from Roberto Rizzo's article 'Psychoanalyse eines pädagogischen Eros', in *Hermann Broch, Neue Studien*, 555.

continued it in the United States.[59] Psychoanalysis also flavoured Broch's memory of his childhood.[60] He also maintained a friendship with Alfred Adler. As Robert Rizzo argues, Broch's 'Self-Psychoanalysis' demonstrates that his ethical and political impulses reflected an understanding of sexuality found in Adler's theories. Broch's lack of engagement with his family in terms of love, combined with his deep and early awareness of his own ego, led to an individual feeling of inferiority and a constant turn to overcompensation. But it was also the source of his persistent democratic tendencies. His individual ego was complete only in terms of its relationship to others. In exile, this axis between the individual and the group (mass society, family, state) became the salient idea in his theory of mass delusion. Rizzo connects this axis directly to the influence of Adler's thought, he points out that Broch's focus on his feeling of duty toward not only family, but society at large was Adlerian not just in theme, but even in its vocabulary of overcompensation.[61] When Broch did engage Freud, he did so not simply to take on Freud's paradigms. He attempted to branch out from Freud's focus on neurosis and sexuality. Broch's theory of the ego for instance did not rest on the division of the psyche into two key drives (Love/Death). He divided his model of the psyche into three specific aspects: the Core-ego (*Ich-Kern*), the Body-ego (*Körper-Ich*) and the psychological ego (*psychologisches-Ich*).[62] He discussed directly his understanding of Freud's theory and his differences from it in his 1936 treatise, 'Remarks on Psychoanalysis from the Perspective of Value Theory'.[63] Mondon summarizes Broch's ego theory as follows, 'The Ego-Source discovers its relationship to the outside world through the corporeal-Ego, while the psychological-Ego appears as

---

59 Broch's analyst in Vienna was Hedwig Schaxel-Hoffer (see Lützeler, *A Biography*, 67) and in the United States Paul Federn (see correspondence between Broch and Federn in Beinecke Library).

60 See Paul Michael Lützeler's biography, as well as articles by Roberto Rizzo, Ch. Mondon and Monika Ritzer in *Hermann Broch, Neue Studien*.

61 Rizzo, 565.

62 See *KW* 10/2, 179–183.

63 Ibid, 173–194.

a facilitator for both entities'.[64] In his model of the mind, the influence was much more Husserlian than psychoanalytical.[65] It was a vision of human consciousness that was close to Sartre's later tripartite division of the mind into 'being for itself', 'being itself' and 'being for others'. It is not surprising that both Broch and Sartre took a humanist approach to the relationship of the human consciousness and the external world and found freedom to be closely connected to duty.

Broch's central concern was to understand the psyche through reference to value theory. He underwent psychoanalysis, and he saw his own sexual relationship in Freudian terms, especially the notions of guilt and sublimation. He even hoped to add to the psycho-sexual vocabulary of analysis with his term *Amphitryonismus*.[66] For Broch, however, the arena of the psyche was not limited to therapy or to the individual. Indeed, cultural criticism, mathematics, literature, even epistemology served a similar purpose to that of his psychoanalysis; they served to reconcile a spiritual, almost mystical vision of the world (in terms of both love and cosmological unity) and an isolated, frustrated experience of the world (seen in the relationship to his family and the limitations of his education).[67] In this way, his psychic theories not only highlight Freud's immense presence in Vienna, but also suggest variability of psychological and cognitive debate there.

Broch tied his opposition between sexuality and rationality to the explicit tension within his own family. He portrayed the relationship in Oedipal terms – in a contest for the attention/love of his mother, he battled

---

64   Monton, 517.

65   Ibid, 516.

66   The term referred to Broch's own sexual neurosis and was characterized by his passionate pursuit 'to reform [his] partner to [an] ideal image', *Psychische Selbstbiographie*, 17; see as well as Lützeler's 'Nachwort' in *Psychische Selbstbiographe*, 167–169.

67   As Mondon states, 'He [Broch] seeks in the image in the mirror to overcome the feeling of inferiority established in his childhood and to regain a lost identity. We have on the one hand the revolt against the standards of the paternal order, the other hand the tendency to over compensation of the Ego. Broch tries in vain his entire life to reach the identity between his Ego and his ideal picture and this apparent, hoped for identity, he was able to reconstruct through the language' (512–513).

and utterly failed against both his father and his brother.[68] The failure left
him with a feeling of inferiority and impotence.

> This is the picture of a terrible feeling of inferiority. That this arose from some humili-
> ation (*Niederlage* – defeat) in early childhood in relation to my father as well as my
> brother with regard to my mother's love, must remain unquestioned. As far back as
> I can remember, I have regarded myself in contrast to these two men as an Un-man,
> as 'impotent'. That I am completely impotent at base, even in the physical sense, is
> a perception that ineradicably accompanied me for my entire life – despite all evi-
> dence to the contrary.[69]

The relationship of Broch to his father, mother and brother in his youth
profoundly affected much of Broch's future life: his physical weakness in
terms of intestinal disease, as well as the accompanying hypochondria, his
dysfunctional relationship to women, and his psychic imbalance in terms
of guilt and obligation. Broch turned these competing psychic forces into
the basis for his own personal sense of tragedy:

> Furthermore, I told you that I am paying too much for everything in my earthly
> life: I pay too much for every relationship, I pay too much for every pleasure, I pay
> too much even for my work – the blanket is too short, and either the feet or the
> shoulders are cold. And so I have to pay with my work for my lust, with my pleasures
> for my human relationships, with my relations for my work, and vice versa: always
> a part is used for payments, and as no accountancies can work without cash, I have
> my additional currency in the pains of my *Bauch* [belly].[70]

Broch's ability, his need, to undercut his own physicality further exposed
a strong sense of impotence in his makeup. He was physically an imposing
figure with a large framed body and strong, handsomely angular face. He
was, however, characterized in letters and pictures as physically frail, his
large frame bent over so that he never reached his full height. Though an

---

68   'The childhood experience that stamped me as an impotent Un-man, in comparison
      with those two men, my father and my brother ...' *Psychische Selbstbiographie*, 17.
69   Ibid, 8.
70   Letter to Jean Untermeyer Starr Hermann Broch Archive. Yale Collection of German
      Literature, Beinecke Rare Book and Manuscript Library.

avid hiker, he was described in his own words as constantly battling to free his mind from the weakness and limitation of his body.

Broch lived the last twenty years of his life on an almost constant death watch. 'I find myself in one of the most miserable periods of my life', he worried in a letter to Hannah Arendt, 'too many years behind me, and too few ahead'.[71] In a memoir focused on his father, H. F. Broch de Rothermann states, 'In retrospect it seems that his whole life was overshadowed and defined by a frantic race with time: I can't remember a moment when I might not hear him say, in a tortured voice, "No time, no time, no time!" ... He wrote a letter to me in Austria (in English) in 1949: "I have no margin for life – I have but a margin for death"'.[72] The tragic aura that came to define him was the outcome of a lifelong neurosis that developed from his early childhood. He would further acknowledge that the neurosis played a significant role in his infidelity and his failed attempts at emotional relationships.[73]

It can be argued as well, and Broch himself implied it, that his sexual neurosis played a significant role in the formation of his intellectual pursuits.

> My life is accompanied and burdened with a permanent moral conflict. [...] Certainly work is for me a very positive thing, and in one way it is 'pleasurable' to me; but this proceeds not only in the form of the most difficult and bitter addiction and enslavement, it can be established only under prescribed and burdensome conditions: one of these is that the magnitude of the task that I set myself mounts beyond my strength, the other of these is that I am also not free in making my choice of tasks, that is, they were laid on me as a superimposed duty. [...] this is the picture of a terrible feeling of inferiority [...] As is the case with all feelings of inferiority, this also led to overcompensations: a) Assurance of masculinity through continually new love b) rejection of

---

71 Letter to Hannah Arendt, 22 January 1947, in Hermann Broch and Hannah Arendt, *Briefwechsel 1946 bis 1951*, edited by Paul Michael Lützeler (Frankfurt am Main: Jüdischer Verlag, 1996), 29.

72 Broch de Rothermann, 2–3.

73 'It goes without saying that all this looms especially large in my relations with people. My behaviour with those near me is timid and shy, and this is to be overcome only with the greatest of trouble. [...] The almost physical torment that I suffered in my connection with my fellow-men has not changed since my earliest youth' (*Psychische Selbstbiographie*, 9).

this sort of assurance – return of original humiliation and then a constant reversion
to asceticism as a chosen form of life c) extending impotence to over compensation
in family relationships d) stretching out family responsibility to every one of my
human relationships, to a collective responsibility for humanity and truth.[74]

Broch employed his own sexual neurosis as a case study for the liberation of
the ego from masochistic cycle of conquest followed by self-annihilation.
He carried with him a sense that he constantly disappointed all those who
loved him. The cycle of disappointment (the lack of emotional access to
his mother, his sexual attraction to 'unfit' lovers such as maids and gov-
ernesses, his divorce and his constant infidelities) followed by outbursts
of over-compensation (his failed attempts of living a dual life, his search
for absolute knowledge, his commitment to rescue efforts during the war
and, again, his constant infidelities) fed a neurosis that eventually led him
to categorize sexual relationships as ephemeral and false.

The symbolic importance of sexuality as a means for conceiving of
abstract notions within the aesthetic, ideological and ethical world of turn-
of-the-century Vienna has been demonstrated by David Luft's work on Otto
Weininger, Robert Musil and Heimito von Doderer. The importance of
sexuality for other intellectuals of the time, such as Freud or Schnitzler, goes
without saying. Through the influence of Weininger and Schopenhauer,
Broch applied his childhood sexual preconceptions to the realm of values
and value construction. The connection between Broch's theoretical and
sexual worlds tells us a great deal about the role male-gendered notions
of thought, especially science, played in the Viennese world of his youth.
Although the neurotic division of love and sex was set out in his childhood household, it would later be reinforced in the Viennese world of the
café house. For, while café houses were the source of Broch's sexual liberation around the time of the war, they were simultaneously the source of
his problematic notions of the separation of mind and body. Broch saw
knowledge, mathematics and science as pure, eternal and ascetic, while he
viewed sexual or emotional attachments as dirty and valueless (in the sense
of *kitsch*). Although Broch did not explicitly tie the untidiness of physical

74   Ibid, 7.

sex to the female – in his own erotic life (as seen through his letters to various lovers) the link was clearly implied.

In his 'Self-psychoanalysis', Broch openly laid out his process of objectification of his partners. He saw his emotional relationships as sources of conflict whose only resolution was to define the relationship through objective, rational criteria. Broch attempted in this objectification to limit the role of sex. He feared the public recognition of sexual motivation: 'These go so far, for instance, that I only want to be seen in public with a tall woman, confessedly because I fear that everyone would know that I had chosen a small one only for pleasure in bed'.[75] Broch, furthermore, acknowledged that he attempted not only to control the parameters of the relationships, but even to conceive anew the nature of the object. 'I plagued myself with the question why only young and lovely women should be the means of arousing potency, why not the old and ugly, yes, why should not the old man (Socrates) have the same purpose, especially as the qualities of soul and spirit have far more objective and enduring worth than the aesthetic ones'.[76] Here he most blatantly pursued a line of logic that separates objectively male and female quantities: the separation of the ethereal realm of the mind from the earthly realm of the body. As he alluded to, the separation of morality and sexuality did not drive him to an ascetic lifestyle, his continued search to prove his potency went on unabated throughout his life.

His sexual experience did not, however, change the ideal of separation. 'I have functioned best in those relationships where I was successful in keeping afar the whole moral muddle, and concentrating myself on the purely erotic'.[77] While Broch attempted to balance the demands of isolation within his intellectual pursuits and his critical humanism, such strict divisions between moral and erotic, dirty and clean, ephemeral and eternal, worldly and spiritual only reinforced his social, class and economic

---

75   Ibid, 12.
76   Ibid, 14–15. He continues, 'and though this has not developed in me as far as homosexuality, I have often enough let myself be chosen by old and ugly women, especially when there was a possibility of discovering in them a Socratic soul or any other spiritual qualities, or to develop in them just these qualities'.
77   Ibid, 15.

tendency for isolation. These psychic and intellectual divisions invited increased intolerance for dirty or empty aspects of Viennese society: mass politics, aestheticism and conflict.

Liberalism

At the foundation of Broch's political theory was a desire for the security of the individual. Democratic societies offered the most humane and ethical principles for allowing the individual the freedom and autonomy to act or negotiate their social world. His theory of total democracy was based on the legal regulation of such negotiations and citizen interactions, that is, punishing citizens who use violence or intimidation against fellow citizens. The dream of a lone ego secured and empowered to pursue its own happiness reflected the emotional striving of a young man attempting to fashion an individual identity in the midst of being a Jew in a Christian Empire and a repressed son in the oppressive world of his father.

Much like David Luft argued for Robert Musil, the explanation for Broch's concern, whether aesthetic or political, for finding an ethical and democratic basis for Central European society is generational. He came of age in a liberal and enlightened culture. His father had come to Vienna during a period of rapid expansion and a high rate of assimilation among Jewish families. This was the period of liberal ascendancy.[78] The liberal generation was marked by individualism and laissez faire economics and by a commitment to democratic, constitutional government. This commitment also meant commitment to bureaucracy and the Court as a vehicle for

[78]   By the time of his son's birth, however, the influence of liberalism as a political force in Vienna had started to wane, and by 1890 the Christian Socialist party of Lueger had gained control of Viennese politics and would hold a position of dominance until 1914. 'German liberalism's brief period of dominance in the Reichsrat came to an end in 1879, and the prospects of liberalism dimmed still further with the emergence of the mass parties in the 1880s' (Luft, *Robert Musil*, 11).

stability. Paradoxically, however, liberalism's commitment to democracy and individualism was exclusive and elitist. Inclusion in the political sphere, which was envisioned and developed during the period of liberal ascendancy, required a commitment to business and to a cultural and bureaucratic society based on Germanic ideals. For Jews, this meant that they would need to assimilate to the German culture. The model for such assimilation was already in place in Vienna within the limited and tightly restricted community of *Vörmarz* Jews. For Hermann Broch, the ties among assimilated Jews, the rising liberal parties and the monarchy would not prove to be a model for his own political engagement. It would, however, inundate his thought with clear links between democracy and individualism. As the relationship between Broch and his father demonstrated, he could reject the underlying importance of economics in such an association, while retaining the notion of the individual as a force for liberation.

At his birth, both the Empire and the city of Vienna were in transition. The demographic shifts in Vienna over the middle decades of the nineteenth century turned the city into a vastly different place, both demographically and ethnically. In size, Vienna grew from a city of several hundred thousand to a city of over one million between 1848 and 1900. The source of this immigration was diverse with Jewish immigration representing more than 20 per cent of the growth. The Jewish population grew from several thousand to over forty thousand during this same period, eventually representing 10 per cent of the overall population. The Jewish population in 1847 was only a couple of thousand in Vienna, but 1910 it was over 175,000. Although the general size of the Viennese population was increasing as well, from 400,000 to almost 2 million, the percentage of Jewish representation grew from under 2 per cent to almost 9 per cent.[79]

Until the nineteenth century, Vienna's Jewish population was contained in the second district (across the Danube channel from the city centre). By the time of Broch's birth, however, the wealthier Jewish citizens had moved into either the first or ninth districts. The expansion of the Jewish population accompanied a major refashioning of the city. In

79   See Rozenbilt, 16–18.

the middle decades of the nineteenth century, the monarchy approved a rebuilding plan designed to modernize the city's appearance and to incorporate the inner city with the outer districts. Until this point, a mediaeval wall and a large military glacis separated the city centre from the outer districts. Vienna appeared and functioned as a mediaeval city. The main thrust of the rebuilding program was the creation of a grand, circular boulevard, the *Ringstrasse*, which served as the main thoroughfare for moving around the city. The building program also reflected the changing political makeup of the city; as Carl Schorske points out, the construction of the Parliament building, city hall, the citizen's theatre and the University along the *Ringstrasse* mirrored the growing influence of the middle class in Viennese politics and commerce.[80]

Like the *Ringstrasse*, the rise of liberalism brought with it the refashioning of the Viennese Jewish community. It seemed to signal a new era in Austrian Jewish history, a movement out of the mediaeval ghetto into the modern metropolis. In reality, it only marked the beginning of a chapter whose tragic ending far outpaced the tragedies of the past. Three times in Viennese history, anti-Semitism led to the expulsion of Jews. The first time was in 1421, when a pogrom led to the execution, expulsion, or forced conversion of the entire population. There is today in *Lessingplatz*, a plaque, written in Latin and celebrating the event. By the middle of the seventeenth century, the Viennese court allowed the re-establishment of a small and highly relegated community of Jews just across the Danube (*Leopoldstadt*). This small community of 'tolerated' Jews (only 500 families) was highly important for the financial operations of the court. However, the visible success of the trans-Danube community increased anti-Semitic feeling. In 1670, Leopold I had the community expelled. The destruction of the Jewish community this time was short lived because of the financial vacuum caused by their absence. In 1693, Leopold reopened Vienna to Jews, but

---

80   This is most clearly seen in the neo-classical architectural allusions to ancient republicanism. See Carl Schorske, *Fin de Siècle* (New York: Vintage, 1980), 24–115.

confined the community to an even smaller section of the city with more restrictions on movement and heavy taxes.[81]

The enlightened reforms of the Josephist Era (1780–1790) initially provided greater legal freedom to Jews within the Habsburg Empire.[82] These freedoms, however, were very limited. When combined with the conservative, Catholic nature of the Metternich era and the Emperors Francis I and Ferdinand I, the *Vormärz* era (pre-1848) reflected a very ambiguous period of Jewish acceptance in Viennese society. Overall, during the period between the Josephist Reforms and the 1848 revolutions, Austria was far behind most of Europe in terms of Jewish emancipation. What developments did take place, took place in the realm of the wealthy banker and merchant class Jews, including an advancement of the German culture (*Bildung*) as the central tool for Jewish assimilation. It was not, however, until the rise of liberal constitutionalism following 1848 and its gaining ascendancy in the 1860s that a broad avenue for immigration, as well as economic and social integration opened for Jewish community.[83]

Although the monarchy had re-established conservative control of the Empire following the liberal revolutions of 1848, the revolutions were not without their effects on subsequent liberals. The new monarch, Franz Joseph I, recognized the new political forces of the bourgeoisie. His policy over the next decades, especially as external military defeats weakened his international position, created a space for liberal political advancement. The liberal parties in Vienna grew up around the remnants of the 1848

81   Robert Kann, *A History of the Habsburg Empire, 1526–1918* (Berkeley: University of California Press, 1974).

82   1781 Tolerance Act and the subsequent 1782 Patent of Tolerance removed many of legal restrictions surrounding schooling, apprenticeship and freedom of movement for Jews. See Berkeley, 30–31. Berkeley also makes clear that some of the Josephist Reforms (the requirement of military service, the adaptation of German last names and abolition of rabbinical courts) had the effect of forcing assimilation on Jews within the Empire, a fact that served to alienate the provincial Jewish population.

83   From 1781 until 1938, Vienna's Jews experienced increasing emancipation, but, with the annexation of Austria by Germany in 1938, the Jewish community of Vienna was once again destroyed, either by forced migration or removal to labour and death camps.

Revolutions. Their basic makeup was parliamentarian, middle class and German.

The political upheavals of the Empire had particular repercussions in Vienna and for young Josef Broch on his arrival in Vienna in the mid-1860s. The weakened position of Austria as a German power and the political effects of that weakness in terms of the Crown's internal power provided liberals with the opportunity for political advancement through coopera-tion with the monarchy. In hindsight, Josef Broch's worldview, his chosen path of assimilation (money and monarchy) offered some shelter from the disillusionment of failed cosmopolitanism. It could not, however, offer any shelter from the terror of National Socialism. And it did not, in the end, offer Hermann Broch a model for his own worldview, though it did instil a sense of duty in Broch that occupied a majority of his energies for the first two-thirds of his life.[84]

From the 1860s, liberal expansion in terms of economics and politics and culture suggested a modernization of Austrian society and established a tradition of progressive, rational governance within large sections of a growing middle class. This expansion was halted by the economic depres-sion of 1873. After 1873, progressive aspects of Austrian liberalism would splinter from the Liberal party itself. Germanic culture, now packaged through nationalism, would also reject enlightened ideas of cosmopoli-tanism, tolerance and assimilation. The Liberal party itself would retain a strong foundation within Austrian politics. It did so, however, through a shift in demographic focus from bourgeois to artisan/farmers and from city to countryside.[85] Within Vienna, democratic and progressive ideas lost traction as the adherents of classical nineteenth-century liberalism isolated them through close ties to the monarchy and exclusionary (anti-democratic) political platforms. The collapse of a democratic, modern political option

84   To be discussed in detail below, Broch's sense of duty was born from a contestation between his attempts to live the life of his father's choosing, while simultaneously pursuing his own desires to be a thinker and artist. Broch would eventually translate the series of approvals and disappointments that marked his life into a theory of potency and impotence.
85   See Pieter Judson, *Exclusive Revolutionaries*, as well as the discussion below.

alienated the generations of young Viennese born between the 1850 and 1900 (including Broch), because they came to recognize that the world in which they were raised was quickly fading. Schorske's thesis on the development of modernism in Vienna effectively expresses the awareness of crisis in the generation of artists and politicians who came of age at the turn of the nineteenth century.[86]

The nature of Jewish participation and assimilation in Vienna over the course of the late nineteenth century demonstrated the influence of two key factors: first, the legacy of *Vormärz* Jewish advancements in the guise of the *Hofjuden* (wealthy, Germanic and assimilationist); secondly, the political relationship between the Monarchy and the rising liberal parties. The preponderance of assimilationist ideology within the Jewish merchant class, to which Josef Broch belonged, can be attributed to the presumed class affinity between Moravian and Bohemian Jewish immigrants and the *Vormärz Hofjuden*. The connection between the Jewish middle class and liberalism on the other hand was the result of political developments in the middle years of the nineteenth century. As Malachi Hacohen states, 'The Austrian *Staatsgedanke* offered a patriotism the underlying rationale of which was not ethnonational but multinational, making Jewish participation unproblematic. It gave Jews an opportunity missing elsewhere for negotiating Jewish and national identity, and this became crucial once rifts opened between them and the Germans'.[87] Friedlander's examination of Jewish politics shows that the last bastion of nineteenth-century liberal beliefs (progressivism, individualism, positivism and cosmopolitanism) came in the guise of the Jewish *Kultusgemeinschaft* as late the middle 1930s. The legacy of such progressivism and cosmopolitanism was still visible in the post-Anschluss world of Viennese exiles, including Karl Popper and Hermann Broch.

---

86   Carl Schorske, *Fin de Siècle Vienna*, 24–112.
87   Hacohen, *Karl Popper*, 49. Steven Beller also acknowledges the close relationship between liberalism, the Enlightenment and Jewish assimilation, 'The Fortunes of the Jewish emancipation were intimately bound up with those of the political expression of the Enlightenment: liberalism' (Beller, *Vienna 1900*, 122).

The exclusion of Austria from Germany only increased the internal problems of the Empire. Since Joseph II's reign, German had been the official language of the Empire, and Germanic norms remained the dominant cultural force within the university, the bureaucracy and the Court. The lack of any role in the establishment of a proper German state within Europe lengthened the divide within the Habsburg lands between German or German assimilated subjects and the non-Germans.[88] German *Bildung* polarized a large portion of the Empire's population between those who saw the German direction of the Empire as chauvinistic and detrimental to Imperial unity (the Magyars, the Czechs, the Ruthenians, the Poles, the Slovenes and other non-Germans) and those who pushed for a union of the Germanic lands of the Empire with the new German state (German nationalists). In this polarized political atmosphere, the liberals, not seeing any contradiction between their ideology of individual freedom and nationalism, turned toward the latter. They set aside their revolutionary, democratic positions and moved closer to one of *Realpolitik* and aristocratic support.

The linkage of Jewish emancipation to liberal ascendency helps explain the failure of Jewish emancipation in the interwar period. The changing political platform of the Liberal Party from the 1890s to *Anschluss*, driven by nationalism and mass politics and fuelled by anti-Semitism, pushed the Jewish political groups, which wished to sustain cosmopolitanism as a goal, closer to the monarchy and the idea of Empire.[89] This left Jewish futures linked to Imperial futures. By the mid-century, Habsburg political

---

88 The loss of German hegemony and the loss of Italy in 1859 added to the internal pressure of the monarchy as well. In 1867 the monarchy and the Hungarians established a compromise (*Ausgleich*) that established the Kingdom of Hungary as an independent state. The kingdom still remained connected to the Habsburg court. Outside of foreign affairs, military operations and currency, it was separate and autonomous from the other lands of the empire. From 1867, the Germanic Austrian lands were referred to as Cisleithania or Austria.

89 For Zionist politicians and anti-assimilationist politicians from the Galician Jewish or Eastern Jewish communities, liberalism itself was rejected outright. See Freidenreich, ch 4.

problems both within and outside the Empire created a new set of political issues that took classical liberalism unawares.

Hermann Broch thus came of age in a Viennese political climate marked by transition and a growing tone of anti-Semitism. His relationship to liberalism was, unsurprisingly, also conflicted. It is clear that the direct political platform of the Liberals did not dominate his thought; nevertheless, key aspects of Viennese liberalism did, that is, the importance of the individual rational actor (the unbound man) and a standard concern for the protection of minority right in a free society. In terms of social status and behaviour, Broch also demonstrated a close connection to the dominant liberal class – the *haute bourgeoisie*. Even if his father had rejected assimilation along the lines of *Besitz und Bildung*, Broch's earlier life style, his apartment furnishings, his dress and cultured manners tied him more closely to the high bourgeois world than to his father's business-oriented lifestyle.[90]

In a sense, Broch took from the liberal tradition in Vienna everything that his father had left untouched. He chose *Bildung* and his father chose *Besitz*. His father was clearly a member of the Jewish merchant class of the late nineteenth century, a class defined by its liberalism and its conservative attachment to the Monarchy; he was not, however, a typical member of the assimilated liberal Jewish class. It is within the realm of culture that Josef Broch deviated from the familiar picture of the assimilated Jew.[91] His

90 The marriage pattern within Broch's family, both his own marriage and the marriage of his father, also deepened Broch's connection to Liberal Vienna, while at the same time adding more isolated, fragmentary pieces to the puzzle that made up his social existence. His father's marriage to Jewish aristocracy, spilt between urban business Jewish family and older more established Jewish families who were imitating more fully the aristocratic rural life. Broch's marriage into a Hungarian, gentile (Catholic) aristocratic family places Broch on the opposite side of the liberal/aristocratic boundary. This furthers the fragmentary nature of his development, while placing him deeper within the liberal tradition. 'Galician Jews ... may have been more devoted than Bohemian, Moravian, Hungarian, or native Viennese Jews to asserting their Jewish identity and living a more consciously Jewish life' (Rozenbilt, 44).

91 Rozenbilt's statistical data suggests that as an industrialist such a lifestyle need not be considered abnormal.

natural inclination was toward stability and money; his son's natural inclination was toward culture and refinement. This did not exclude Hermann from enjoying the trappings of his privileged economic position;[92] he did so, however, from an aristocratic stance in which he differentiated money from lifestyle. He makes this difference clear in an open letter from 1920 entitled *Die Strasse*, where he states: 'Possessions possess me, not at all' (*Keinerlei Besitz besitzt mich*).[93]

The eclectic nature of liberalism's influence on Broch reflected an eclecticism in the tradition itself, which grew out the political crisis of liberalism in last decades of the nineteenth century. In his book on Robert Musil, Luft clearly articulates the cultural tension created by the Vienna's liberal mandarins. For Luft, the tension underlining Vienna's intellectual milieu at the turn of the century was twofold. First, there was the tension within liberalism; it was a political tension between the liberal's close ties to the Habsburg aristocracy, what Luft describes as 'the distinctive feature in the ideological inheritance of the Austrian liberal: the social and cultural emulation of an aristocracy [...] of display, cultivated pleasures, and social grace',[94] and the developing political forces of nationalism and mass parties, forces developing under a liberal parliamentary inheritance. The second tension was intellectual. It was a tension between the Viennese commitment to scientific materialism and their growing attachment to philosophical irrationalism, the former being heightened by the basic function of the latter. As Luft argues:

> Indeed, the post-Kantian tradition was generally resisted by Austrian intellectuals before 1900; although Viennese liberals were proud of their German culture, they were strongly influenced by French and English traditions of liberalism and by the German classicism and humanism of Lessing, Goethe, Schiller, and Wilhelm von Humboldt rather than by the familiar figures of post-Kantian idealism. In this context, what was emphasized after 1848 was primarily the liberation of the unbound man from the interference of the state in the development of capitalism and from the

92   Broch's lifestyle, which was the embodiment of the dandy, was a testament to his close alliance to aristocratic activities and tastes.

93   Broch, *KW* 13/3, 30.

94   Luft, *Robert Musil*, 11.

authority of the Roman Catholic church in education – and the new opportunities for men of property and education to participate in a representative political process.[95]

The contorts of liberal individualism described here were basic to Broch's upbringing and his social education. By early twentieth century, however, the freedoms provided by liberalization found less and less ground on which to take hold. Conflict breed disillusionment and political intransigence, crisis outpaced freedom as the catchphrase of modernization. The First World War and the collapse of the Empire would simply confirm it. Nevertheless, the liberal tradition of the autonomous actor in a political sense found expression in democratic ideologies of the 1910s, especially in Austro-Marxism and the cultural idea of cosmopolitan remained central to institutions like the Jewish *Kultusgemeinschaft*. It was through these liberal descendents that Broch would bend his own cultural criticism towards the general political notions of democracy and individualism.

The example of Hermann Broch and his connections to the liberal, progressive traditions of the nineteenth century was not isolated. The work of Malachi Hacohen on Karl Popper traces a similar cultural legacy for the progressive tradition. Much of Hacohen's *fin-de-siècle* Vienna is a familiar one, seen in both Schorske and Luft, vis-à-vis liberalism. But Hacohen highlights the progressive, reformed-minded culture of Viennese liberalism – a culture that Hacohen argues survived the late nineteenth-century crisis of liberalism and the rise of Christian Socialism and ethnonationalism in at least a limited fashion. The eventual rise of fascism would sound the final death knell for this culture at the end of the First Republic, but not without fostering an intellectual and cultural legacy for Austrian exiles such as Popper.

Hacohen is an important contribution to the way we conceive the crisis of liberalism in *fin-de-siècle* Vienna, for he suggests that the legacy of liberalism within the intellectual world of the early twentieth century should not be seen simply as a failure. With both Popper and Broch, we see that aspects of the liberal tradition continued to inform political

95   Luft, *Eros and Inwardness*, 7.

thought not only in the First Republic, but even into the exile of thinkers of the generation of 1905. That is not to say, however, that the influence was uniform and constant. Broch was not a clear and obvious member of Hacohen's progressive *Spätaufklärung*. Broch's Jewish identity was more complicated, his assimilation more tied to business and social standing than to Austrian-German cultural markers. Broch was not *Gymnasium* trained. He converted to Catholicism and married into an aristocrat family. He was a businessman and a manufacturer. Furthermore, Broch's political theory rested more heavily on the balance of rationality and irrationality than did that of Popper's.

Born in 1886, Hermann Broch was clearly not a representative member of Schorske's liberal generation or even his generation of rebel sons. His key influences in his youth were liberal. His father, a businessman and assimilated Jew, was dependent on the Emperor and the aristocracy as a means for legal protection and economic security (his speculations and his factory production were supported by government contracts). The close ties between the aristocracy and the Viennese Liberals made the aristocracy necessary, but the aristocracy also remained impenetrable for the haute bourgeoisie, especially the urban Jews. Broch's thought and his political stance did not reflect an extreme commitment to liberalism, in fact, his socialist-tinted democracy and his close connections to the thought of Otto Bauer and Max Adler, made him much more an Austrian Marxist than a liberal. Broch's liberalism was not pragmatic; it did not link to specific political platforms or social movements, like Popper's cosmopolitan, progressive liberalism described by Hacohen or the more conservative, pro-business, pro-Monarchy brand of his father. Yet, the influence of liberalism, especially its influence within assimilated Jewish culture must be recognized. He did develop his political thought around three key aspects of the liberal *Gründerzeit*: 1) democracy as the basis for political institutions, 2) the unbound individual and 3) bourgeois, assimilated lifestyle.

From assimilation to liberalism, his experience in turn-of-the-century Vienna left a lasting mark on his political and ethical approach to life. He lived in the world of the *haute bourgeoisie* and feared the destruction of his own social identity and economic security. Yet, he rejected the vacuous ethics and aesthetics of his own class because of his deep commitment to values and duty. In the next chapter, I examine how his failure to overcome the contradictions between his value theory and his cultural conservativism alienated him from deep critical engagement with the massive political upheaval of the Austrian First Republic.

CHAPTER 2

Politics of Disengagement, 1918 to 1932

The aestheticising man deserves to be killed.[1]

The idea of Broch as a political thinker is not new and the idea does not lack for primary source evidence. Nonetheless, classifying his political worldview remains an ongoing and somewhat contested process. In the last chapter, I suggested how Broch's early biography supplied much of the intellectual concepts for his political theory. But, in another way, his early biography obscures our understanding of his political thought, because from the First World War until the publication of his first novel at age 46 Broch subordinated politics within his intellectual agenda. My goal in this chapter is to explain why he remained fundamentally disengaged from politics during the Austrian First Republic.

His experience of assimilation in late nineteenth- and early twentieth-century Vienna created the merger of a conservative, Baroque cultural chauvinism with a modernist critique of materialism and reactionary traditionalism. Such a cultural identity helped promote an elitist fear of mass politics and explains his lack of political engagement. By the late 1930s, the growing dangers of totalitarianism and Central European fascism challenged Broch's apolitical attitude. The annexation of Austria by Germany in 1938, and Broch's arrest the next day, drove him head first into political engagement. In this new context, Broch would nonetheless bring to his political theory many of the ideas he cultivated under the Austrian First

1   Hermann Broch, *Das Teesdorfer Tagebuch für Ea von Allesch*, ed. Paul Michael Lützeler (Frankfurt: Suhrkamp Verlag, 1998), 47.

Republic, including a fear of mass culture, an anti-Soviet bias, progressive
views of state-protected individualism, and a commitment to ego-based,
idealistic ethics that would often complicated the efficacy of his political
activism in exile.

My focus in this chapter is the period 1919 to 1934, a period where new
political ideologies challenged liberal democracies, especially the newly
founded republics of German Central Europe. It is a disingenuous claim
to say that Broch lived through this period without any signs of political
engagement. In the immediate post-war period, he was active in the local
politics of Lower Vienna, but these activities did not extend beyond 1920
and did not express any ideological platform for sustaining democracy
or progressively structuring the post-Imperial Austrian state. And by and
large, Broch turned completely away from pragmatic politics, which he
described in 1918 as 'the last and most evil flattening of the people. [It is]
the prime example of radical evil as a necessary consequence of the dogma
of morality'.[2] Though seen by some as a political criticism of politics, the
dismissive tone of this statement reveals more about Broch's alienation
from the politics of revolution and mass culture than about his rhetorical
engagement with contemporary events.[3] And when connected to his other
comments on politics in the 1920s, it exposes a current of conservativism
and intellectual elitism that separated Broch from deep engagement in the
First Austrian Republic.

To establish my claim, I examine two explicitly political essays from
the immediate post-war period,[4] along with his letters and a *Tagebuch*

2   '*Die Straße*', an open letter to Franz Blei, was published in Blei's and A. P. Gütersloh
     journal, *Die Rettung*, vol. 1/3, 20 December 1918, *KW*, 13/1, 3–4.
3   See Wendlin Schmidt-Dengler, '"Kurzum die Hölle": Broch's Early Political Text
     "Die Straße"', in Paul Michael Lützeler, ed., *Hermann Broch: Visionary in Exile: The
     2001 Yale Symposium* (New York: Camden House, 2003), 55–66.
4   '*Die Straße*' and '*Konstitutionelle Diktatur als demokratisches Rätesystem*', published
     in *Der Friede* 3/64, 11 April 1919. See also '*Konstitutionelle Diktatur als demokratisches
     Rätesystem*', *KW 11*, 11–23.

written to his Ea von Allesch in 1920–1921.[5] In the third chapter, I examine his first published novel (written between 1928 and 1932) in terms of its message of social activism/engagement. Through these sources, a clear pattern of concerns and objectives develops, and a clear conclusion can be made about Broch as a political activist in the interwar period, that is, Broch sustained a strongly disengaged relationship to politics. He chose aesthetic goals over political ones and allowed social and personal concerns to outweigh political action.

From these sources, I chart the following characteristic of Broch's intellectual worldview during the Austrian First Republic. 1) His actions were in tune with the liberalism co-opted by Austro-Marxism, a democratic voice for the workers, but controlled within a larger parliamentary system. 2) His concern for education and physical improvement of his workers exemplified his progressive liberal roots (via *Bildung*) and the contemporary Austro-Marxist platform that carried them into the 1920s. 3) His business interest and his cultural distancing of the middle class from the proletariat, as well as his tendency towards universalist social constructs, his concern for private enterprise, and even his soft peddled anti-Semitism, all mediated the reformist possibilities of his liberalism qua socialism. 4) Any ideological commitments suggested in his liberal or social democratic leanings are repeatedly set aside for personal concerns or intellectual commitments to epistemology and aesthetics.

The significance of politics to Hermann Broch's thought has received scholarly attention since the late 1950s, when Wolfgang Rothe established Broch's *bona fides* as an anti-fascist democratic reformist.[6] His writing on human rights, especially from the 1940s to his death, only reinforced this progressive image. In the early 1970s, however, Karl Menges and Heinz Osterle questioned whether this political image had not been overly defined

5   Hermann Broch, *Das Teesdorfer Tagebuch für Ea von Allesch*, Paul Michael Lützeler, ed. (Frankfurt: Suhrkamp Verlag, 1998).
6   Wolfgang Rothe, '*Hermann Broch als politische Denker*', *Zeitschrift für Politik* 5 (1958), 329–341.

by a sense of encomium, setting off the 'affirmative/critical debate'.[7] The
Menges/Osterle critical school suggested that conservativism, bordering
on pseudo-fascism, better characterized his political views, stressing his
anti-revolutionary and anti-Marxist ideas.[8] Dagmar Barnouw and, most
recently, Uwe Dörwald have also argued for the conservative and anti-
democratic nature of Broch's interwar writings – arguing for a universalist,
organic traditionalism and an anti-populist fear of revolutionary political
ideologies, respectively.[9]

The critical claims of scholars such as Menges did not, however, override the characterization of Broch as a democratic reformer; in fact, they
simply prompted more scholars to examine his early work in order to
challenge such claims.[10] The debate over how to understand his political ideology generated a thematic focus on engagement and consistency
in his thought. Paul Michael Lützeler entered the 'affirmative/critical
debate' in 1973 with a direct study of Broch's early political views. In his

7   For examples of their criticism see Heinz D. Osterle, 'Hermann Broch, *Die
     Schlafwandler*: Revolution and Apocalypse' *PMLA* 86/5 (1971): 946–958 and
     Karl Menges, 'Bemerkungen zum Problem der ästhetischen Zeitgenossenschaft
     in Hermann Brochs *Der Tod des Vergil*.' *Modern Austrian Literature: Journal of the
     International Arthur Schnitzler Research Association*, 'Special Hermann Broch Issue',
     13/4 (1980): 31–50.
8   Osterle states: 'Broch may have dreamed of the corporate state, a basic idea of inter-
     national Fascism. His reactions show that the collapse of the Danube Monarchy was
     a profound shock for him as for most other Austrian writers' (Osterle, 'Revolution
     and Apocalypse', 954).
9   Dagmar Barnouw, *Weimar Intellectuals and the Threat of Modernity* (Bloomington,
     IN: University of Indiana Press, 1988) and Uwe Dörwald, *Über das Ethische bei
     Hermann Broch: Kritische Historiographie zur ethischen Intention und ihrer Funktion
     bei Hermann Broch* (Frankfurt am Main: Peter Lang, 1994).
10   See Friedrich Vollhardt, *Brochs geschichtliche Stellung: Studien zum philosophischen
     Frühwerk und zur Romantrilogie 'Die Schlafwandler', 1914–1932* (Tübingen: Max
     Niedermeyer, 1986), Paul Michael Lützeler, *Hermann Broch, Ethik und Politik:
     Studien zum Frühwerk und zur Romantrilogie Die Schlafwandler* (Munich: Winkler
     Verlag, 1973), Ernestine Schlant, *Hermann Broch* (1978, repr., Chicago: University of
     Chicago Press, 1994), and Joseph Strelka, *Poeta Doctus Hermann Broch* (Tübingen:
     Francke Verlag, 2001).

study, he argued that the ethical structure of his writings from 1908 to 1933 implied a political humanism that aligned most directly with an Austrian social democratic worldview. Furthermore, he claimed that Broch's ethical humanism functioned through its social commentary as a form of political engagement. Lützeler's work established a strong foundation for seeing Broch's worldview as democratic and progressive, and opening the door to arguments for an identifiable consistency in political outlook.[11] Ernestine Schlant, in her examination of Broch's early work, suggests that a form of Platonic, ethical humanism functioned as an intellectual constant in his artistic, epistemological and political goals.[12] Although Schlant argues that Broch is, in fact, disengaged in pragmatic politics during the period from 1919 to 1932, nonetheless, she helps to reinforce the claim that his earlier philosophy established a politically viable foundation for political progressivism.[13] My position is, in fact, close to Schlant's. I, however, stress more forcefully his political withdrawal during the interwar period and the radical nature of Broch's re-evaluation of politics in the middle 1930s.

Joseph Strelka would crystallize the notion of continuity and engagement suggested in the affirmative school with his characterization of Broch as *poeta doctus*. He makes a blatant claim for seeing Broch as a politically engaged artist from the late 1920s to the middle 1930s (starting with his composition of *The Sleepwalkers*, 1928–1932). Strelka argues that Broch lived as a '*poeta doctus*', who hope to 'influence' the political actions of his readers and to open their eyes to the 'related risk' of fascism and totalitarianism.[14] Strelka quotes a letter from Broch to Daniel Brody (7 June 1935),

11　I examine Lützeler's book in more detail below.
12　See Ernestine Schlant, *Hermann Broch*. Though she examines Broch's work from the early decades of the twentieth century for its philosophical and not its political significance, her linkage of Broch's exilic political theory to his philosophy of history in the 1920s implies a political consistency. The implication reinforces the image of Broch as actively shaping the struggles for political power.
13　Both Schlant and Strelka provide well-documented biographical discussions of Broch and acknowledge that he cannot be called an active political figure in the 1920s and early 1930s.
14　Strelka, *Poeta Doctus*, 28.

in which Broch expresses 'a burning ambition to intervene in this world'.[15] The letter, however, suggests to me both an acknowledgment of years of disengagement, as well as a late arrival to the concern about a world 'that had become so abominable'.[16] Broch wrote the letter more than a year after the bloody defeat of the Social Democrats with whom he supposedly shared deep commitments, but about whose defeat he was silent.[17]

Though I agree with the intellectual genealogies of 'affirmative' scholars such as Lützeler and Schlant, I come to a very different conclusion on how to define and understand Broch *als Politiker* in the interwar period. Lützeler concludes that Broch's ethical focus defines him as politically engaged, while I conclude that Broch's actions and ideas demonstrate a distance from politics, a position I define as disengaged. In some ways, the difference can be attributed to the definition of political. Lützeler's general use of the term comes very close to cultural criticism or social theory. Because the goal of Broch's ethical program was the renewal of European society, his ideas and writings are defined as political. I use the term in a more limited sense to mean observation, theorizing, or action on policy or events connected to the polis or state.

Furthermore, I challenge Lützeler's comparison of Broch to writer/activists such as Zola; such comparisons suggest a depth of social engagement that is out of place in terms of Broch during 1920s.[18] Broch was clearly too absorbed in his own mind and his own personal issues to have written anything that would resemble '*J'accuse*'. His aesthetic work and his philosophy of history did aim at critical humanism, but to call that

15   Ibid, 30.
16   Letter to Daniel Brody, 7 June 1935, quoted in Strelka, *Poeta Doctus*, 30.
17   Hartmut Jäckel provides a more extensive list of letters making similar claims to political engagement and a sense of moral duty. But, as with Strelka's evidence, it all comes from the period after 1935. See Jäckel, 'Hermann Broch and Politics' in *Hermann Broch: Literature, Philosophy, Politics,* 93–106.
18   See Lützeler, *Ethik und Politik*, 14. Hartmut Jäckel argues that Broch's relationship to such literary/political figures fails on a second level, at least in Broch's exilic work, because Broch abandons his literary efforts for a political agenda, which is full 'of the frequently too insistent zeal that seeks not only to instruct the reader but also to convert him' (Hartmut Jäckel, 'Hermann Broch and Politics', 99).

critical humanist stance political misunderstands Broch's withdrawal from the pragmatic world of politics in the 1920s. His withdrawal was a critique of the political impotence and cultural emptiness or aestheticism of the Austrian First Republic.[19] As he stated in 1918:

> Politics is the prime example of the uncontrollable. [...][It is] the prime example of radical evil as a necessary consequence of the dogma of morality. In short, it is hell. I know you, dear friend, will say this is a requisite mopping up process, in order to prepare the faith, a reawakening of the knowledge of the communion of all things metaphysical. Maybe.[20]

Broch disengaged from the political change going on around him, and he retreated into an ivory tower intellectualism through which he attempted to play the role of social reformer qua intellectual.

Broch's Political Agenda in his Own Words

Broch's *Tagebuch* to Ea von Allesch in the immediate post-war period is a combination of intellectual history with personal diary. Broch described its purpose in the opening lines: 'Since it is a diary, it must be completely candid – otherwise it would be meaningless; it is only right that you have it, it is part of my belonging to you. There is, indeed, no greater proof [...] many others than I have written *to you* [...] this will be a diary written *around you*.'[21] By 'written around you', Broch meant that the journal was not exclusively about their love – not a simple declaration or memorial; it was, instead, about how her presence in his life affected his understanding of the ego or self. At the time, Broch's major intellectual project was a historical philosophy that addressed the possibility of value construction

19   Against Schmidt-Dengler, *'Kurzum die Hölle'*, 55–66.
20   *KW* 13/1, 34.
21   *Teesdorfer Tagebuch*, 9.

in the modern world. As he read Kant, neo-Kantianism, Dilthey, Marxist philosophy and modern literature, all in an attempt to map the cognitive boundaries of the individual ego, he recorded the development of his ego under the irrational influence of Allesch's presence in his life. The journal allows one to see Broch's basic reactions to the political and social worlds around him in an unguarded and intimate way.[22]

By examining a short passage from the *Tagebuch* (8 July 1920), we can see the depth to which Broch's mind enveloped multiple worlds. It also demonstrates the degree to which he was able to immerse himself in the Viennese world of the café and the intelligentsia, while maintaining a full schedule as a husband and businessman:

> To the office, the hair salon, the dentist, to Halm and Goldman [antiquarian], visit with [Paul] Schrecker, to Gonzaga [street – family apartment in Vienna], then to Café Central, a visit with Fischer (painter), then to Kuppitsch [bookstore], then the Cotton union – meeting with Schwankhöffer, to you for 2 short hours, it has not gone well with you and I have since then a repeated, terrible worry about you. Something must be done, my love, sweetie.[23]

Passages such as these, along with discussions of family and money, predominate in the journal, but Broch's political views and even his immediate political activities are also on display. We know from other autobiographical sources that his war efforts and his post-war leadership positions showed a strong commitment to community and state in years between 1914 and 1921:

22   The focus of the journal is on Allesch's and Broch's relationship; it was in one manner a de facto series of love letters to Ea from the early part of their relationship (from July 1920 until January 1921). What Manfred Durzak describes as 'Liebeslektion.' Manfred Durzak. *Hermann Broch* (Stuttgart: Metzler, 1967), 20. Broch met Allesch at Café Central, where she was known as the local muse. Broch's son described her as the archetype for 'oppressive-dominant women, but long-suffering martyrs, the manipulative, professional victim type [...] and combined this with a sharp intellect, broad learning in a number of fields [...] an original sense of humor, and a quick mind. Physically she was attractive in a direct, hard-to-miss way: she had fiery red hair, slender, sylph-like figure, and that indefinable quality known as "chic"' (Broch de Rothermann, 30).
23   *Teesdorfer Tagebuch*, 24.

I had entered industrial work in 1908. [...] I gained a range of economical perceptions. [...] I was able to gain important insight into the relationship between industry and workers as well as into overall social mechanisms. [...] I held different official and semiofficial positions, as I was involved with the committees for 'the preservation of the worker's peace', [...] as well as 'the reorganization of worker's rights', and finally on 'the efforts for fighting unemployment'. [...] [T]hese activities, with which I was occupied at the time, were without a doubt uncommonly instructive.[24]

This commitment may have been the consequence of his experience of community leadership as director of the Teesdorf war hospital or of his social and economic position as business leader in Lower Austria.[25] Whatever the incentive, he worked on several boards that oversaw disputes between labour and ownership, including his work on Conciliation Commission of the Lower Austria and a member of the Industrial District Commission in Wiener Neustadt. His success in these efforts was recognized by the state and, as Lützeler states, 'after this experience, he toyed with the idea of becoming active in politics'.[26]

Within his own factory, Broch demonstrated a progressive political agenda that aligned with a larger post-Imperial move to the left and towards democracy and greater class equality. He made significant improvements in working conditions and health, including 'a free lunch each day for needy children and ... a library of four thousand books ... a gymnasium ... and swimming pool'.[27] If one considers Broch's work for both ownership and labour in the period from 1919 to 1922, one cannot but conclude that Broch was amenable to socialism and a shift towards greater democracy.[28] From an

---

24 *Psychische Selbstbiographie*, 86–87.
25 The Teesdorf factory, with over 800 employees, was located in one of the centres for Austrian industrialization and power production, especially hydroelectric. Broch published an article on the hydroelectric power during this period to a clear sign of his involvement in the industrial rebuilding of the Austrian economy in the immediate post-war period.
26 Paul Michael Lützeler, *A Biography*, 59.
27 Ibid, 48 and *Teesdorfer Tagebuch*, 37, fn 22.
28 Unlike Adler's and Bauer's Social Democratic policies, Broch's policies at his own factory were purely about providing some economic self control and cultural/ social improvement – it did not extend to real political power. For discussion

intellectual point of view, the Austro-Marxist ideology that characterized Red Vienna also aligned very closely with his own views on social justice.[29] Based on his book reviews of Austro-Marxist writers such as Bauer and Max Adler, as well as several on neo-Kantianism, he clearly supported the philosophical, ethical viewpoint of Austrian socialism. But, his political leanings were most in line with the conservative wing of Austrian Social Democracy. He supported the political development of a social democratic state as long as that state pursued a gradual integration of shared governance between owners and workers.[30]

His connections to Social Democracy were more than theoretical, however. As his *Tagebuch* reveals, in 1920, he considered running as a candidate for the Social Democrats, though he uses the term Bolshevism.[31] Journal entries from 16 and 20 July 1920 discuss the idea of running for office in support of 'Bolschewimus'. Lützeler suggests that a telephone call mentioned in the same journal entry refers to a conversation with Benedikt Kautsky (son of Karl), who was the secretary for Otto Bauer, head of the Social Democrats. The entry also indicates that his ideas were not in lock step with the party and that preconditions would be necessary. Though Broch did not explain what these preconditions would be, the general political attitude presented in the *Tagebuch* suggests that he would have found even the moderate wing of the Social Democratic party too radical in its push to elevate worker's council and its possible relationship to international movements, like the Hungarian Communism Republic under Bela Kun.

The journal suggests that his relationship to the party was minor. He questioned whether as a representative he would have the power to sway

<hr>

of the relationship between the Social Democratic leadership and the *Räte*, see Anson Rabinbach, *The Crisis of Austrian Socialism: From Red Vienna to Civil War 1927–1934* (Chicago: University of Chicago Press, 1983), 23.

29   Schlant also describes Broch's intellectual position as close to Austro-Marxism, especially on the issue of peaceful transition and ethical necessity of political actions; see Schlant, *Hermann Broch*, 32.

30   This notion of a gradual historical shift to socialism is best seen in his 1919 essay, '*Konstitutionelle Diktatur als demokratisches Rätesystem*,' *KW 11*, 11–23.

31   *Teesdorfer Tagebuch*, 40.

options to his thinking or would simply 'afterwards show that he had been right'.[32] He shared some intellectual goals and had direct contact with the Social Democrats, but comments such as these show that his overall relationship to Austro-Marxism was conditional and somewhat dismissive. What is more significant in the passage, however, is that his entire discussion of playing an active role in the Social Democratic party appears to be nothing more than empty rhetoric. He may have been having conversations with lower officials in the party, but in the context of the journal, it is clear that Broch's commitment to a socialist agenda was weak.[33] Within this passage alone, the weakness of his commitment can be seen by the priorities he lays out in regards to parliamentarian elections in 1920. It must be remembered that Central Europe from 1919 to 1920 was in the midst of constant revolution, revolution that inevitably brought violence in its wake. Austria itself was on the edge of violent revolution and the leadership of Austro-Marxism was at that time struggling with the path forward; would they follow in the footsteps of German Social Democracy and ally with the Right in order to put down Leninist rebellion? Or work to secure electoral victories and control of Vienna, while accepting a diminished role in national politics?[34]

In July 1920, the political stakes for a democratic Austrian First Republic reached a height not seen again until 1934 and the defeat of Social Democracy. The extreme nature of politics between 1914 and 1922 can be seen in the Friedrich Adler's (son of Austro-Marxist leader, Victor Alder) assassination of Count Karl von Stürgkh in 1916.[35] Yet, for Broch, the priorities were vastly different. In his *Tagebuch*, he discussed a possible

32   Ibid, 40.
33   Who initiated such conversations is unclear, but it does suggest that Broch's position as a factory owner with democratic leanings made him attractive as a Social Democratic candidate.
34   See Martin Kitchen, *The Coming of Austrian Fascism* (London: Croom Helm; Montreal: McGill-Queen's University Press, 1980), 30–34 and Rabinbach, 11–24.
35   See Howard M. Sachar, *Dreamland: Europeans and Jews in the Aftermath of the Great War* (New York: Random House, 2007), 178.

candidacy in the context of his relationship to Allesch, and most pressingly
their chance to spend time alone together at the Karlsbad Spa:

> The only question now, in terms of how to bring about the sale of the factory, is on
> what will we live, if we should expect Bolshevism [a Social democratic victory] ... I
> only hope that Bolshevism is not established until after Karlsbad. It must be consid-
> ered whether my candidacy with regards to Bolshevism – although only under certain
> preconditions – may still not be prudent. On the one hand, the preconditions may
> not be fulfilled, because I do not have the personal influence to push my opinions
> through, rather I can only prove afterwards that I was right, on the other hand, it
> would make going to Karlsbad impossible, so we have to leave the issue as is for now.
> I am so happy with the thought of Karlsbad – happy is still the right expression – yet
> I have a terrible fear of rejoicing.[36]

Broch priorities were clear: 1) vacation at Karlsbad with Ea, 2) sell the factory, 3) run for political office. He even hoped that the Social Democrats
did not win anytime soon, for he feared the impact it might have on his
ability to sell his factory.[37]

Broch's dismissive tone was further emphasized in an entry from 23
July, when describing his impression of a public furniture exhibition.[38]
The exhibition was clearly seen by Broch as a political event in that it was
attempting to link artistic expression to political ideals – in this case furniture and republicanism. His reaction to the exhibition and the crowd
(*Masse*) that attended was highly critical. In just three lines he clarified
several key aspects of his political views:

> I find nothing of note, beyond, the idea that they should once again decorate castles
> with it [the exhibited furniture] and allow monarchs to live in them. Any 'public

---

36   *Teesdorfer Tagebuch*, 40.
37   Paul Michael Lützeler discusses Broch's focus on the theme of vacations with von
     Allesch as an intellectual process and as fantasy construction. He sees it as part of
     Broch's intellectual exploration of both the ego in a psychological and Kantian sense
     and the balancing of the 'I' with the concept of the 'you.' See Paul Michael Lützeler,
     Die Entropie des Menschen, 138–141.
38   See *Teesdorfer Tagebuch*, 47. Presumably Broch attended the exhibition in connection
     to the fashion journal, *Die Modern Welt*, for which he was a regular contributor.

collection' is really a scandal, for it requires both the capability for art enjoyment and more particularly the presence of the crowd. Everything associated with 'pleasure' (*Genuß*) – including even the socialist idea of 'Comrade' (*Genosse*) – is absolutely ethically reprehensible.[39] The aestheticising man deserves to be killed.[40]

In a footnote to this passage, Paul Michael Lützeler observed Broch's subtle conservativism and his push back against the republican rhetoric of democracy.[41] Broch clearly saw the idea of democracy merged with the crowd here and saw the purpose as propaganda, not artistic education.

The artistic activity was vacuous because it had a common, pragmatic purpose – sway the crowd. The disdain and the danger Broch felt at mass politics, even if democratic, are seen in the vitriol of the statement, 'The aestheticising man deserves to be killed'.[42] Broch's language in the midst of real death from political violence suggests a false bravado characteristic of elitist detachment.

His journal entry of 26 July 1920 announces the end of his brief consideration of a run for political office. It may be that the initiative for such a run was brought to him and that he did not seek it, which would help explain the tentative and dismissive nature of his comments on the idea throughout the journal. Nonetheless, by the 26th, political candidacy was obviously no longer viable. And an increasingly negative tone towards 'Bolshevism' reached its apex here. 'The political (plan) would have some allure, if one could achieve something in terms of the "violation" of the people, and at the same time hold the empirical baggage in check. That is, of course, no program, rather so-called idealism'.[43] Broch may have supported the rhetoric of democracy and freedom in Austro-Marxism, but he feared the pragmatic consequences of inflammatory language, such as violation/ rape (*Vergewaltigung*) and the dangers of radicalizing, mass politics. The

39   Broch is making a pun on the shared root for pleasure and comrade.
40   *Teesdorfer Tagebuch*, 47. From the context of the *Tagebuch*, this last line of this passage ('It may not fit for the modern world') probably refers to the usefulness of reviewing the display in the journal, *Die Moderne Welt*.
41   Ibid, 51, fns 2 and 3.
42   Ibid, 47.
43   Ibid, 49.

passage supports ideas presented in the essay 'The Street' (1918), where he justified his rejection of leftish, mass agitation.[44] The discussion of 'empirical baggage' refers to the general conservativism of his democratic inclinations. He had deep concerns, some for personal reasons, of violence on the streets and attacks on private property and economic resources – a fear for the loss of economic autonomy for the non-working class.

Beyond the conservativism of Broch's class identity, what was most surprising in his conservativism was a cultural anti-Semitism. The self-hating Jew paradigm that has explained the presence of anti-Semitic remarks in writers such as Otto Weininger and Karl Kraus has been suggested as an explanation for similar comments in Broch.[45] I do not think the term is useful for my discussion, because we are not dealing with published treatise on the value of Jewish thought or language or the biological difference between Jews and Gentiles, as could be assigned to Kraus or Weininger. In fact, what I label as anti-Semitic in Broch was his use of class and political based language in an offhand manner, and in each case the remarks indicated class difference or the east/west divide between nineteenth-century Jewish émigrés.

There are several instances in the journal where he made unfaltering and spiteful remarks about Jews.[46] On 30 July 1920, he wrote: 'travelling 3rd Class to Vienna. A terrible old Jewess in the seat next to me explained everything about the pogroms'.[47] In this brief line, Broch's upper class expectation and prejudices are on full display. A dandy on all accounts, he was not surprised to find in the third class carriage an unsophisticated, backward-looking woman. The trivial and bothersome nature of her very presence is sharply displayed. The comment, however, suggests much more about his social identity. For her presence is bothersome not because of poverty, but because of her ignorance, that is, her failure to embrace cosmopolitanism

---

44   Lützeler makes the same connection between the journal and the earlier essay; see *Teesdorfer Tagebuch*, 51 fn 3.

45   Lützeler makes this claim in regards to the *Tagebuch*, see *Teesdorfer Tagebuch*, 56, fn 6.

46   Ibid, 20, 54, 56 and 77.

47   Ibid, 54.

and modernity. The fact that she is Jewish heightened the disdain because it created an even greater divide between him and the old woman. It was an internal Jewish divide, materially wealthy assimilated Jews versus non-assimilated Eastern Jews. The divide was material in the sense that geography, wealth, occupation and dress were visible signs of the Western Jewish versus the Eastern Jewish communities in Vienna.

One could argue that the tone of distaste was here shorthand for material, class difference. Yet, the material difference contained an ideological difference, as well; assimilated Western Jews connected their economic and political autonomy to the key features of modernity: Enlightenment secularism and cosmopolitanism, which required a shared language of German *Kultur*, industrialization and its economic prosperity and liberal ideas such as limited suffrage and constitutionally based citizen rights. Much of the anti-Semitism of Western Jews towards Eastern Jews was the fear that the presence of a 'pre-modern' Jewish culture would endanger the viability of an assimilated Jewish culture. In his comment, Broch expressed both a material and an ideological bias towards the 'terrible old Jewess'.

The connections among Jewish identity, status and modernity are furthered in an entry concerning Rahel Varnhagen from 7 July 1920. With a clear sense of irony, Broch referred to Varnhagen's correspondence (love letters) to her husband and feigned offence because her letters anticipated the literary value of his own *Tagebuch*. The presentation of a bound edition of Varnhagen's letters to von Allesch emphasized a similarity in the two women's writing style and intellect. In making the comparison, he found it necessary to remark on Varnhagen's (née Levin) Jewishness: 'But for all that, she is a Jew, which incidentally one finds worthy of note'.[48] Though this is an offhand remark, it points out a pattern in Broch's characterization of Jewish traits. He saw positive attributes in Jewish intellectual and artistic activity, but negative attributes in the cultural expression of Jewish traditionalism.[49] Broch found value in connecting his own Jewish identity

---

48   Ibid, 20.
49   Jewish mysticism is a clear exception for Broch and many other 'Western' Jewish intellectuals at this time.

to that of Varnhagen – an enlightened Jewess, poet and *salonnière*, who came to symbolize the cosmopolitan culture of Berlin, Moses Mendelssohn and the *Haskalah*.

The duality in Broch's Jewish commentary can also be seen in his comment from 19 August 1920: 'Left at 10, travelled (by train) with a horrible group of Jews, who make every Horthy understandable'.[50] A more caustic and unfeeling statement from a Jew about the political assassination of other Jews would be hard to imagine. Horthy, regent of Hungary from 1919 to 1944, headed the Hungary counterrevolutionary forces that overthrew the Communist government of Béla Kun in 1919. As the military leader during the White Terror, Horthy explicitly supported the shift from a 'philo-Semitic' national culture to an anti-Semitic one.[51] Horthy's later connection to Nazism and war crimes in the Second World War should not be read into Broch's statement, but the Jewish pogroms that accompanied the anti-communist violence between 1918 and 1920 created deep concern within the international Jewish and non-Jewish communities.[52] For Broch, living in the former Habsburg Empire and deeply engaged with Hungarian intellectuals in Vienna (including an affair with Edit Rényi) such sardonic humour exposed a deep callousness towards Jewish alienation and endangerment. It must be remembered that Broch conceived of his journal as a literary undertaking, and one should not dismiss such language as private or humorous in a self-referential matter. Such comments make one question his political awareness and engagement in the immediate post-war period. As argued above, his supposed social democratic leanings and political support looks very weak when placed beside such politically naïve statements – even if they were personal and private ones. His offhand reference to the murder of thousands of Jews and socialists, just months after the events, suggests a prejudice (clearly born of class and political ideology) in line with the casual anti-Semitism of upper middle

50   *Teesdorfer Tagebuch*, 77–78.
51   See Ezra Mendelsohn, *The Jews of East Central Europe Between the World Wars* (Bloomington, IN: Indiana University Press, 1987), ch 2, 'Hungary'.
52   Ibid, 97.

class and aristocratic conservative culture of the Empire. More importantly, it suggests that Broch's political thinking was so disengaged or distracted by personal and class concerns that he could not see the movement of pogroms from East to West, from tsarist Russia to the more liberal lands of his own assimilation as frightening or dangerous.

Political Essays

At the same time as the *Tagebuch*, Broch wrote several essays directly addressing the political situation of post-war Austria: 'The Street' (*Die Straße*, published as an open letter in 1918) and 'Constitutional Dictatorship as Democratic Soviet System' (*Konstitutionelle Diktatur als demokratisches Rätesystem*, published in 1920). These two essays, along with several book reviews, represented the only direct and public proclamations of Broch's views on politics in the First Republic, and both works asserted idealized intellectual support for a gradual socialism, while also showing a clear distrust for the dangers of a Bolshevik style mass movement.[53] Broch's central intellectual activity at the time, a philosophy of history, directed most of his political theorizing towards the issue of transition in state structures and epistemological possibilities. Thus, revolutions (turnings) were a central theme and his conservative nature preferred a gradual revolution driven primarily by cognitive and artistic shifts, not by political, mass revolutions of the Russian Soviet type.

'The Street' was a personal justification of Broch's 'flight' from the mass demonstrations in Vienna on 12 November 1918. One day after the end of the war, the socialist Red Guard under the leadership of Egon Erwin Kisch held protests and attempted to seize control of parliament. The event, described as a coup by some, failed and resulted in the death of two people

53   *Teesdorfer Tagebuch*, 33.

with almost fifty more injured.[54] Lützeler argues that Broch sympathized
with the popular desire to join with Germany; Broch did not, however,
approve of Franz Werfel's or Egon Erwin Kisch's action on 12 November.
He did not reject the enthusiasm of the political goal, but he rejected outright the occurrence of mass hysteria.[55]

In 'The Street', he criticizes politics as a relative value system that had
the potential to morph into an oppressive, valueless system.[56] Democracy as
a simple political notion of freedom did not work for Broch;[57] his conservative and spiritual character demanded a law by which to direct action. He
remained concerned with the autonomy of the individual, but he did not
assume ethics flowed directly from freedom. He saw a complex relationship among the individual, rationality, knowledge and history. His political
theory demanded that these factors remain operative in both theoretical
debate and pragmatic street demonstrations.

In tone and intent, the letter is an apologia, a defence of Broch's anti-
revolutionary position within the political left. Anyone suggesting democratic reform in 1918 (even a centralist Wilsonian idealism) had to come
to terms with the role of revolution in such a model. Broch's connections
to the Social Democratic party in Lower Austria meant his democratic
concerns could not be addressed without forcing him to make pragmatic
decisions about violence, mass demonstrations, coups, demagoguery and
the like. These conflicts were clear from the discussion of the *Tagebuch*

54   See Harold B. Segel, 'Introduction' in Harold Segel, ed., *Egon Erwin Kisch, The
     Raging Reporter – A Bio-Anthology* (West Lafayette, IN: Purdue University Press,
     1997), 23–25. For a fictionalized depiction of events see Franz Werfel, *Barbara oder
     die Frömmigkeit* (Frankfurt am Main: Fischer Verlag, 1996). Werfel was a leading
     figure in Kisch's Red Guard activities at the time and a friend of Broch.
55   Lützeler, *Ethik und Politik*, 43–44.
56   Schmidt-Dengler's discussion of the cooption of Broch's phrase, 'Politische die letzte
     und böseste Verflachung des Menschen' (first used in *Die Straße*), argues that Franz
     Blei and Heimito von Doderer misemployed the phrase to express a notion of politi-
     cal disengagement that Broch never intended. See Schmidt-Dengler *'Kurzum die
     Hölle'*, 62–64.
57   Broch developed this theme more fully in *The Sleepwalkers*, see Chapter 3, this volume.

above, and the published essays defined the background to the undefined preconditions mentioned in the *Tagebuch* in July 1921.

In the essay, Broch wanted to be seen as engaged and supportive vis-à-vis Social Democracy. He made a direct declaration of his support for Social Democracy in the opening lines: 'I have agreed from the beginning with every kind of communist economy, as it attempts to construct a better world'.[58] But, that support was conditional, and turned on the issue of the social stability. 'Dear friend, it is clear that I recently fled in the face of the masses (*Volksmasse*); you know this, but I fled not because of a particular social antipathy, but out of depression and despair'.[59] In this way, 'The Street' is an expression of the central debate of the Social Democratic party: would their political platform be rightist (parliamentarian) or leftist (Soviet led dictatorship of the people). Broch argued here for the right-wing Social Democratic position.

Yet, even his support of right-wing Austro-Marxism is out of step with Bauer's and especially Friedrich Adler's aggressive rhetoric against reactionary and nationalist forces. Such rhetoric would expand throughout the 1920s and early 1930s as fascism became the all-encompassing term for all anti-democratic and repressive political activities. Broch, however, revealed a naïve evaluation of right-wing, nationalist politics in the essay. While he fled in the face of left-wing radicals, he showed some acceptance for the vitality and community of nationalist gatherings.[60] In the end, all mass movements were 'disgusting' and valueless for him because they were ethically vacuous. But, it is only the left that received direct reprimand in his essays. He continued a similar pattern in *The Sleepwalkers*, where he criticized reactionary politics from the point of view of Romanticism and culture, but criticized Marxism and capitalism through examples of morally failed actions. Overall, he maintained an awkward silence in terms of the evaluation right-wing political movements until well after Hitler's rise to power in 1933 and the destruction of Social Democracy in Austria in 1934.

58   *KW* 13/1, 30.
59   Ibid, 30.
60   Ibid, 31–32.

Several scholars have examined the political importance of 'The Street',
along with his essay on constitutional dictatorship, in order to illuminate
Broch as a political figure in the Austrian First Republic (as well as interwar
Central Europe and the United States). The tendency in the scholarship is
to see the essays as examples of political engagement, even with their apolitical language. Wendlin Schmidt-Dengler sees the article as searching for
an intellectual position equal distance from all criticism, but not in order
to 'flee' politics, rather to condemn politics as a method for addressing the
decadence of post-war European society.[61] Schmidt-Dengler does acknowledge that there was 'at least a hint of deviation from political correctness'
vis-à-vis Broch's discussion of Judaism and socialism.[62] The contradictions
in his democratic tendencies and its effect on his relationship to the Jewish
community and to Social Democracy are, however, too deep to be seen
simply as signs of sophisticated political commentary.

In March 1919, Béla Kun established a communist government in
Budapest and shortly after that Bavaria declared its own communist state.
For Austria, daily violence and the threat of civil war was ever present. The
central issue revolved around the political role of the Worker's Councils
(*Räte*) and later Soldier's Councils. Following on the example of the
Bolsheviks in Russia, the *Räte* movement pushed for political control. By
April, Communist party demonstrations on the streets of Vienna were
routinely turning violent: buildings set on fire and both demonstrators and
army units (*Volkswehr*) killed. By July 1919, the Communist party gradually
diminished in influence as Austrians showed their preference for stability
over revolution.[63] Nevertheless, in April 1920, when Broch published his
second political piece, the issue of how socialism and communism would
develop in Austria was far from a settled matter.[64]

---

61   Schmidt-Dengler finds the article to be a significant contribution to the understand-
     ing of interwar Viennese literary directions and concerns.
62   Schmidt-Dengler '*Kurzum die Hölle*', 55.
63   See Freidenreich, 22–47.
64   In November of 1918 when he published his open letter, 'The Street', members of
     both the right and left splinter groups clashed in front of parliament. For details see
     Lützeler, *Ethik und Politik*, 43–44.

In the context of political unrest, Broch called for stability and an end to mass hysterical activities. Even though he supported some of the political aims of those involved, he questioned whether the political goals of either side in the street fighting could produce positive results. On the one hand, he opposed the materialism of the bourgeois classes. Democracy in an economic system of unchecked capitalist control equated to oppression. He expressed his ideological agreement with the democratic impulse of open dialogue for the working class. Furthermore, Broch argued against the danger of special interest in politics, what he called 'Indulgence' (*Genuß*): the misuse of public trust for the advancement of a limited number of citizens. One can see in these early political tracts seeds of his later critique of democracy in the United States, where he questioned the exclusionary impulses of the ideas of the pursuit of happiness and its pragmatic equivalent the American Dream.[65]

In his later essay on the 'Constitutional Dictatorship as Democratic Soviet System', he made a more involved argument for both his support of Social Democracy (its eventual dominance of the state) and his conservative fear of rapid social change. The main argument of the essay turned on the issue of historical changes, where Broch used the shift from the Old Regime authoritarianism to parliamentarianism as a historical example of how change progresses, but should do so at slow pace. The theme of slow change over rapid revolution exemplified his fundamental conservativism.

In the 'Constitutional Dictatorship as a Democratic Soviet System', Broch made several dogmatic claims. 1) Soviet-styled socialism based on worker councils cannot be democratic and should be rejected by Austria. 2) Democracy should be based on social justice that incorporates all economic classes, not just the workers. 3) Parliamentary power and elections are the only possible solution to the end of Empire. 4) If a 'depoliticized' world is going to development, which is the end game of Marxism, it can only do so in the future. In short, a liberal democratic, electoral system is the only way to avoid the 'debasement of man' (*Entwürdigung des Menschen*).[66]

65   See Chapter 5, this volume.
66   *KW* II, 22.

Ernestine Schlant sees the political lesson of the 'Constitutional Dictatorship' essay as a straightforward confirmation of Broch's utopian idealism, and she implies that one can find a consistent political position here – protection of human life and avoidance of violence.[67] Such a reading is, in fact, too generous. There are three aspects of the intellectual historical context that need to be addressed. First, Broch's call for a slow parliamentarian shift to social democracy need not be, and I do not believe it was, connected to his later political position of the preservation of human life. His position as articulated in the article was, in short, a mainstream Social Democratic position. It was the position of the Social Democratic leadership and the leadership of the Republic. It was a liberal position, but Social Democracy was the only liberal (i.e. enlightened, progressive, constitutional) party in Austria in the interwar period.[68] Non-violence was clearly a concern for Broch from his earliest writing until his death, but in this case, non-violence was the not the driving factor, it was a politics based on economic interest and a political platform where victory through parliamentarian election was chosen over usurpation of power through the workers' councils.

The opening lines of his essay warned that Russian style soviet state structures would manifest themselves pragmatically in the very way their rhetoric suggested. I read Broch's essay as the definition of the unexplained 'preconditions' from the *Tagebuch*, the preconditions necessary for him to pursue candidacy as a Social Democrat. Precondition number one: democracy as the will of *all* people. He took the Marxist definition of a period of transition, the dictatorship of the proletariat, to be a new form of absolutism – an abandonment of democracy and progress. The second precondition was the freedom of the individual, without which there is no rule of law. But, he saw the socialist notion of a state with maximal freedom for its citizens as an idealized, contradictory concept that wanted to unite complete democracy with complete dictatorship. It was an idea that only works if all citizens share the same ideas or values. Broch found

67   See Schlant, 31–33.
68   See Freidenreich, 22–47.

such idealism to be historically out of place. And he lacked support for the
idea of totality in terms of government authority. He reversed that position in the mid-1930s when he truly placed the protection of human life
in front of the demands of individual freedom. In his later political theory,
he trusted more fully in the possibility of empowering the state in order
to regulate social interaction.

Broch's commitment to democracy in the essay was clear and, as
Lützeler points out, the choice of publication made this evident.[69] It was
also clear that Broch connected the reforms of Social Democracy to the
building of a post-Monarchy republic. His direct references to Kautsky,
Bauer and Fr. Adler support such a claim. His commitment to democracy,
however, should not be read as a commitment to Marxism. His discussion
of Kautsky, Bauer and Adler all appear as rhetorical devises in his argument for restricting the influence of worker councils (*Räte*) in the new
Austrian state. He uses prominent names from non-Marxist Leninist theory
(Kautsky, Bauer and Adler) because they share similar goals and similar
critiques of Soviet styled socialism.

To align, however, his view with that of Bauer's and Adler's, as Lützeler
does, seems to go too far. When one reads Broch's use and interpretation
of these thinkers with the view that they were written by a factory owner,
writing in a centrist, republican journal, and by someone who less than a
year later would refuse to run for office as a Social Democrat, it is a fair
conclusion to make that Broch chose to reference Kautsky, Bauer and Adler
because criticizing Bolshevism through the medium of Social Democratic
leaders was more effective than having a democratic leaning factory owner
arguing for the protection of industry and property rights. In his journal
entries from 1920 and 1921, he linked directly the danger of Bolshevism to
his own economic security, personal desires and aesthetic activities. In two
entries from July 1920, he feared the victory of left-wing Social Democracy

---

69   See Lützeler, *Ethik und Politik*, 52–53; The journal *Die Friede (The Peace)* was a 'one
     of the most critical and democratically engaged political blotters of the post War
     years […] and strike […] a decidedly anti-monarchist and pro-republican-democratic
     tone' (52). The journal is, however, not a decidedly Social Democratic organ; it
     reflected peaceful and democratic views from left and centre.

(*Bolschewismus*) because they would prevent him from finishing his book on value construction and from getting a divorce.[70]

It was over the rebuilding of the Austrian economy and the avoidance of civil war that Broch and Bauer and Adler agreed. The necessity to pursue change through elections was also in common. But, the depth of Broch's commitment to a 'de-politicized' proletarian future has little overt evidence. In his essay on worker councils, he conceded the goal of a stateless, end of history. But, the depth of that commitment was questionable, and the vehicle of such a historical change was not to be placed in the hands of the Social Democratic party or an enlightened proletariat. As Lützeler himself acknowledges, Broch seemed to hope that political reformation could be apolitical, led not by parties and mass movements, but by 'unbound intellectuals'.[71]

In 1950, Broch forcefully asserted that intellectuals needed to guide the humanizing process. His writings from the 1920s, however, placed stability and individual freedom ahead of humanizing politics. His essay on worker councils was not about Social Democracy, it was about democracy, defined here by the rule of law and the expansion of individual freedom. The criticism of bourgeois aestheticism and the personal rejection of materialism did have a socialist ring; they were not, however, backed up by Social Democratic commitment.

This left Broch in an odd political position. Social Democracy under the philosophy of Bauer and M. Adler was ethically the closest political ideology to his own Kantianism, and since Kantian ethics required individual freedom, moderate Social Democrats like Bauer were also the closest ideology to his democratic beliefs. In the context of the battle within the Social Democratic party this was a conservative position, and one that suited well both Broch's liberal and Baroque upbringing in Vienna. He took a conservative approach to democratic state building. But, a commitment to balanced parliamentarianism had no pragmatic possibility in a world where oppositional forces on the right showed no real indication

70   *Teesdorfer Tagebuch*, 19 and 31.
71   Lützeler, *Ethik und Politik*, 14.

of maintaining compromise and moved more and more towards authoritarian and oppressive governance. It was the far right that perfected the aestheticization of politics and joined the rule of law to physical force.

Broch's plea in the essay, backed up in *The Sleepwalkers*, was to tap the brakes, to allow history to catch up to the meaning of its first sea change (from monarchy to democracy), and only after ethical norms for democracy were established could a state proceed to a post-political world. In the meantime, Broch was working hard on the guidelines for such a redefinition of ethical norms through his aesthetic and epistemological work. What he seemed to want in the interwar period was enough peace and stability to pursue these aims. History, however, did not stand still for him, and he soon realized that liberal democracy and stable industrial economies were not givens in the post-war political culture. They had only looked like they were in comparison to the dangers of mass political revolution on the left.

The limitations of Broch's social democracy remains inferred and not stated in all of his writings from the immediate post-war period. While Broch may have supported democracy as political goal and may have called for labour reform and some empowerment of workers, he stopped well short of the 'ending of history'. He did not envision a political endpoint that was supra-national or classless. By and large the tone of the essay is marked by materialist concerns – the repeated use of the term '*Mittel*'. Economic concerns underlay all of Broch's thoughts in the essay. As he argues, 'sites of production' are central loci for political activity, and thus they cannot be limited to the voice of only one aspect of that process, that is, workers' councils. The 'Entrepreneur', 'the director', 'the clerk', must be given as much consideration as the 'worker'.[72]

The conservativism seen in Broch's *Tagebuch* and his essays highlighted the legacy of the classical liberal period of his adolescence in nineteenth-century Vienna. Paradoxically, his attraction to Social Democracy and then his rejection of it came from the same Viennese liberal roots. The attraction was driven by commitments to *Bildung* and cosmopolitanism, while his rejection of politics and leftish mass movements was driven by

72   *KW* ii, 17.

a strong sense of classism (including anti-Semitism) and a commitment to order and stability (including protection of property, tradition and the interests of wealth). The point here is that his notion of political activism was strikingly upper middle class Viennese in its expression. He conceived of politics from the point of view of a café intellectual, he tied political action directly to aesthetics, and then set out to rectify political crises through epistemology and individualism. Inherent in this approach was a social conservativism and an assimilationist distrust of the masses. His political inclination was democratic and committed to security and law. The key influences for his earliest political thought were Kant, Austro-Marxism and a fundamental conservativism, which reflected his individual social and personal development.

Broch's democratic tendencies were moral in their justifications and showed the influence of Kantian ethics. 'As Hermann Broch in his open letter expressly demonstrates, politics has to be value oriented'.[73] His attack on both bourgeois and social democratic politics of interests was consistent with much of the neo-Kantian thought in Germany and Central Europe. His notion of an ethical humanism, however, was endangered by the breakdown of social control. In both 'The Street' and 'Constitutional Dictatorship' essay he stressed the need for rational, controlled action. His political solutions suggested that real advancement in the social and political realms took place in the context of control. The notion of security foreshadowed here Broch's later concerns for the security of the individual.

Broch suggested in these essays that politics too easily reflected vacuous phrases designed to win theoretical debates; yet, these empty phrases also took on real and dangerous meaning when co-opted by the masses. 'The Street' and 'Constitutional Dictatorship as Democratic Soviet System' were attacks on the idea of politics itself. Though Schmidt-Dengler argues that Broch engaged the political by elevating the political beyond the realm of the everyday, these articles represent a conservative approach to political transition that lacks a political platform or even a critical stance toward

---

73   Monika Klinger, *Hermann Broch und die Demokratie*, 41.

the formation of a new Austrian state. They represent, instead, personal concerns and class bias.

Schmidt-Dengler sees Broch's use of the imagery of 'The Street' as connected to a 'central topoi of [post-war] Austrian literature', in which the street was seen as an extension of the mob. It was a dirty and dangerous place, where even the 'undead' operated.[74] Schmidt-Dengler aligns Broch with writers and artists such as Otto Dix, Karl Kraus and Heimito von Doderer, in that all these intellectuals show deep reservations about *die Straße*: 'The street is filled with the mental ill, and it is the street that causes mental illness'.[75] In Broch's later novel, *The Death of Virgil*, he gives us an elaborate description of the dangers of the mob in the streets of ancient Brundisium:

> this bawling, yelping, compelling male laughter had nothing in common with the female laughter of Misery Street, no, this laughter contained something worse, terror and awe, the awfulness of the matter-of-fact that did not concern itself with the human, neither with him who looked on and comprehended here from the window, nor indeed with any human being.[76]

The imagery of the street was here a cultural and intellectual concept. In the context of Vergil's coming death, the imagery highlights the growing division of the spiritual and the material world; as the novel progresses, the emptiness of the material world becomes more and more evident. In both literature and politics, Broch understood the street, the masses and mass action as unworthy of intellectual occupation, as well as dangerous and to be avoided. The juxtaposition of spiritual/intellectual/evaluated to material/political/grounded suggested a bunkered mentality and an atomized view of society. It was a cultural viewpoint that also mirrored his psychic self-image.

Several other scholars have agreed with the notion that Broch could be defined as political, if by political one means critically involved with the

---

74   Schmidt-Dengler, '*Kurzum die Hölle*', 60.
75   Ibid, 61.
76   Hermann Broch, *The Death of Virgil*, Jean Starr Untermeyer, tr. (New York: Pantheon Books, 1945, renewed Vintage International, 1972), 115.

definition of the social value construction. Scholars like A. H. Perez and
Uwe Dörwald, however, help support my contention that Broch's critical
modernism was by and large an expression of conservative, if not elitist,
cultural criticism. Perez argues that Broch's political thought was a development of his confrontation with pluralism in Vienna and should be seen
as a 'reintegration of the individual and society and the reestablishment of
harmony between man and nature'.[77] He further argues that Broch worked
for social reform, but only in the sense of social and psychological interaction, not political or institutional change. 'There was yet a third way open
to perceptive Austrian minds of the period: redeem the self by redeeming
society. This option should be understood in the Neo-Freudian sense of
humanizing politics and social life by ameliorating its evils and accom-
modating and canalizing the irrational forces in man'.[78] Perez, in effect,
recognized a political activism operating within a Schorskean paradigm of
internal, psychological politics, and he explored that shift in Broch through
his investigation of his Freudian influences. Perez, however, argued that
Broch, like Schorske's Hofmannsthal, viewed the irrational side of politics
through the lens of instinctual unity, that is, through the traditional values
of the Austrian aristocracy: *Schlamperei* and the Baroque.

Perez argued that Broch was influenced by the Austrian Baroque in that
the idea of wholeness and catholicity was implied in the authoritarian push
for religious and governmental hegemony. There was a cosmopolitanism
implied in the Baroque period as well, from its lack of national identity and
from the multinational identities of its rulers. Perez claimed that Austria,
in opposition to Germany, developed a religious, cosmopolitan cultural
identity, whereas Germany developed a nationalistic, individualistic and
revolutionary one:

> Viennese theatricality, in all of its political, social, and cultural ramifications, was
> but the outer foliage of an organic view of the universe that was at root religious.

77   Arvid Henry Perez, 'The Disintegration of Values: A Social and Intellectual Study
     of the Austrian Philosopher-Novelist Hermann Broch, 1890–1930' (Dissertation,
     University of California, Los Angeles, 1970), 19.
78   Ibid, 16.

> [...] In Austria, right down to the beginning of the nineteenth century – past the Enlightenment, therefore – there was a persistent identification of aristocratic rule with a cosmic vision which was the cosmic vision of the Counter-Reformation.[79]

Indeed, Perez captures an important characteristic of Broch, that is, the degree to which he was enmeshed in the aristocratic mores of bourgeois, assimilated Vienna at the turn of the century.[80] His activism, however, was still a critical activism and not a reactionary flight. He sought in Catholicism and the Baroque, not a recoverable past, but a stable, jumping off point towards a new future. In the end, neither Catholicism nor the Baroque provided him with a path for reintegration of modern values.

In examining Broch's anti-intellectualism, Uwe Dörwald argues that his conservative nature made his relationship to pragmatic politics difficult and paradoxical. Dörwald hints at what I believe to be the correct historical interpretation of Broch as disengaged in this period (disinterested is the word Dörwald uses).[81] 'The Street' plays a key role in Dörwald's analysis. He sees 'The Street' and later *The Death of Virgil* as metaphorical statements of Broch's conservativism and disinterest in politics. The symbolism of separation (eternal and chthonic) that Dörwald highlights fits well Broch's internal struggles with ego psychology, his contested identity in terms of vocation and assimilation, and his political withdrawal of the 1920s. It was from the balcony, high above the masses and the materialism of the street, that he, as a poet, could conceive in a new way the ethical values that link to an absolute worldview. On the level of the street creativity became aestheticism, a product of the unthinking crowd or a manipulation of the crowd for political or economic gain. Broch referred to this as bourgeois philistinism in the *Tagebuch*.

What the *Tagebuch*, 'The Street' and the 'Constitutional Dictatorship' essay demonstrated was that Broch's political disengagement was more than intellectual, and only later did his position find a fully developed (anti-bourgeois, anti-communist and revolutionary) theory. His decision to

---

79   Ibid, 28.
80   To be discussed below.
81   Dörwald, 141.

reject pragmatic politics through the Social Democratic party, to promote an anti-revolutionary politics and to ignore (or subtly elevate) conservative positions such as class divisions and tradition, grew out of his social positioning as businessman and cultivated member of the upper middle class. This conservativism can be seen in two key areas: his anti-Semitism and his failure to see nationalist movements as equally as dangerous as communist ones. This was a result of his own security within the cosmopolitan, Catholic world of the Empire, which became defined, for progressive thinkers, through German *Kultur*.

Challenging the Historiography of Engagement

Carl Schorske's work *Fin de Siècle Vienna* and William Johnston's book *The Austrian Mind* established the question of social engagement as a dominant theme in Austrian intellectual history.[82] Broch studies has taken up that theme and made it a central feature in understanding his political legacy. This section points out a historiographical distinction in the way we discuss engagement in regards to Broch's social and political actions between 1918 and 1934. The historiographical tendency in evaluating him has been to follow Johnston's sociology, which examines social engagement beyond the political or ideological arena:

> Some Marxists pontificate that to be worthwhile a thinker must be engagé; anyone else may be dismissed as 'decadent' or 'aesthetic' or 'irrational' [...] What counts is whether the motive for opting out is ideological, as in the case of Nietzsche or Kraus, or purely disinterested, as in the careers of countless Austrian literati and theorists. However justified it may be to evaluate a publicist by his flair for mobilizing society to change, such a criterion can only caricature someone who spurns politics. Because

82   Carl S. Schorske, *Fin de Siècle Vienna* and William M. Johnston, *The Austrian Mind: An Intellectual and Social History, 1848–1938* (Berkeley: University of California Press, 1972).

> Austria [...] abounded with such adamantly apolitical figures, it is indispensable to segregate Marxist sociology of engagé intellectuals from the more inclusive sociology of thinkers.[83]

Under the rubric of 'sociology of thinkers', Broch and almost any *fin-de-siècle* intellectual can be characterized as 'engaged'. The problem for understanding Broch and much of the literati of the Austrian First Republic through this definition of engagement is twofold. First, it allows one to pass over in silence how Broch's social or cultural values guided his political tendencies. Secondly, it allows one to treat his experience of the First Republic as a *tabula rasa*. His position as an 'adamantly apolitical figure' invites a reading back into the vacuum of Broch's political voice, a voice of social engagement defined by his commitment to social theories such as vitalism or ethical humanism.[84]

The second tendency is heightened by the fact that Broch became 'adamantly political' in the context of the failure of the Austrian First Republic, the rise of National Socialism and his exile. The divergence between his deep political engagement from 1936 to his death in 1951 and his political quietism during the First Republic has led many scholars to develop false claims of consistent progressivism or consistent conservativism, or suggest the consistency of ethical duty and humanism somehow override political inconsistency. Broch published his first novel at the age of 46. Until the age of 40, industry and the culture of aristocratic imitation defined his life as much as cultural criticism and intellectualism. He received a technical education in textile manufacturing and business, and from the time of his graduation (1909) to the selling of his factory (1927) he lived a dual life – businessman by day, intellectual by night.[85] Taking this biographical and historical context into account, I conclude that the historiography around Broch simply ignores the most direct explanation – he changed

---

83   Ibid, 4.
84   Such a situation helps explains the deep divisions in the understanding of Broch's politics found the 'Affirmative/Critical Debate.'
85   The Broch family owned a textile factory in Lower Austria; Broch managed the firm along with his brother for close to 20 years. See Lützeler, *A Biography*, 31–61.

his mind. Driven by historical circumstances, he was forced to overcome a culturally conservative position of disengagement and reject the elitist commitment to epistemology and aesthetics as pragmatic social forces.[86] Such a position became difficult to discern because of Broch's sharp criticism of Viennese aestheticism in his 1948 essay on Hofmannsthal. His *Hugo von Hofmannsthal and his Time* obscured for many Broch's embeddedness in the metropolis of kitsch.

In arguing for a re-evaluation of Broch as political thinker during the Austrian First Republic, I am examining the conclusions of authors such as Paul Michael Lützeler, Ernestine Schlant, Joseph Strelka, Karl Menges and Dagmar Barnouw. In the case of all of these scholars, Broch's intellectual activity during the Austrian First Republic has been defined as political. Lützeler, Schlant and Strelka saw him through a liberal lens of political theory, while Menges and Barnouw characterized his work as reactionary or pseudo-fascist. The basis for any political worldview (even agenda) in Broch comes from two essays written in immediate post-war period (1918–1920) and his novelistic work of the early 1930s, as well as his short reviews essays on contemporary political theorists, such as Otto Bauer and Max Adler. These works seem to comprise a sufficient amount of political discussion to warrant the title of a political program. As argued above, I do not think they do. In fact, the two seemingly strongest political statements, 'The Street' and 'Constitutional Dictatorship as Soviet System', were in fact apologias for Broch choosing not to engage politically in the First Republic.

Broch's focus on politics after 1936 was obvious and understandable; but, before that date, the question of how to understand him politically resulted from a paradigm shift in Broch studies. Lützeler narrates this shift in the introduction to his own work on Broch's early politics. What Lützeler describes is the confluences of new material with a desire to move beyond the limitation of formal literary criticism. In this moment, social commentary and politics became the new vehicle by which to measure the

---

86   This historical flip-flop is further complicated by Broch's embracing again the centrality of cognition to his political work on mass hysteria in the 1940s.

importance of Broch's work. This new paradigm was strongly historical and biographical in its character, and the result was a flood of critical studies that claimed to see Broch as more than an artist, rather as someone deeply engaged in the social and political challenges of his world. This development in Broch criticism led to the merger of social criticism with political thought, as evidenced in Lützeler's work, where he uses the term political almost interchangeably with the idea of social commentary.

Such a paradigm shift, however, did not equate to a unified view on Broch's newly discovered political awareness. In fact, interpretations ran across the political spectrum from progressive to pseudo-fascist. The reactionary interpretations of Broch put forth by Karl Menges and Heinz Osterle played an important role in shifting the discussion of Broch's political thought from his late Austrian and his exile period to his earlier works (1910s to his novel *The Sleepwalkers*). Both scholars read Broch into the intellectual historical context of interwar Central Europe and found deep similar among Broch and thinkers such as Carl Schmitt. Dagmar Barnouw furthered this interpretation by linking Broch to a Weimar literary scene in which idealistic and utopian disillusions prevented intellectuals (including not only Broch, but also Benjamin, Mann and Jünger) from critically engaging in society. Most particularly for my argument, she suggests that these intellectuals had a naïve relationship to power politics.

The connection of Broch's thought to reactionary ideologies of the interwar period prompted scholars like Vollhardt and Lützeler to examine Broch's early work. In their examinations, they argue that his earliest intellectual works lacked any direct or indirect similarities to reactionary ideologies (from life philosophy to totalitarianism). Yet, ironically, Lützeler's description of Broch as politically engaged through his stance as 'unbound intellectual' comes very close to the ideal of 'negotiable detachment' Barnouw wanted the failed intellectuals of Weimar to take.[87] Ernestine Schlant's examination of Broch's political theory during this period offered a similar take away on his liberal and humanitarian *bona fides*, though she is much more direct in clarifying a lack of political continuity in his

---

87   Barnouw, *Weimar Intellectuals*, 30.

thought. The value of Schlant's, Vollhardt's and Lützeler's work is that they demonstrated decisively that Broch's philosophical and aesthetic values were humanist and progressive. Their work fits in well with the development of the theory of critical modernism from Viennese cultural history of the early 1990s, which leave one with little doubt that Broch was a keen observer of cultural development in the First Republic, but neither theory necessitates equating such cultural criticism with politics.

By examining Lützeler's study in more detail, I am able to trace out a pattern of historiographical assimilation of Broch's cultural criticism into political action. Lützeler concludes that Broch has a Kantian ethical position that forms the centrepiece of 'a *Gesellschaftskritik* in its various *tagespolitischen*, philosophical and artistic expressions'.[88] Lützeler stresses Broch's cultural criticism (a Krausian 'Pathos') over *tagespolitisch*. Though, he does examine the interaction with Marxism in a more directly political matter – pointing out Broch's sympathy for trade unionism and his anti-revolution stance. He links Broch's political conceptions with those of Max Adler and Otto Bauer based on a shared concern for Kantian ethics. He argues that Broch's literary critical essays from 1919 to 1922 are 'evidence of Broch's socio-critical engagement'. He defines, in the end, Broch's political agenda as that of the unbound intellectual, whose goal is to show the positive and negative utopias of the current age and to suggest a novel post-Kantian, post-Christian ethic for a new humanity. Broch was a 'representative of the party of the unbound, critical intellectual whose job it was under the current social conditions to work for the *Humanisierung* of political affairs'.[89]

Lützeler argues that it was Kantian idealism, especially the universal structure of the categorical imperative, that allowed Broch to move beyond the cultural pessimism and life philosophy of Nietzsche, Schopenhauer and Weininger. Lützeler points out that Broch's moral imperative was not metaphysical in its ethical concerns, but concerned with historical theory. In finding Kant, Broch had an idealistic and universal model that could

88   Lützeler, *Ethik und Politk*, 12.
89   Ibid, 14.

sustain rationality and individualism. Lützeler goes on to claim that the moral aesthetics of Kant were political.[90] He does not, however, provide any similar quotations from Broch that would suggest Broch attempted to apply Kant in a political fashion. In fact, at this very time, Broch is making statements about the moral impossibility of politics.[91] And even though Schmidt-Dengler went to extremes to show that his essay 'The Street' was a literary statement on the value of politics, the essay fits more into a classical form of apologia, as well as a simple apology for his abandonment of pragmatic political action in the midst of both internal and external attacks on the liberal democratic position of Austro-Marxism. I do not deny the intellectual affinity of Broch to Bauer and M. Adler, but Broch lacked an ideological position. He lacked a concern for state, especially coming from an Austrian context where the state did not exist as a simple, and probably not a central, political entity.

Lützeler correctly identifies Broch's attraction to Kant as driven by Broch's philosophy of history. It is a philosophy of history that is somewhat unique to him. As a Viennese and an autodidact, he blended his philosophical understanding from a variety of Central European sources. We find a cyclical structure to his model of historical movement similar to the modelling (decadence and rebirth) found in the philosophies of cultural pessimism to which he was attracted in his youth. For Broch, however, it was not an organicist model, but one that cycled through the opening and closing of social value systems. The opening or closing was defined by a society's ability to incorporate developments in knowledge. Here Broch's fundamental liberalism tended towards linear progression in human understanding, but without the concomitant social development along a similar linear and upward path of progress. His philosophy was also somewhat Hegelian in its understanding of historical transition as dialectical in the sense of conflict creating the foundation for a new open value system. Here again, however, his philosophy of history lacked the progressive directionality of Hegel and, more importantly, any teleological

---

90   Ibid, 38–40.
91   See *KW* 12/1.

clarity on the end of history. It was not until well into Broch's American exile that he identified a politically defined historical goal.

During the First Republic, his historical model still hinted at the eternal reoccurrence of value systems through death and rebirth. Thus, he retained a focus on the will of the individual as a primary mover in human history (though universalist in the Kantian sense and not subjective). The creative ethical human endowed with aesthetic and cognitive insight into the structure of the universal could express and direct the 'style of the age'. Broch may have abandoned the cultural pessimism and the anti-systematic claims of philosophical irrationalism, but he did not embrace an enlightened model of history where political philosophy drove the creation of freedom and progress. Broch, as a Central European, was much more historicist and idealist than that. He understood history as unique in its own context and focused on the individual as free to create values based on the uniqueness of his/her own context. This was why he adopted Kant, as a means of getting out of the historicist problem of relativity of values. Kant allowed him to have an autonomous, willed individual as the centrepiece of the value construction process that undergirded his philosophy of history. Through Kant, Broch overcame the anarchy of Nietzsche's anti-systematic individualism and the Machiavellianism of relative values suggested by German historicist tradition, and did so without justifying historical progress through the state or nation. Even in the Anglo-French liberal models of history, political developments remained the primary driver of historical change through the agency of individual freedom. Broch's philosophy of history based on Kant's cognitive model of willing and autonomy could operate in a political status quo. For a Central European intellectual, especially a subject of the Habsburg Empire, this was the only viable non-political position to take. Like Kant, Broch's beliefs in rationality and freedom tied him to the liberal tradition of popular sovereignty and allowed Broch to see democracy as a logical outcome of secular European society. But, more importantly, it detached ethical activity from political activity by severing the historical development from the importance of the state or, as Lützeler also claims, from humanity as a whole.[92] It is Lützeler who introduces the idea that Broch's social reality could be called political, not Broch.

This left Broch in the position of seeing only individuals as the designers of a new value system; by the 1920s, however, the radicalism of mass politics and the development of relative, closed value systems had endangered the capability of such individuals to accomplish the task. The sense of pessimism in his first novel (*The Sleepwalkers*, 1932) reflected his desperation in the face of political violence and street demonstrations. He excluded the masses from history. He elevated the ethically creative to a position of opening paths for the turning of history from closed to open. In his theory, the closing of history occurred as a result epistemological limitations on the power of a centripetal value to account for new developments in knowledge. The transitional periods were the only places where the masses could enter into history, and since they entered into history during phases of value disintegration or in the midst of the conflict of relative value systems, they operated during a period of fear and instability. It was here that both individuals and masses appear as historical agents, but not as fully conscious ones. They entered into twilight consciousness and set the stage for mass aberration. Lützeler argues that Broch's philosophy of history should be seen as political because it was concerned with evaluating historical development and social praxis. But there was little room left for Broch to imagine historical change as political. The notion of the state or the statesman was absence, and an ideology of materialism or vitalism or aristocracy was also absent. Of the three, the aristocratic preference for status quo and apolitical politics characterized him best. His repeated use of the term Machiavellianism suggested that even politics in the form of humanism could be unacceptable to him.

Lützeler's examination of Broch and Austro-Marxism seems to be on firmer grounds vis-à-vis politics. His argument about Austro-Marxism, however, covers over a critical difference between Broch and Alder or Bauer, the difference between real and fictional. Lützeler claims the only difference between Alder and Broch, in terms of their shared belief that

92   See Lützeler, *Ethic und Politik*, 42–43.

socialism should aim for a sociological attempt to merge Kantian morality with socialist community building, was that Broch 'under the influence of Vaihinger' expressed his theory hypothetically, and Adler saw the develop-ment of 'sociological laws' through morality as real and necessary.[93] Such a conclusion only makes the reading of Broch as politically disinterested or naïve more understandable, and left Broch once again in a situation where he could remove the historical agent of change from the material realm to the metaphysical realm and from the masses to the elites.

In Lützeler's discussion of the essay on 'Constitutional Dictatorship', he finds even more ground upon which to construct an image of Broch as political. As with 'The Street', Lützeler's argument relies on the necessity to paint Broch's political engagement with the colours of those he resembles intellectually. First, because Broch shared Kant's concerns for the ethical reconstruction of society through a rational 'good will', and Kant made the claim that this was expressively political, Broch was thus expressly political. Secondly, because Broch reviewed socialist thinkers who have an ethical sociology that was amenable to Kant, Broch was somehow engaged in the socialist struggles of the immediate post-war period. Lützeler says Broch associated himself with the ideas of Alder, but these ideas were *geistliche*, not political.[94] Broch, in fact, was simply 'standing near' these political figures and agreeing with their intellectual suggestions for sociological research, not political action. And just as 'The Street' was an apologia, which justified Broch moving further away from the political battles in which these men took part (even if here participation equals opposition), his 'Constitutional Dictatorship' essay extended that apologia into the theoretical justifications for slow, conservative action in the material realm of politics.

Broch's affinity to the Social Democrats cannot be denied, but the alignment of his democratic sympathy and his socialist actions in regard to his own factory should not lead us to conclude that these verbal affinities went much below the surface. His relationship to socialism as a political ideal was limited to a period in 1919/20; at this time, he felt compelled

93   Ibid, 50.
94   Ibid, 49.

to address the dangers of revolution and the economic weakness of the Austrian economy. In doing so, he chose to embrace a democratic platform, really the only democratic platform, by embracing Social Democracy. But, the embrace was reluctant. His Kantian beliefs about ethical creativity allowed him to see Bauer and Max Alder in very positive terms, and the historical reality that world war had made the Socialists a leading party led him to combine his economic position of job provider and owner of the means of production with his intellectual view of democracy. But, in his only theoretical essay on politics during the Austrian First Republic, he called for moderation.

Once again, Lützeler suggests a deep sense of engagement in Broch by two means: 1) the simple fact that a factory owner supported a socialist cause, and 2) by making the claim that Broch's essay somehow represented a challenge to the conservative political thought of Spann. Such a claim has no support in Broch's essay. The simple fact that the essay was published while Spann was active at the University of Vienna and because Broch's ideas oppose Spann's program should not equate to the conception of opposition. It was not clear from anything Broch wrote that he even saw Spann as a threat to the Austrian state or to democracy. It is a curious conclusion to draw that we should see Broch as a crusader against the growing danger of fascist or corporatist politics and an ardent supporter of social democracy, when he said almost nothing in terms of the former, and a great deal that is unflattering about the latter. The pattern of proving Broch's liberal democratic *bona fides* through association continues in Lützeler's direct examination of the essay.

Lützeler does say that one cannot attribute a political journalistic activity to Broch during the period of the 1920s.[95] He builds, however, an argument (suggested in his title) that leads one to the conclusion that Broch's ethical position during the Austrian First Republic (Kantian and historically based) allows us to characterize Broch as politically engaged. Even more, he leads the reader to understand Broch's political position as democratic and socialist in the progressive sense of ending bourgeoisie

95   Ibid, 59.

aestheticism and its barrier to greater social integration. Indeed, Lützeler effectively demonstrates Broch's democratic commitment and his individualism as an extension of his Kantian position. Broch's positive reviews and associated values in terms of key Austro-Marxist thinkers are also well established. But, in the end, Lützeler's argument, later expanded by scholars like Strelka, obscures the political nature of Broch's mind and biography. Lützeler over sells Broch's activism by building an argument based on the affinities of ideas. Karl Menges makes the same mistake in his logical connection of Broch to thinkers like Carl Schmitt.[96] Lützeler can illuminate shared intellectual and epistemological positions, some of which have inherent political implications, and then leave the reader to imagine the political engagement of undeniably activist thinkers like Max Adler, Otto Bauer, Thomas Masaryk, and even Emile Zola as Broch's.

What we lose in this process is a historical understanding of Broch's apolitical cultural mentality, and thus ideas like critical modernism and modernist humanism take on political overtones, which they, in fact, lacked in much of the First Republic's cultural crisis. Broch was engaged; but his engagement was seen in his commitment to a Central European notion of cosmopolitanism and not in a politically engaged question of nationalism, socialism or democratic rights. He sought solutions through metaphysics and fiction; and in so doing, he failed to understand the real stakes for political dangers in interwar Central Europe. The kind of political engagement and democratic theorizing that Broch gets credit for in arguments like Lützeler and Strelka only occurred in his exile and after a realization of the true dangers to individualism, as well as a deeper sense of being Jewish.

Lützeler quotes from one of Broch's letters in order to suggest that his novel *The Sleepwalkers* represented a point of continuity with his political agenda from exile and that he was not part of the aestheticizing culture he so effectively described and condemned in *Hofmannsthal and His Time*.[97]

96   The connection to Schmitt is based on the notion of a total state, the removal of the division between citizen and state through total power and the connection of the state to an essence of the *Volk*. Broch shows no signs of having an über-individual objective in mind when he creates his theory of human rights and dignity.
97   Lützeler, *Ethik und Politik*, 67–68.

My attempt to highlight Broch's intellectual biography from the 1920s is to suggest that in point of fact, this idea of continuity needs to be questioned to some degree. I conclude that, in fact, the basic impulses for democracy, human rights and ethical action were consistent across Broch's experiences, but that his distancing of himself from the political, because it was unethical and bourgeois, did not represent a heroic attempt to produce cognitive means for ethical rebirth, rather they represented a fundamental naïveté. His relationship to the notion of reality suffered from intellectual a priorism, cultural elitism and psychological conflict driven by his rejection of the physically intimidating material world for the higher more approachable world of spirituality.

Through Kant, Neo-Kantianism and Vaihinger, Broch came to build a philosophy of history that was idealist, based on the creation of a fiction and the exclusion of the masses. It was a fiction that allowed for social change and historical development, without the need for a deep sense of political commitment. His attraction to Austro-Marxism in the immediate post-war period shows a lingering liberalism defined by notions of secularism and cosmopolitanism, but based on the rational individual. Since this point of view suggested a democracy, he ended up close to the only democratic and liberal political entity of the 1920s: Austro-Marxism. However, he could not commit to even that because the socialist movement was involved in an internal conflict that endangered in Broch's mind its very democratic foundations.

Broch's philosophy of history aligned directly with that of Nietzsche in that it was not a politically based philosophy. The discussion was about historical epochs, values and styles. Like Nietzsche, Broch seemed to see the world as an aesthetic phenomenon. The dominant Central European tendency in the philosophy of history from Kant to Hegel to Droysen and the Prussian school to Marxist historians and cultural critics, even to the sociologists like Weber, was to conceive of history in explicitly political terms. The structures of nation, bureaucracy, class and leadership were the centrepieces to all of these narratives of historical movement. Though some blend an idealistic notion of mind or God into the forces that shape historical trajectory and goals, their narrative were primarily secular (in

an Augustinian sense) in their emplotments.[98] Broch lacked any sense of
these structures in terms of trajectory or goals. Both *The Spell* and *The
Death of Virgil*, two novels often seen as having a political interest in their
storylines lacked any attempt to struggle with direct political conflict.[99]
The final scene of interlocution between Augustus and the dying Vergil
relegated politics to pre-modern discussion of patronage and friendship.
The only scene that truly depicted a secular, human experience was Vergil's
trip through the streets of Brundisium. This was a human experience, but
again not a human political experience. If anything, Broch portrayed the
poet's conveyance as a cultural conflict based on socio-economic difference.

In *The Spell*, we are again closer to pre-modern conflicts surrounding
knowledge and spirituality than we are to the modern political experience.
The modern political experience, even for Kant and Hegel in their political philosophy, was characterized by mass society and ideas of revolution.
Broch's novel set in the Alps, in a small village, seemingly left behind by the
modern world and connected to mythologies such as Demeter and chthonic
forces, failed to awaken in his reader any sense of modern political dangers
of the 1930s. Mythology as a part of the aestheticization of politics was a
fully developed idea by the time Broch wrote the first draft of his novel.
But, the efficiency of fascist mythology, even where *Blut und Boden* ideas
played a central part, operated with the tools of technology and modernization. The mythological power of politics was found in the city and on
the subway, not in the infertile mines of an abandoned Alpine mountain.
As I argue in this chapter and in Chapter 3, the absence of politics can be
seen both in Broch's cultural identity and cognitive concerns of the 1920s
and 1930s, and in the technologically barren world of *The Sleepwalkers* and
its progressively vanishing modern terrain.

Lützeler's concluding claim that Broch's political engagement must
be understood as a political decision to redefine politics through a sense

---

98   For a discussion of German historicism's political activism and its religious model-
      ling of historical progress, see Robert Southard, *Droysen and the Prussian School of
      History* (Lexington: University of Kentucky Press, 1995).
99   Against see Patrick Eiden, *Das Reich der Demokratie*.

of being 'unbound' is suggestive, but I think understood out of context. In the context of the Austrian First Republic, this was a position of disinterest, not activism. There are specific areas where disengagement can be identified: 1) Broch's dismissive relationship to Social Democracy during the height of its struggle for political control and survival; 2) The conservative and elitist rejection of mass political action, based on Broch's preference for stability and protection of his own propertied interests; and 3) Broch's expressions of anti-Semitism that reflect a commitment to a classical liberal sense of classism. Broch's decision to forego repeatedly the pragmatic world of Austrian politics in its deepest moments of crisis (1919, 1927 and 1934) were not the actions of someone searching for a political solution. They were the actions of someone naïve to the realities of political power.[100] All of this, in the context of the 1920s, emphasized Broch's conservative commitment to stability and the propertied class, a fear of leftist revolution and blindness to the dangers of nationalist mass politics. All of these positions characterize an intellectually conservative tendency to embrace social control through the universalist ideals of the Catholic Baroque and imperial tradition.

Conclusion

The examination of Broch's *Tagebuch* suggests that what prompted his political engagement in the years immediately after the war was personal. It related above all to the protection of his economic position and stabilization of the Viennese cultural milieu to which he hoped to integrate with

100 Osterle argued that such 'unpolitical' activities represented a reactionary position, in
     which Broch hoped for a corporate stabilization of society as a solution to the dangers
     of socialist revolution. Though, I agree that Broch's fear of Bolshevism pushed him
     away from political engagement in 1919/1920; he did not do so because, 'Democracy,
     especially social democracy was anathema to him at the time' (Osterle, 'Revolution
     and Apocalypse', 954).

more fully. What he seems to have been concerned about was the process of 'socialization': the control of the economy by the state – whether a slow process involving partnership of capital, workers, consumers and state or a rapid expropriation of industry and property from private hands. He feared that socialization would undermine his own position in Austrian society. It was clearly a private motivation, but it stood behind much of what he said politically between 1918 and 1920. I do not find it a coincidence that his period of direct political engagement ended in 1920, at the same point that Socialist control in national politics ended. Social Democracy ruled in Vienna and Broch could agree with much of what it did and stood for (especially what Rabinbach calls Social Democracy's '*Bildungs-ethos*').[101] Like the Socialists, Broch chose to forego immediate pragmatic politics and focus on cultural education and epistemological preparation for a better tomorrow.[102] Christian Socialism, however, had control of the national agenda and that meant that the dangerous aspects of Social Democracy, its radical forms, would be put in check. Broch's worldview fit securely in the political development of Social Democracy and Christian Socialism in the first four years of the Austrian First Republic. From that point forward, the 'critical' nature of his modernism returned to an epistemological basis and remained focused on cultural criticism and aestheticism until the mid-1930s. Broch's later admission that concerns for aesthetic ideals in the midst of fascist terror was immoral carried a good bit of self-conscious criticism.

There was also a dismissive rhetoric vis-à-vis the pragmatism of current politics and social activism. This reveals a contradiction in image of Broch *als Politiker*. On the one hand his essays and book reviews from the 1920s supported an ideal model of gradual, ethical socialism, ideas which he briefly pursued publicly and pragmatically. On the other hand, however, his letters of the 1920s and *The Sleepwalkers* displayed a cynicism towards any real or material expression of the political. This presents us with the picture of an alienated and disconnected intellectual, an individual marginalized by his

---

101 Rabinbach, 30.
102 As Stephen Colbert suggests in his political satire – 'building a better tomorrow, tomorrow'.

class and Jewishness to the point that his world closed in on itself, leaving Broch blissfully unaware of the mounting dangers around him. He became locked into a universal idealism that bred pessimism because he lived in a world where materialism and relativism reigned. In *Hofmannsthal and his Time* (1947), Broch levelled a severe critique of the aestheticized world of interwar Vienna. And though he did not, in the 1920s, gaily celebrate the collapse of European culture, he failed to engage the most imminent forces of its destruction. Like Nietzsche's 'men of Goethe', Broch failed to get angry and to act; he fell into an intellectualism that could condemn the emptiness of contemporary culture, while simultaneously being able to separate itself from the instability of 'Rousseauian men'.[103]

Intellectual immaturity and personal instability created in Broch an antagonism towards the political left and an obtuseness to the dangers, especially to Jews, of the political right. This political characterization is what I have labelled disengaged. This is not to say that he pursued an unengaged life of quietism or fled into the garden of the aesthete. He did not. Broch was very much a public intellectual during the First Republic, he published articles and reviews in fashionable magazines, *avant-garde* and mainstream journals, he attended salons and cafés, he studied at the university, and he pursued literary and epistemological work whose central goal was social improvement. Broch believed in social engagement, yet he dismissed pragmatic politics as insignificant, bothersome or dangerous. Where Broch failed in his understanding of politics seems to have been his ability to distinguish the bothersome from the dangerous.

From the middle 1930s, he was a politically engaged intellectual and someone fully aware of the pragmatic dangers to Jewish culture and identity, as well as someone who directed his intellectual energies primarily at combating fascism. This image, however, does not correlate with the Hermann Broch of the 1920s, and we must avoid the tendency to understand the immediate post-war Broch through this later image or to argue

103 See Friedrich Nietzsche, 'Schopenhauer as Educator', in *Nietzsche Untimely Meditations*, Daniel Breazeale, ed. and R. J. Hollingdale, tr. (Cambridge: Cambridge University Press, 2013), 125–194.

for a consistency between his actions under the Austrian First Republic and his later exile. Broch's *Weltansschauung* during the Austrian First Republic reflected personal and intellectual concerns that relegated politics to a secondary or tertiary importance. By examining his statements on politics, personal and public, I am correcting the historiographical fallacy of continuity and teleology in defining Broch's political nature.

Having been educated in the world of *fin-de-siècle* Vienna, Broch was a humanist, an individualist and a democrat. He lived the assimilated life implied in his father's liberal, bourgeois world. But, politically he was limited in his choices owing to his own rejection of money and the anti-Semitic turn of the Christian Socialist and the pan-Germanists. Austro-Marxism at the turn of the century was certainly attractive to Broch on many levels. He knew, read and admired the central intellectuals behind the movement. Austro-Marxism, however, had limits in its attractions. By the end of the First World War, these limits had led to a clear rejection of Soviet-style Marxism because of its materialism and its exterminationalist rhetoric vis-à-vis the middle class.[104]

It may appear that in this chapter I have held Broch up to an extremely high standard of social responsibility and then criticized him for being human in the midst of it. In fact, I have. My intention, however, was to use such criticism as a way of clarifying the historical context of his intellectual activity during the Austrian First Republic. To do so effectively, it was necessary to demonstrate that the model of political engagement and social responsibility, which Broch created for himself during his exile and which scholars have too often read back into his early work, needed a more critical lens to be properly viewed. In the next chapter, I further examine the political implications of Broch's thought in the First Republic through a political interpretation of his novel *The Sleepwalkers*.

104 See Lützeler, *Ethik und Politik*, 33–58.

CHAPTER 3

The Sleepwalkers and Modernity

> Eternity must be comprised in a single existence, in the totality of a single
> work of art, and the nearer the work of art comes to the frontiers of total-
> ity, the greater its possibility of survival.[1]

In this chapter, I examine the theme of dystopia and modernization in
The Sleepwalkers. My examination argues for a sense of pessimism in the
novel that strengthens the previous chapter's image of Broch as disengaged. As I will argue in Chapters 4 and 5, pessimism followed Broch into
exile, but as Broch shifted to a more directly engaged political position
optimism became the dominant theme of his mass delusion theory and
his political essays. In a sense, during the Austrian First Republic and in
The Sleepwalkers, a politically disengaged Broch buried his optimism in a
foregrounded pessimism. But, in exile, he presented his political theory as
an optimistic solution to the horrors of the contemporary events. In the
novel, he shows the decadence of his time and the dangers of political and
economic change, but he fails to provide a path forward in the overcoming of these dangers. He, instead, maintains a false hope that the forces of
totalitarianism and mass society can be checked by an intellectual revolution in ethical creativity. Broch's literary work did not exclude him from
being critical in his modernism; but, his aesthetic and cognitive solutions
to value disintegration maintained a sense of elitism and disconnection
in the face of dangerous mass cultural behaviour. His acknowledgement

---

1   Hermann Broch, 'Joyce and the Present Age', in John Hargraves, tr., *Geist and Zeitgeist:
     The Spirit in an Unspiritual* (New York: Counterpoint, 2002), 90.

of these dangers dominated the narrative of the novel and thus promoted an aura of pessimism. His critical modernism did not translate to practical or engaged solutions to the challenges of technological advancement and modern mass society. Within the elite, traditional world of Vienna, critical modernism could become in the hands of intellectuals like Broch a toothless, idle concept.

Both Ernestine Schlant and Joseph Strelka argue that Broch's turn to politics came in the early 1930s. With the completion of his first novel and several essays on ethical art, Broch set out an intellectual program for exposing and delegitimizing aestheticized politics.[2] Though there are clearly parallels between Broch's ideas on kitsch and the work of thinkers like Walter Benjamin, Schlant gives Broch too much credit for the political significance of his cognitive and aesthetic essays of the early 1930s. These works may seem to open the road for social stability through epistemological progress, but the historical philosophy of *The Sleepwalkers* was clearly pessimistic about any cognitive breakthroughs occurring, and as Broch watched the destruction of the liberal idea (which had been in retreat for his entire life) in the late 1930s and early 1940s, his historical pessimism about the ability of aesthetic activities to produce ethical outcomes only heightened. It was the pessimism and despair of the late 1930s that produced a visible shift in Broch in terms of politics. To read that shift into the epistemology and literature of the 1920s and early 1930s mischaracterizes the political insight and engagement of Broch.

My last chapter helps to make the idea clear for the period from 1918 to 1927; my discussion here pushes the period of disengagement to the middle 1930s. Schlant's quotation of a letter from Broch, in which he mentions the 1934 February civil war helps to make the point.

---

2   Schlant writes, '[Broch's essays] were charged with political relevance. [...] Broch sees the poet's cognitive mission as the only justification of literature in catastrophic times. Without proper regard for this conversion of cognitive efforts into ethical achievements, and of ethical achievements into political statements, the entire political dimension of these essays is lost. Broch's insistence on *Dichtung* as the only means left to assuage man's metaphysical anxieties and thereby to become a political force was never again as pronounced as in the first half of the 1930s' (69–70).

> Yet there are several external or quasi-external reasons for this sterility: (a) my constant financial worries, due to my various obligations, and increased through large repairs on our house in Vienna – one more reason which turned me so abruptly to write for the theatre – financial worries consume a tremendous amount of time; (b) the extremely complicated situation in my personal life which – seen from the point of view of productivity – also is part of the external hindrances; (c) the political events in the world in general, those of February and July in particular, events which, after all, went under my skin; (d) the interruption through the premiere in Zurich, which came at an extremely inconvenient time.[3]

The mention of the civil war suggests a link between Broch's essayistic and literary work and contemporary politics. Broch did mention the civil war in his letter, but he mentioned it third, behind money issues and personal relationships. If one compares other Austrian intellectuals, even Stephan Zweig, and their reactions to these same events, the relative disinterest of Broch is evident.

One basic starting point for my discussion is that Broch's cognitive theory and his literature from *The Sleepwalkers* to *The Death of Virgil* should not be read as political in any direct sense. One can, as Schlant does, suggest that his essays of the early 1930s and his unfinished novel *The Spell* represented a politically engaged Broch, but that is an overly generous reading of him and his political pragmatism. For Broch, direct political involvement occurred only from 1936 to his death in 1951, and only from 1938 to 1947 in a fully committed sense. Schlant, in fact, agrees with my general conclusion that Broch's truly engaged relationship to politics started in 1936 and his essay on the League of Nations. 'With the "Resolution" Broch resumed a practice he had abandoned in 1919, after his contribution to the post-First World War economic and social situation in the essay on "Constitutional Dictatorship". In direct response to political events, he sought to chart a practical political solution inspired by maximum respect for individual man'.[4]

The Sleepwalkers, written between 1927 and 1932, represented Broch's most focused intellectual work in his pre-exile period. It was a work that

3   Letter quoted from Schlant, 74–75.
4   Ibid, 89.

was primarily apolitical, and where it was political, politics were shown as ineffective. They represented failed solutions – kitsch and aestheticism. In this way, the novel was a carrying forward of the disengaged political position seen in his writings of the early 1920s. By examining the novel's interface with modernity, especially in the themes of technology and industrialism, one can see that while he examined modernity in a direct way in terms of its manifestations, his solutions to its effects were only epistemological. The novel was cognitive and aesthetic, not politically pragmatic. Industrialization could not be addressed politically because Broch's political disengagement of the 1920s still held sway.

Broch's novel, the high point of his intellectual activities in the Austrian First Republic, was explicitly pessimistic about the usefulness of pragmatic politics and viability of contemporary Central European society. It was a position that wanted to project some notion of hopefulness at the end of the work, but overall the novel's final volume presented a new reality for modern Europe that lacked both forceful protestations of modernity's danger and solutions to its effects. Instead, Broch simply begged the political question at the end of the novel and hoped that his cognitive theory, implanted in the final volume, would suggest a new direction for positive value construction (*Wertwillen*) and a new creative ethics. Though one should not criticize the novelist for using the novel as his vehicle for social engagement; one can question whether Broch's commitment to cognitive theory and aesthetics in the declining years of social democracy and parliamentarianism in Austria and the rise of the Hitler in Germany was not fostered by the hollowness of his political acumen.

One word in regards to the affirmative/critical debate is worth a mention at this point.[5] Much of the work examined by those who wished to see Broch's writing as tinged by reactionary thought and connected to thinkers such Carl Schmitt came from the his work during the 1920s and early 1930s. My work, although critical of the affirmative nature of the interpretation of his work for its political value, does not agree with the claims of the critical school. I do not find comparisons of Broch to Schmitt valuable,

5   See Introduction for discussion of the debate.

because my claim is that Broch lacked the central understanding or even concern to address problems in the functioning of the state or nation. I do argue for a sense of pessimism in his understanding of modernity, but I do not read that pessimism as apocalyptic; and thus, I do not connect Broch to degeneration theorists like Spengler or to palingenetic political movements. As Vollhardt, Lützeler and Schlant effectively argue, Broch's early work was too deeply engrained in individual freedom and humanism to connect to any of the reactionary or ultra-conservative activities of the early twentieth century. Nonetheless, if one charts his intellectual agenda with enough care in terms of its political value, one can be more critical of his political failures and blind spots during the 1920s and 1930s.

In writing *The Sleepwalkers* Broch hoped to create a scientific art that merged rationality and spirituality. It was not a conservative ideology or theory of degeneration that most accurately explains his criticism of modernity as valueless and destructive, but a neo-Kantian attempt to link the real and the ideal. In the context of fascism in the 1930s, it made him a passionate liberal democrat. In the 1920s, however, the image suggested to us by the documents was a disengaged intellectual attempting to overcome the antinomies of idealism and pragmatism – trying to build an ethical art that would allow for an ethical value system that would produce real social unity.

Such idealism was clearly connected to his attraction to Kant and Plato, but it was also the expression of his alienation within Viennese society. And in a sense it was a double alienation. Having been alienated from the world of Jewish *Bildung* until his forties, Broch failed to secure a solid platform from which to engage with the political world around him. Yet, assimilated into a world of wealth, comfort and leisure, he closed himself off from the world of pragmatic politics, cutting that relationship fully with the sale of his factory in 1927. From that point until the rise of National Socialism, Broch lived and work in a world apart, a world of the interior ego and the world of the transcendental universality of art and ethics. He recoiled from the real and material world around him and distanced himself from his own socialism by demonstrating its filthy and dangerous nature. At the same time, he turned a blind eye to the growing dangers of reactionary politics. He conceived of such politics as a hollow nationalistic attempt to build *Gemeinschaft*. He believed such efforts were vainglorious and romantic, and ultimately impotent. In all, Broch unknowingly positioned himself as liberal in a purely idealistic (non-material) sense. It was in *The Sleepwalkers* that all of these political positions coalesced.

The Sleepwalkers was Broch's first novel, and he envisioned the three-volume novel as an aesthetic warning about the dangers of European modernity, by which he meant industrialization, mass culture and 'the destruction of values' (*der Zerfall der Werte*). He illustrated this historical process of value destruction through the story of three protagonists (Pasenow, Esch and Huguenau). In each story, the backdrop of industrialized, mass culture directed and enhanced the loss of a universal set of social values for organizing communal interaction and giving meaning to life. Broch used a poly-historical narrative to present this process over three generations in German history (from 1890 to 1905 to 1918). Each volume focused on an individual character and his struggles to stabilize his social, political and economic position in a rapidly changing world. Each historical period defined the struggle for stability differently, based on the forces of modernization in play. For Pasenow in 1890, the forces of modernity represented a clash of old regime values with the developing autonomy and power of wealth found in the urbanization of Berlin. For Esch in 1905, modernization represented the expanding influence of industrialization and capitalism in the new urban settings of the industrial city of Mannheim. Mannheim, as a centre of political radicalism connected to modernizing ideas like liberalism and as the central symbol of German industrialization from late nineteenth century to the Second World War, embodied the growing impact of capitalism at the turn of the century on a broader section of German society: from the aristocracy to the middle class to Marxist revolutionaries to immigrants. For Huguenau in 1918, Broch paradoxically shifted the narrative from an urban to a rural setting. In so doing he was not fleeing modernization; he was, instead, charting the deepening penetration of modernity to all levels of German society. In the setting of the rural village, Huguenau showed the triumph of the business for business sake value system of capitalism and completed the slow descent into hyper-individualism that defined the struggles of Pasenow and Esch.

Paralleling these modern, socio-economic battles, however, were the subjective and psychological conflicts of the protagonists. These conflicts were more internal and metaphysical, defined by explorations into sexual identity, spirituality and existential happiness. The overall structure of the novel allowed Broch to merge the external socio-economic landscape of European modernization with the psychological narrative of hyper-individualism. Through these agonistic narratives, he outlined the failure of competing values systems and demonstrated the modern tragedy of a value vacuum that offered no set of rules or beliefs that could, in the context of modernity, integrate the individual and the communal.

In the following discussion of the three protagonists, I argue that the idea of industrialization provides an important medium for conceptualizing Broch's discourse of *der Zerfall der Werte*. My argument is that his discussion of the disintegration of values is inexorably linked to his critique of mass, industrial society, and that in observing this link we can better appreciate the intellectual concerns of post-1914 German art. Broch's contribution to the discussion of how European culture adjusted to the world of industrialization and the political and psychological dangers it brought forth opens a new perspective on the intellectual debate over the crisis of liberalism, the role of aesthetics and the conflict between rationality and irrationality. In the novel, we find a severe critique of autonomy and liberalism alongside a hopeful plea for re-directing art towards individual creativity and a universal commitment to the Enlightenment project. In offering this reading of the novel, I acknowledge Broch's critical humanism and social commentary, but simultaneously I question the isolation of the human mind from the grit and grime of human existence. Simple human existence was under severe pressure during the time of the novel's composition from problems such as the Great Depression, political violence and militarism. Yet, the protagonists of the novel show very little awareness of the deprivation and violence on a physical level. Their suffering is internal and even their window seat to other's suffering is distant and unengaged. Because the novel was conceived of as a novel of cognition, such distancing is expected. But, the failure of all three protagonists to recognize the cognitive dead end of their historical epoch and to act upon that awareness makes one wonder how Broch could conceive of the novel as a tool of social reform. Even, if one argues for Bertrand or the narrator of the final volume (perhaps the same character) as the true protagonist of the historical odyssey through German ideology, one finds scant traces of an actionable worldview to guide such thoughtful readers.

The Sleepwalkers and Industrialization

The interpretation of *The Sleepwalkers* as a novel of industrialism and its dangers has received little attention in scholarship. Unlike many modernist works of the post-1914 period in German art and literature, *The Sleepwalkers* lacked a fully external expression of the physical dangers of a technological modernity, especially in comparison to works such as the dystopias of Kafka and Čapek or the nightmarish visions of dehumanizing technology found in the *Neue Sachlichkeit* paintings or the technologically dangerous world of Fritz Lang's *Metropolis*. In the first two volumes of the novel Broch presented a world that was by and large urban, capitalist and industrial. The damage this world brought to its inhabitants, however, was not physically manifested, nor could the solutions to the damage be found in practical issues of ownership of the means of production or changes in the control of political power. Suffering took place in the individual consciousness of Broch's characters, and the source of the suffering was an existential angst about the lack of a credible value system. As the story advanced chronologically, the visibility of industrialization and its symbols (the city, the train, immigration) faded and were replaced by the psychological cost of modernization.

The layout of the novel argued for the importance of the internal over the external, especially the restructuring of the novel just before its publication.[6] In the spring of 1930 Broch made the decision to expand his

6   See Breon Mitchell, *James Joyce and the German Novel, 1922–1933* (Athens, OH: Ohio University Press, 1976), 'manuscript evidence shows conclusively that he did in fact revise and greatly expand the third section of his novel, after reading *Ulysses*. Broch began writing *Die Schlafwandler* in 1928, and by early 1930 the novel was in

novel from a single volume book, which united *Pasenow* and *Esch* with a brief epilogue. This decision changed *The Sleepwalkers* into a trilogy, with the epilogue expanding into the 300 plus page third volume, *Huguenau or the Realist*. In its restructured form, the balance of the novel shifted from volumes one and two to volume three. Now the longest of the three volumes, it also brought together the leading figures of volumes one and two. The renovated third volume shifted from the modern, industrialized landscape to the rural village. The stories, however, retained the urban intrigues of sex, violence, crime and revolution developed in the first two volumes; business, entrepreneurship and manufacturing also remained a constant motivation or source of unease for all the characters.[7]

With the newly expanded *Huguenau*, however, the visibility and importance of industrial society shifted. No longer a simple narrative about the impact of industrialization, it shifted the setting from the city to the small town, it weakened the direct confrontation with – urbanization, technology, capitalism and science – and instead began to explore the impact of industrial society through epistemology. It also forced Broch to restructure volumes one and two in order to balance out the architectonic relationships of the three stories. One of the key results of this change was that the disintegration of values became more and more central to the

---

what he then thought be its final form. It consisted of two sections "Pasenow" and "Esch" (of approximately equal length) and a short "epilog"; he intended to publish them together as a one-volume novel. It is clear that at this point he considered *Die Schlafwandler* finished, and had no intention of altering it significantly' (154–155). See also Broch's letters to Daniel and Daisy Brody, H. G. Meyer, Frank Thiess, and Willa and Edwin Muir. From these letters, one can reconstruct not only the chronology of Broch's expansion of the novel, but also gain insight into his intentions, especially his claims to a new novel form, the epistemological novel, that could balance the hypertrophy of rationalism with a scientifically defined irrationalism, *KW* 13/1, 177–188.

7   See Mitchell, 159–160, for a discussion of the key additions in *Huguenau*. These additions helped make the third volume the most inventive and experimental volume in the novel in terms of narrative structure. Broch added to the stylistic aspects of philosophical essayism, poetry, theatrical staging, as well as presenting a named narrator for at least portions of *Huguenau*. Many scholars have been very critical of the narrative impact of these changes; see Barnouw, 241–245.

narrative structure, and the immediate presence of industrialism faded from the reader's view.

Nevertheless, we should not see this shift as an abandonment of Broch's concern for modernization. Instead, we should understand this restructuring as a new strategy for educating the reader about its true danger.[8] In line with other early twentieth-century literary modernists, Broch presented industrialization in a paradoxical manner. He deconstructed the physical attributes of modernization and used abstraction and symbolism to express a deep sense of dislocation and intrusion. Pursuing a similar pattern in *Huguenau*, Broch ultimately abandoned narrative flow and logicality.

The epistemological redefinition of the novel addressed Broch's observation that science and philosophy had lost step with the metaphysical needs of society. Hyper-rationalism could not approach the totality of human existence, and literature had an ethical duty to open human consciousness to this cognitive totality.

> The age of philosophical universality, which was also the age of the great compendiums, was brought to an end by philosophy itself, which became obliged to withdraw its most burning questions from the realm of logical discussion or else, as Wittgenstein has put it, refer them back to the mystical. It is at this point that the mission of literature begins; the mission of a cognition that remains above all empirical or social modes of being and to which it is a matter of indifference whether man lives in a feudal, bourgeois or proletarian age; literature's obligation to the absoluteness of cognition, in general.[9]

In accordance with the aesthetic demands of the post-war world, he created in the *The Sleepwalkers* a novel of cognition (*Erkenntnisroman*).

Realist and naturalist narrative approaches could no longer provide a style appropriate to the hyper-rationalism and anti-mysticism of the modern *Zeitgeist*. Even the modern inventiveness of Joyce and Musil, who at least attempted to understand the relationship with the rational and irrational, had failed to find a truly 'scientific' style for integrating human irrationality in art and values. Broch claimed that once the totality of knowledge or the

8   See letter to Daniel Brody, 19 July 1932, *KW* 13/1, 201–203.
9   Broch, 'Joyce and the Present Age', 88.

universal was questioned, it left art in a position of permanent invention.[10] In such a situation of epistemological relativism, taste and morality could be abandoned. As Broch stated:

> The farther step taken beyond the monotheistic cosmogony has been taken almost imperceptibly, and yet it is of greater significance than any preceding one: the First Cause has been moved beyond the 'finite' infinity of a God that still remained anthropomorphic, into a real infinity of abstraction; the lines of inquiry no longer converge on this idea of God (they no longer converge on any point, one may say, but run parallel to each other), [...] every solution is merely a temporary solution, and that nothing remains but the act of questioning in itself.[11]

Many modernist and post-modernists thinkers have viewed this relativism of knowledge as an opportunity for redefining art as experience, a new and powerful social tool for levelling modern society. Broch's work in the early 1930s, on the other hand, remained much more conservative, and instead struggled to demonstrate the dangers of the autonomous value systems produced by epistemological anarchy. He struggled to put the genie back in the bottle by laying the foundation for a new universal value system that would direct the 'style' of an age towards totality. It was with *Huguenau* that Broch confronted industrial society most explicitly from the point of view of its impact on the totality of cognition, creating in the process a re-examination of modern views on freedom, individualism and autonomy.

Broch suggested that fiction even when minimizing the physical presence of industry and technology, nonetheless could attempt to explain the relationship of humanity to inhumane forces of the modern, industrialized West. In this case, he denuded the human environment of industry to recapture the socially constructive force of human agency. His project was an enlightened one that refused to indict the technology of the modern world. Instead he indicted the individual and her or his hysterical commitment to autonomous value systems. He argued in effect that robots and bombs did not threaten the freedom and progress of Western society, thoughtless,

10 See Louis Kampf, 'The Permanence of Modernism', *College English* 28/1 (Oct. 1966), 1–15.
11 Broch, *The Sleepwalkers*, 426.

distracted and bored humans do. The limited success of modernist literature with this message of enlightened self-awareness presaged the intellectual history of the 1930s and 1940s, where rationality, the Enlightenment project and human agency became more and more challenged.

Although the literary depiction of industrializing Germany clearly suggested that industrialism and modern relativism were dangerous and alienating forces, the novel as a whole operated as an aesthetic solution to the breakdown of universal value systems and ethical anarchy. Broch claimed that the art of the modern age had regulated aesthetics either to the position of simply describing the past or to the position of dehumanizing the power of art through abstraction. Art was stripped it of the power to enact social improvement. His interwar work indicated a caesura in European thought: modern aesthetics and positivism excluded classical and Christian values as sources for modern creativity, yet prophets of irrationalism championed the overthrow of enlightened secularism. The novel constructed a literary image of modernity that recognized the dialectical nature of reason and the limitations of individual autonomy in the face of the modern society. Yet, it also celebrated key enlightenment ideals, such as the commitment to industrial urbanity, democracy and individual agency.

The novel suggested a redefinition of individualism and freedom designed to create a new absolute value in the wake of secularization and rationalism; simultaneously it rejected Romantic irrationality and its conservative embrace of the past, as well as the socialist reshuffling of the material relationships of production. Although the novel failed to adequately define this totalizing cultural force, it represented an attempt at saving and reforming an enlightened future for European society. Broch's progressive view of enlightened self-awareness, however, reinforced the image of him as politically disengaged. His decision to internalize the modern experience highlighted the naïveté of his political understanding of mass politics and nationalism. Just as in his later novel draft, *The Spell*, he challenged seemingly large political issues (revolution, mass aberration, anti-Semitism, labour unrest) from a rural setting with a vague and unidentified national space. One cannot help but conclude that Broch's focus on the internal, cognitive aspects of modernity operated without internal reference to institutional influences such as nations or parties. The combination of withdrawal from the urban, mass culture and the aestheticization of politics that accompanied it confirmed an interwar worldview in Broch that failed to grasp the real sources of violence and murder operating in the political milieu. Huguenau, as the unpatriotic, vaguely French/German, war profiteer who fled the modernizing tendency of industrialization for a small village (a theme Broch repeated multiple times in his novelistic work from the early 1930s and which mirrored somewhat his own biography of the same period) failed to embody in any effective way the brutality and inhumanity of the moment, which Broch asked him to represent. As a rapist, a murder and a saboteur, Huguenau's actions lacked the pathos of real cruelty. One saw the same distancing of human outrage and concreteness in Esch's abuse of his wife at the end of volume two. The price of cognitive focus was engagement with social reality. It was a price Broch was not just willing to pay, but chose to pay because it fit his own emotional and intellectual disconnection vis-à-vis the political world of the Austria First Republic.

The Sleepwalkers

In the first volume, *Pasenow or the Romantic,* the story revolves around Joachim von Pasenow, a Prussian military officer and the son of a minor aristocratic landowner. Similar to earlier realist novels and the other modernist novels Pasenow's story lacks a compelling plot. The intrigue of the novel takes place in the mind of Pasenow with his psychological battles. His mental conflicts cover a wide range of topics: Who to love? Where to live? What duty to pursue? The desire for a concrete and universal value system, however, remains dominant in his search for answers. Pasenow relies on the past to define his value system. He embraces the conservative aspects of the aristocracy and the Old Regime – blood, land and the military – and he stubbornly maintains the conviction that these values still hold promise for building a prosperous and intelligible society.

Broch defined this conservative, backward-looking worldview as Romantic, and Pasenow's Romanticism was most clearly defined through the cult of the uniform, a new cult that would replace the universal value production of the Church.

> Once upon a time it was the Church alone that exalted as judge over mankind, [...] And as once it was only the garments of the priest that marked a man off from his fellows as something higher [...] so when the great intolerance of faith was lost, the secular robe of office had to supplant the sacred one [...] And because, when the secular exalts itself as the absolute, the result is always romanticism, so the real and characteristic romanticism of the age was the cult of the uniform, an idea which did not really exist and yet was so powerful that it took hold of men far more completely than any secular vocation could [...] the man who wears the uniform is content to feel that he is fulfiling the most essential function of his age and therefore guaranteeing the security of his own life.[12]

Romanticism signified an empty value system because it claimed an absolute position of leadership but lacked any pragmatic social authority. One only 'feels' secure by covering oneself in symbols whose value came entirely from their pre-modern origins. As a value system outside of its own time, it could not serve as a guide to modern society; it was what Broch described as a 'closed value system'.

Pasenow's experience of urban life and his relationship to the character Eduard von Bertrand exemplify Broch's negative view of the closed value system of Romanticism. Bertrand and the city represent the antagonistic values of industrialization. Bertrand is an aristocratic friend of Pasenow from the army. Bertrand, however, quits the army to take up the life and clothing of a businessman. For Pasenow, his friendship with Bertrand becomes a neurotic obsession, for Bertrand's mere existence in the world undermines the stability of his antiquated value system. As the personification of capitalism and industry he represents insecurity. Bertrand did not

12   Ibid, 20.

know the world of the rural simplicity, and thus had no notion of what he was destroying.

> It was seldom that he [Bertrand] visited this outlying villa suburb, [...] although only rich families accustomed to a permanent equipage could live here without being keenly aware of the disadvantage of its distance from the city [...]. This comfortable neighbourhood with its castellar edifices in the most excellent Renaissance, Baroque and Swiss styles, surrounded by carefully tended gardens [...] all this breathed out a great and insular security [...]. [T]he daughters of these families could devote themselves to their pianos in complete security: theirs was a safe and gentle existence, [...] yes, if Bertrand had grown up on the land he would not be spreading insecurity, and had they allowed Joachim himself to stay at home he wouldn't have been so susceptible to this feeling of insecurity.[13]

Bertrand was for Pasenow a threat and an instigator. He had traded in the world of simplicity and clarity for the chaos of industrial society. He became, 'A mere adventurer, in fact! And Pasenow cast a glance round the restaurant, feeling embarrassed to be sitting there with an adventurer; yet there was nothing else for it but to see it through: "So you're always travelling, then?" "Oh, it's only on business that I travel – but I like travelling about. Of course a man should always do what his demon drives him to". And with that the cat was out of the bag; now he knew; Bertrand had quitted the service simply to go into business, from mere greed, mere avarice'.[14] This contradiction between Pasenow and Bertrand characterized the world of the late nineteenth-century German Reich as a world in a conflict of values. Bertrand in his civilian clothes represented the activities and values of capitalism, industry and the globalizing economy. Pasenow in his uniform with its rigid regulations and fixed relations of colour and shape promoted a sense of timelessness and conservativism.

Furthermore, Broch contrasts Pasenow's Romantic attachment to the uniform and the land with the industrial world of professionalization, which in this case is the urban setting of Berlin. Although the city is the capital of the Reich and symbolically linked to the aristocratic Hohenzollern family,

13   Ibid, 31–32.
14   Ibid, 27–28.

in *The Sleepwalkers* Berlin appears as a modern, urban environment.[15] The city appears to Pasenow as a dangerous and unsettling place, a counter paradigm for social organization. The danger, however, is not crime, disease, overcrowding or even autonomy – the standard fears associated with the rapid urbanization of the industrial age. It is the failure of the city to represent something eternal; it is its novelty, which suggests change and even progress, that so unsettled Pasenow.

> [B]ut here in the actual centre of the city everything seemed hostile to Nature:
> above the noisy light and the innumerable shop-windows and the animated life of
> the streets, even the sky and the air seemed so urban and unfamiliar that it was like
> a fortunate and reassuring, yet disconcerting, rediscovery of familiar things when
> he found a little linen shop, in whose narrow window lace, ruches and half-finished
> hand-worked embroideries picked out in blue were lying, and saw a glass door at the
> back which obviously led to a living-room.[16]

Pasenow contrives to replace industrial nature of the city with the pre-industrial world of cottage industries and simplicity. Yet it is the civilian businessman Bertrand who appears in the first volume as engaged and powerful, and it is only in the city that Pasenow himself demonstrates vitality and potency.

The theme of potency overwhelms the first volume of the novel. The theme is most fully explored through Pasenow's sexuality. Broch creates an urban world where Pasenow feels impotent and drained of life; yet, it is only in the city that he embraces a vital and open relationship to sex. Thus, Broch ironically reverses the Romantic metaphor of rural fecundity; the city becomes the promoter of sexual vitality. Only by Pasenow assigning sexual activity and sexual partners social and moral values based on an aristocratic social system can he ignore and overcome the contradiction Broch established. The final scene of the novel clearly demonstrates the conflicted nature of sexuality and potency. Pasenow, having quit the city and returned to the countryside, is unable to consummate his marriage

15   See Paul Michael Lützeler, *Hermann Broch und die Moderne* (Munich: Wilhelm
      Fink, 2011), Chapter 1.
16   Broch, *The Sleepwalkers*, 31–32.

with his new, aristocratic wife, Elizabeth. The inability of either character to communicate to the other in sexual terms pervades the scene.

Pasenow, who had consummated a sexual affair with an immigrant showgirl, Ruzena, while in Berlin, is now trapped by his own mental linkage of sexuality with the city (the ultimate symbol of Germany modernity). Since his marriage to Elizabeth represents his Romantic connection to the land and past, he is unable to separate on his wedding night the insecurity of the city/sex pairing from the security of the countryside/marriage image. Trapped in a closed system of Romanticism, he impotently retreats into the pre-packaged value system of the uniform.

> She [Elisabeth] had moved a little to the side, and her hand, which with its befrilled wrist was all that emerged from the bedclothes, rested in his. Through his position his military coat had become disordered, the lapels falling apart left his black trousers visible, and when Joachim noticed this he hastily set things right again and covered the place. [...] The candles flickered; first one went out, then the other. They lay motionless and gazed at the ceiling of the room [...]. Then Joachim had fallen asleep.[17]

The scene ends in failure; the marriage is not consummated. The scene communicates to the reader the oppressiveness of social categories in the world of late nineteenth-century Europe, but it also communicates the oppressiveness of Romanticism as value system. Joachim Pasenow's uniform functions for him as an artificially constructed value system and it forces him to withdrawal from his humanity.[18] In a world where values and spirituality were so clearly separated by manufactured relics of the past, the result was impotence.

Had Pasenow never experienced the insecurity of the city, his value system may have worked. Consummation of the marriage could have proved a source of security linked to the ancient notion of land and fecundity. What Broch suggests in the novel, however, is the separation between urban and rural cannot be maintained. In fact, the city is becoming the sine quo non and the countryside a piece of antiquarianism. He reinforces

17 Ibid, 158.
18 See Monika Ritzer, *Hermann Broch und die Kulturkrise des frühen 20. Jahrhunderts* (Stuttgart, 1988), 239–246.

the transition through the image of the suburb. The suburb is a new space somewhere in between the rustic simplicity of Old Regime Europe and the barren uncertain landscape of the industrial urbanity. Like the uniform, the suburb could only produce a surface level simulacrum, for it was only a false covering. The city lurked below the suburb; it served as its provider and ultimate foundation. Pasenow refuses to recognize his dilemma, but nevertheless Broch suggests his backward-looking Romanticism is untenable. Pasenow looks in at the modernizing world of the city, while he hides in the rural world of the past. But, even he recognizes the ultimate falseness of the uniform as a simply covering. Like the description of the Berlin suburb above, whose existence relied on its proximity to the city, the uniform was a manufactured replacement for a lost time, a mere mirage of a regulated world.

Broch's focus on the uniform and its Romantic symbolism functions well in terms of character development and the construction of the novel's architectonics (as the three main characters move historically towards confrontation in the final volume). But, when read in connection to the political questions established in my second chapter, Broch's obsession with the uniform as a symbol of the past exposes his distance from the intellectual tradition of German political Romanticism in turn-of-the-century Central Europe. In particular, it exposes the absence of national identity and the lack of understanding of nationalism's role within the Romantic movement. This is particularly ironic as Broch chooses to end his novel in the most contested region of German/French national antagonism imaginable – Alsace. It is surprising that his own focus on historical philosophy did not expose him to the historical Romanticism of the German historiography, where the narrative of German nationalism emerged out of a blending of German idealism, the Prussian Reform Movement, and the Romantic development of a *Volksgeist*. By the turn of the century, German historiography, especially the Prussian School, had linked this Romanticism not only to a national *Kultur*, but more importantly to a Prussian militarism. In this tradition the uniform did not look anti-modern or futile.

The second volume, *Esch or the Anarchist*, transports the reader to the turn of the twentieth century. It shifts the actions of the novel from Berlin and the lands of Eastern Prussian Junkers to the capitalist, industrialized world of the Mannheim and the Rhine valley. August Esch, the central figure of this volume, represents a world defined by money and trade; his occupation is an accountant, he works for a shipping merchant and even his understanding of right and wrong is characterized by double entry bookkeeping. Early in the second novel, Broch links volumes one and two through the reappearance of Bertrand. Esch takes a clerk's position with Bertrand's company. The reintroduction of Bertrand does not simply link the action of the first novel with that of the second; it also forces the reader to transfer the conflict of values (rural vs urban, capitalist vs agrarian) onto the actions of the second novel. It forces the reader to understand value conflict in a polyhistorical matter; the intrusion of modernity 15 years later appeared as an ever creeping and pervasive power that has migrated to deeper levels of society. It hints to the reader that Bertrand's value system has taken root and expanded, positioning Pasenow's Romanticism as stagnant. The second volume replaces the simple conflict of aristocrats debating the embrace of innovation with an intra-urban and intra-capitalist debate of workers, entrepreneurs and owners over the source of value in a more fully modernized society.

Esch's existence is unquestioningly urban. The choice between the rural and the urban seemingly lost in the world of 1903. Esch exists in the uncomfortable and imposing world of the city, which Pasenow attempted to deny. Even when he quits his job in Mannheim, disillusioned by Bertrand and capitalism, he flees to another city. Furthermore, Esch recognizes the disintegration of a universal value system under the pressure of modern, capitalist society. Esch is unable to be a Romantic, a point made clear in an exchange with a friend, Lohberg, 'Lohberg answered: "Herr Geyring is a victim of the poison that's destroying the world. Only when they get back to nature will people stop hurting each other" [...] "Only in God's good air, that lifts our hearts up, are men's nobler feelings awakened". Esch said: "That kind of thing has never got a single man out of jail yet".[19] In this passage and many others it is clear that Esch recognizes his world as modern.

19   Broch, *The Sleepwalkers*, 213.

Nevertheless, he finds no comfort in the modern, technological and capitalist world of the city:

> A hatred of commercial methods stirred again within him, hatred of an organization that behind its apparent orderliness, its smooth corridors, its smooth and flawless book-keeping, concealed all manner of infamies. And that was called respectability! Whether head clerk or chairman of a company, there was nothing to choose between one man of business and another. [...] He would have liked to go straight down to the counting-house and tell the blind fools there that they too should break out of their prison of hypocritical ciphers and columns and like him set themselves free.[20]

The history of the disintegration of values shifts in the second volume from the death of a universal value to the failure of any other value system to step in for a deceased God. The novel narrates a story of failure. It is the failure of the urban experience: capitalist greed in conflict with socialist utopianism, both of which prove unable to explain the meaning of life. Once again Bertrand symbolizes capitalism, this time its failure. When Esch discovers that Bertrand orchestrated the false arrest of Martin, Esch's friend and a socialist revolutionary, he quits his job and abandons the comforts of a world defined by success and security. Later in the novel, Bertrand's own suicide further indicts the value system of the industrialist, since it cannot even accommodate its most successful adherent.

Socialism, the obvious alternative to capitalism, fairs no better in the novel. Anger over Martin's false imprisonment, Esch contemplates his own radical pursuits. He writes a letter implicating Bertrand in police bribery and attempts to publish the letter in a socialist newspaper, but the editor of the paper rejects Esch's heroic offer.

> 'Have Bertrand locked up'. The editor laughed more than ever. 'That would just about put the lid on it'. 'And why?' asked Esch with irritation. 'He's a decent chap, friendly and sociable', explained the editor amiably, 'a first-class man of business, the kind of man one can get on with'. 'So you can get on with a man who's hand in glove with the police?' 'Heavens above, of course the employers work with the police; if we were

20   Ibid, 217.

on top we'd do exactly the same'. 'And you call that justice?' said Esch indignantly. The editor raised his hands in amused resignation.[21]

Esch's experience with the impotent stance of the Marxist editor leads him to equate capitalism and Marxism as vacuous value systems. 'Nothing else was different, and his incursion here seemed all at once so wholly superfluous that even his article, which had sounded powerful and sinister, suddenly appeared lame and superfluous too. The same crew everywhere, thought Esch with fury. The same crew of demagogues, living everywhere in the same disorder'.[22] Having rejected both capitalism and socialism as spiritually vacuous, Esch turns to a more spiritual source for his value system.

He hesitatingly shows sympathy for a Christian worldview but rejects it because he cannot reconcile it with his modern, urban lifestyle.[23] At the end of the second volume, he marries Mother Henjten in the hopes of finding some shelter from the dangers of a valueless world. He pursues a conventional, but ultimately extremely particularist solution to his need for redemption.[24] While the marriage proves somewhat successful, the narrator clearly suggests that his salvation is a false one. It does not provide Esch with a value system capable of easing his fear of death:[25]

---

21 Ibid, 230.

22 Ibid, 229.

23 In *Huguenau*, Esch returns to Christianity driven to a hysterical insecurity by the destruction of the First World War. Christianity, however, fails to provide him with a cognitive model for understanding his fellow citizens. It also fails to aid him in establishing any workable, pragmatic system of social values.

24 'Esch, reborn in newly awakened longing, knew that he was at his goal, not, it was true, that final goal in which symbol and prototype return to their identity, yet none the less at that temporary goal with which earthly mortals must rest content, the goal that he termed love and that stood as the last attainable point on the coast beyond which lay the unattainable', Broch, *The Sleepwalkers*, 316. Broch makes the individual nature of this relationship even more clear by emphasizing the age and lack of fertility of Mother Hentjen, Esch's wife.

25 The omnipresence of mortality in the production of social value systems is central to Broch's theory of cognition and its relationship to art in the early 1930s. 'At the side of the truly religious man, as also at that of the creator, there is always death, exhorting him to fill his life with ultimately attainable significance, in order that it

Nevertheless he knew that these hunted creatures, seeking the imperishable and the absolute in earthly things, would always find no more than a symbol and a substitute for the thing which they sought, and whose name they did not know: for they could watch others dying without regret or sorrow, so completely were they mastered by the thought of their own death; they furiously strove for the possession of some woman that they might in turn be possessed by her, for in her they hoped to find something steadfast and unchangeable which would own and guard them, and they hated the woman whom in their blindness they had chosen, hated her because she was only a symbol which they longed to destroy in their anger when they found themselves once more delivered over to fear and death.[26]

In the third volume of the novel, the First World War magnifies the spectre of death and places even more pressure on individuals like Esch who have failed to find a viable universal value system.

Esch plays an important role in the discussion of fiction and the industrial age for he accepts the role of technology and industrialization in German culture. Esch works within the culture and seeks both profit and status within the urban, capitalist world he has inherited. In this way, *Esch* presents European culture at its industrialized height and its optimistic hegemony. In particular, his actions highlight the growing sense of freedom linked to technology (movement and travel) and linked to social values of liberalism. Esch exemplifies the paradox of Broch's 'sleepwalking', that is, technology and freedom sap bourgeois culture of its vitality, it does not animate it. Esch's dissatisfaction with his life ultimately comes from the freedom granted by industrial society. The failure of any value system to replace God suggests that the promise of the Enlightenment, industrialization and progress cannot be a panacea for the modern, Godless West.

---

may not have been lived in vain. If there exists a justification of literature, or a supra-temporality of artistic creation, it is to be found in a totality of cognition such as this. For the totality of world comprehension as striven for by the work art, in Goethe's sense at least, concentrates all knowledge of humanity's endless evolution into one simultaneous act of cognition: eternity must be comprised in a single existence, in the totality of a single work of art, and the nearer the work of art comes to the frontiers of totality, the greater its possibility of survival' (Broch, 'Joyce and the Present Age', 90).

26   Broch, *The Sleepwalkers*, 325.

Progressive, bourgeois, capitalist values are found wanting in terms of providing a rule for right and wrong.

Esch ends up in the same place as Pasenow, simply by another route. In the third volume, then, it is not surprising to see Pasenow and Esch, now living in the same town, drawn to each other and to a dream of Christian redemption. Their hopes, however, like the town they live in, will be liter-ally and figuratively burned down by the realist Huguenau with his relative values and new moral order.[27] Pasenow attempted to ignore modernity; Esch attempted to fit novel situations into conventional boxes; both failed to find an adequate solution to the moral and social disruption of the industrial age. The uniting of the Pasenow narrative with that of Esch in the third volume demonstrates the spiritual limitation of Christianity, sug-gesting that in the modern world there is no requiem from the onslaught on mass, urban culture and its value vacuum. The failures of Pasenow and Esch, thus, paved the way for the protagonist of the third volume, who saw no value in even attempting to regulate the tools of modern world; he simply used them for his own advantage.

The story of Esch is most revealing about Broch's conservativism and his intellectual elitism (described in Chapter 2), for Esch is present and even active in the conflict of capital and labour. He has the moral indigna-tion and the psychological instability to represent what Broch would later describe as 'twilight consciousness'. Yet, instead of becoming activated to protect or destroy the material sources of happiness/fear, Esch chooses to act half-heartedly. He makes bold claims, but he never follows them through. His most direct and aggressive actions turned out to be only dreams. Here we see a stark difference between Broch's idea of *sleepwalking* and his post-exile discussion of mass aberration, that is, action. He invented a world in *The Sleepwalkers*, where real world consequences felt unreal. Cheating, political corruption, rape and murder produced little affect on the reader, because he infused these events with a sense of kitsch and aestheticism. Like his political writings of the early 1920s, the haziness of action and conse-quences reflected a distancing of Broch from the masses and 'the street'.

---

27   Europe's fate in the First World War is a clear parallel.

He chose to identify revolutionary conflict and mass politics as valueless and then to challenge it by operating outside of its influence. Broch moved actions from the external to the internal, from the political to cognitive. But, in so doing, he shut himself off from any real social commentary and held out aesthetic solutions for failed aesthetic values. In his mass aberration theory, he maintained the internal source of change, but he tied it to a new 'here and now' activism.

In the third volume, *Huguenau*, the narrative moves 15 years ahead and examines the world of Germany in the final year of the First World War. The protagonist of the novel, Wilhelm Huguenau, presents the reader with a completely new figure in terms of the conflict of value systems. Unlike Pasenow or Esch, Huguenau shows no sign of conflict or existential unease. For this reason, he displays vitality in his actions, a psychological calmness and a definable value system. This does not mean, however, that he represents the solution to the disintegration of values; in fact, historically Huguenau represents the culmination of the process and nadir of European culture.

Huguenau, age 29 at the outbreak of the First World War, was a successful businessman. In 1917, he was drafted and sent to the Front. It was there that he saw the world for what it truly was 'grey, worm-eated and completely dead in a silence that was inviolable'.[28] With this new knowledge, he promptly deserted his post and set off to pursuit his fortune in business. Over the course of the remainder of the novel, the deserter Huguenau would instigate social unrest, commit rape and finally commit murder. Yet, all of his actions go unpunished as Hugeunau is protected by the legitimacy of professional success. He himself does not recognize his crimes as improper. They are simply the by-products of his logical pursue of business; they exist outside of morality. The cold and calculating nature of Huguenau's value system can be seen in his interaction with Frau Esch. Having raped Frau Esch and, unbeknownst to her, murdered Herr Esch, Huguenau nonetheless takes a position of moral probity in his business relationship to her.

28   Broch, *The Sleepwalkers*, 346.

Dear Madam,

Hoping that this finds you well as it leaves me at present, I take the opportunity of reminding you that according to our contract of 14.5.1918 I am in control of 90 per cent of the shares of the 'Kur-Trier Herald', [...] Since I am anxious to avoid having any dispute in the law-court with the amiable wife of my late respected friend Herr August Esch [...] I beg to propose that we should compound our affair by mutual agreement, which would be all to your advantage, considering the legal position. The simplest way of doing this would be for you to buy back from me [...] our 60 per cent of shares in the business, [...] I offer them to you for the half of the original price, reckoned in francs at par.[29]

Huguenau cannot conceive of a world where values link to universal struc-tures; relativism defines his world. He no longer understands values in terms of ends, but only in terms of means. Consequences no longer matter. There is nothing to be lost or won, only a logical process to be followed.

Huguenau represented a new source of value, where individuals freed by both the destructive nature of the war and the progressive claims of the Enlightenment sought to secure their autonomous value systems at all cost:

in this fashion, in this absolute devotion to logical rigour, the Western world has won its achievements, – and with the same thoroughness, the absolute thoroughness that abrogates itself, must it eventually advance ad absurdum: war is war, *l'art pour l'art*, in politics there's no room for compunction, business is business, – all these signify the same thing, all these appertain to the same aggressive and radical spirit, informed by that uncanny, I might almost say that metaphysical, lack of consideration for consequences, [...] this, all this, is the style of thinking that characterizes our age.[30]

The result of this new European worldview was not the psychological iso-lation and torture seen in Esch, but Huguenau's rational justification for murder. Broch goes further in the final volume by suggesting that these autonomous value systems will by necessity come into conflict as they develop upon parallel tracks.[31]

---

29   Ibid, 629–630.
30   Ibid, 446.
31   'And the infinite remoteness, the inaccessible noumenal remoteness of that point towards which all lines of inquiry and chains of probability were now destined to strive, rendered impossible at one stroke the binding of all single value-systems to a

The individual freed through the logic of liberalism becomes an autonomous agent; the individual driven by a progressive commitment to science
and logic need not struggle to find his or her value system. Logical commitment to a defined goal produces a fully contained value system. What
Broch claims in the final volume of *The Sleepwalkers* is that post-war solution
to the disintegration of values is much more destructive than the earlier
manifestations of this conflict. In 1918, European culture simply stopped
looking for a truly universal value system and found comfort and stability
in pursuing autonomous, closed value systems, for one could justify these
systems logically. The abandonment of the ends to the means seemed like
a small price to pay in a world that had the technological ability to anni-
hilate itself. Again, the polyhistorical, psychological examination of values
becomes in the end a statement on modern, industrial society and its cost.

It is reason and an over-commitment to reason that initiated the disintegration of values. Industrialization played a central role in the novel
as a source for breaking down the absolute value system of pre-industrial
Europe. However, the modern value system represented through industrialization, capitalism and the bourgeoisie could not sustain itself as an
absolute value system. Its materialism failed to give meaning to human
action; even the Marxist materialist critique of bourgeois capitalism came
out simply as another form of failed materialist values.

Broch's epistemological novel suggested a pessimistic view of the
modern world, but at the same time it did not employ aesthetics as a mere
medium for politic stability or mass delusion (art in that sense is kitsch).[32]

---

central value; the abstract ruthlessly invaded the logic of every single value-making
activity, stripping its content bare, and not only forbade it to deviate at all from the
form determined by its function, insisting on purely functional structure, [...] but
has also radicalized so thoroughly the single value-systems that these being thrown
back on themselves and referred to the Absolute, have separated from one another,
now run parallel to each other, and, since they can no longer combine in the service
of a supreme value, claim equality one with the other: like strangers they exist side
by side, an economic value-system of "good business" next to an aesthetic one of *l'art
pour l'art*, a military code of values side by side with a technical or an athletic, each
autonomous, each "in and for itself", each "unfettered" in its autonomy', ibid, 448.

32   See Hermann Broch, 'Evil in the Value System of Art' in *Geist and Zeitgeist*, 13–40.

His literary work decentred the technological dangers of industrialism and urbanization and argued that the locus for positive and negative change should be the mind of the individual. This was clearly an enlightened view. However, Broch adjusted his views on individualism and agency in the light of the Romantic critique and the development of mass culture. This re-imagined Enlightenment required the individual to limit his or her belief in complete freedom. The individual had to recognize that logic when applied fully to a single terrestrial goal closed off the individual in an autonomous value system. Such systems blinded the individual and society from fundamental communality. Autonomous value systems thus allowed societies to accept all consequences as equally justified.

In a clearly anti-conservative manner, Broch suggested in the *Pasenow* section of the novel that Romanticism held little hope in these regard. For Romanticism relied on a denial of the present and future. Materialism as well had little chance to overcome the value vacuum because it inevitably led to competing, autonomous value systems that required the annihilation of opposing systems. In this sense, Broch's interwar work defined a 'no longer not yet' moment, where the past was impotent and optimistic progression illegitimated.[33] Social values in the modern world would have to be created from whole cloth.[34]

Moreover, the danger of the inability of modern society to provide a value system was only heightened by the liberating force of modern capitalism. The liberal value of freedom unchained the individual from the past, but for Broch the result was not a democratic or libertarian utopia, but

---

33 See *KW* 11, 11–25 for 'no longer not yet' theory in Broch's *Theory of Mass Delusion*.
34 While Broch remained committed to a democratic political structure, he saw the European and American traditions of democracies as deeply flawed and in need of restructuring. Karl Menges has suggested that Broch's Platonically tinged theory of a universal good, when applied to politics, suggests clearly fascist tendencies in his work. On the basis of Broch's biography and his anti-fascist activities and writing of 1930s and 1940s, I find this position difficult to support. One must admit, however, that Broch's radical attempt to build a new vision of social values by rejecting key aspects of the Enlightenment, liberalism and even Marxism leaves him in position of trying to define his own 'third way' characterized by a commitment to totality.

the anarchic release of autonomous values and actions. Only by overcoming the delusionary belief that materialism and positivism in the hands of the individual can create values in society could Europe recover from its disintegration of values.[35] In pursuing these problems, Broch engaged in the crisis of liberalism debate of the post-war period, which was most clearly defined by Max Weber in political terms.[36] Broch's engagement was aesthetic and epistemological.

The Sleepwalkers represented one of German-speaking Europe's most intriguing and subtle engagements with the impact of industrialization on German culture in the aftermath of the First World War. Until 1914, the twin forces of optimism and positivism extended the desirability of

35   What exactly Europe should embrace as a universal value is only vaguely suggested in *The Sleepwalkers*, which is by and large diagnostic in its structure. In his epistemological and aesthetic writing of the same period Broch attempts to define a new absolute source for social value construction, unfortunately his discussion remains vague and often contradictory. In the end, Broch calls for a modern version of the Platonic ideal. For a discussion of Broch's view of this new ethical absolute see Schlant, who provides a somewhat favourable reading of Broch's Platonism, and Karl Menges, *Kritische Studien zur Wertphilosophie Hermann Brochs* (Tübingen, 1970), who provides a negative critique of it.

36   For a discussion of the rise of a crisis in liberal ideology see Brett R. Wheeler, 'Modernist Reenchantments I: Liberalism to Aestheticized Politics', *The German Quarterly*, 74/3 (Summer, 2001), 223–236. Wheeler succinctly defined the crisis of liberalism in German culture that marked the turn of the twentieth century. 'No issue more wracked the consciousness of late nineteenth-century and *fin-de-siècle* Europe, and Germany in particular, than the crisis of liberalism. It was a crisis fuelled by a generational shift from institutional to cultural concerns, from the foundation of a unified state and the establishment of its institutional structures and practices to a fear of the cultural consequences that such institutionalization of political and social life would bear. Feelings of fear and revulsion toward liberal institutions found their most remarkable expression in the powerfully and enormously influential voice of Friedrich Nietzsche, whose virulently anti-democratic and especially anti-liberal rhetoric came to define the sentiments of two generations to come. Liberalism, he insisted, was an oxymoron. For liberals believed not in liberty and liberation but in its static, statist structures that actually constricted the possibility of freedom rather than expanding it' (223). The critical engagement with liberalism in German culture is continued by thinkers like Weber, Lukacs and Broch.

freedom, democracy, rationality and free market capitalism to larger and larger sections of society. Certainly these ideas did not go unchallenged in the pre War period. In German culture, Nietzsche's characterization of liberal bourgeois culture and positivism as life denying and decadent supplied later German thinkers with a severe critique of modern society.[37] The centrality of Romanticism in the formation of German national identity also supplied central Europeans with a means for rejecting enlightened, liberal society, and many scholars have linked the increasing importance of irrationalism in the politics of the Third Reich to the Romantic tradition.[38] Finally, the growing importance of Marxism and Freudian theory in Central Europe led to a further questioning of enlightened values and the instrumental dangers of rationalism.[39]

Broch's modernist novel traced 30 years of German history (1890 to 1918) and described that world as demoralized, aimless and violent. The action of the novel was internal; it was driven by the individuals and their struggles with their consciousness. Industrialization was clearly present in the culture, but it did very little in terms of activity. *The Sleepwalkers* demonstrates that modernization defined European cultural views beyond the question of technological reordering of the physical environment; in this way, it shows that fiction's role in defining the importance of industrialization for Europe should be seen not only in the works of science fiction, fantasy or realism, which focus on the technological, physical manifestation of industrialization, but also in cerebral, barren landscape of the modernist novel. It was not, however, that modernist writers ignored the question

---

37 Though it is not until the twentieth century and especially after 1914 that Nietzsche's ideas become integrated into more popular cultural movements. See Steven E. Aschheim, *The Nietzsche Legacy in Germany, 1890–1990* (Berkeley: University of California Press, 1992). Though not Nietzschean, Oswald Spengler's *Decline of the West* pursued similar ideas on decadence. Oswald Spengler's *The Decline of the West*, Charles Francis Atkinson, tr. (Oxford: Oxford University Press, 1991).

38 There is a large historiography around the 'German Sonderweg' that pursues this relationship, see Liah Greenfeld, *Five Roads to Modernity* (Cambridge, MA: Harvard University Press, 1992), 275–402.

39 In the 1930s, the Frankfurt School would combine the Freudian and Marxist critiques of enlightened modern society.

of industrialization; it was that they have shifted their attention from the expression of industrialization, that is, the footprint of industrialization on our physical environment, to a new focus on the relationship between the individual and the seemingly unending complexity of modern social patterns. The First World War served as a key breakpoint for this shift in literary focus. As the destruction of the war suggested to the modernist artist that what was broken or dangerous in modern society was not simply technology, but the moral apparatus of the individual who employed the technology. Machine guns did not kill people, people did.

Such a view placed Broch in an expected literary position vis-à-vis modernism. Howard Kaye's concise discussion of Broch's 'novel of cognition' suggests that the novel created an inventive position in modernism by allowing Broch to dismiss both the failures of positivism and the Romantic individualism of Nietzsche.[40] He created a form of literature that could criticize the ethical emptiness of the modern world without putting 'forward the turbulent, asocial claims of the self'.[41] Broch's cognitive novel challenged the failures of science and demanded of the reader an ethical commitment, a will to value. Kaye's position is representative of the general assumption that Broch's call for a new language of cognition and the distancing of himself from the failures of Nietzschean vitalism, German expressionism and Romantic heroism equated to deep societal engagement.[42] Kaye, however, comes very close to my own conclusion in his final line, where he characterizes the impact of the novel with words that are suggestive of the disengagement and intellectualism described in my previous chapter. Kaye writes, 'Broch's attempt to use literature in the pursuit of action-compelling knowledge was, as he soon recognized, a profound and noble failure'.[43]

40 Howard L. Kaye, 'Hermann Broch's *Sleepwalkers*: Social Theory in Literary Form', *Mosaic* XV/4, 79–88.
41 Ibid, 79.
42 Kaye stops short of such a direct claim, but scholars such as Lützeler, Strelka and Schmidt-Dengler come to this conclusion (see discussion above and my ch 2).
43 Kaye, 88.

The point of this chapter was to highlight the internalization of industrial society within *The Sleepwalkers* and to use that point of departure as a way of seeing more fully how much of Broch's intellectual activity between 1918 and 1933 grew out of such an intellectual position. This position, thus, reinforces my biographical analysis of Broch's political worldview under the Austrian First Republic. It does not undermine Broch's position as a critical modernist, as a humanist or as a committed progressive; it does, however, allow one to question whether these intellectual positions have any relevance to understanding Broch's political engagement during the same period.

I conclude that attempts to paint Broch's intellectual production during this period as politically engaged, even as what Lützeler refers to as the politics of the 'unbound intellectual', fail to recognize a naïveté as well as an intellectual elitism appropriate to someone so deeply influenced by the Austrian Baroque, Platonism and Kant. As Kant suggested, social change did not require political action in any direct or pragmatic sense. In fact, stability and order are far more important. The role of scholars and public reason make historical progress possible, not political action, especially not revolution. As Kant states: 'Argue as much as you want, over whatever you want, but obey!'[44]

Broch's pessimism was an expression of his historical philosophy; the no longer, not yet moment of European aesthetics created a situation where art was either kitsch or became a symbol for the 'disconnectedness' of the historical moment of value disintegration. In this way, he suggested a moment of impotence in terms of centralizing values, but such a situation did not equate to panic. The sensation of the unfamiliar lacked immediate connections to political unrest or violence. Broch was happy to wait out the no longer, not yet moment within his historical model, and in so doing passively accepted a political middle road, which in the context of the Austrian First Republic meant at best the acceptance of a shift to the right.

44 Immanent Kant, *Beantwortung der Frage: Was ist Aufklärung?*, Gutenberg Project Ebook (2009), <http://www.gutenberg.org/files/30821/30821-h/30821-h.htm> accessed 13 November 2013.

With *The Sleepwalkers*, Broch addressed modernity as a product of cognitive confusion dressed up in the clothing of industrialization and urbanity. His descriptions of violence and criminality (from domestic violence to rape to murder to revolution) lacked a corporeal tangibility. He found plenty about which to despair, but such despair took place in the drawing room of one's mind. The image of the sleepwalker was an apt one as the action of the novel played out in a foggy and vacuous world of the dream. Even the ending focused on an epistemological plea for hopefulness, but it was only a plea, a prayer, not a pragmatic examination of citizen rights, constitutions and economic structures of ownership and poverty, the kind of ideas Broch began to address directly only in 1936 with the 'League of Nations Resolution and most directly in 1940 with his work on the *City of Man* project. I examine these ideas in Chapters 4 and 5.

CHAPTER 4

Politics of Engagement, 1936 to 1951

> Democracy cannot abandon its foundation, the concept of a human soul
> and of human dignity.[1]

There are two geographical orientations to this study; in the first three
chapters the orientation was Viennese and European. For the remainder of
the book, I examine Broch's political thought in an American context. This
second context is, however, more complex than simply American. During
the 1930s and 1940s, the United States became the centre for democratic
political theorization and did so under a strong influence from European
thinkers. Many European intellectuals replaced the concept of 'European'
with that of 'Western' in their ideologies of state, civilization and empire.
The notion of 'the West' had existed in European intellectual thought well
before this point, but that idea of the West functioned more as an anti-
pode to the invented idea of the East – the product of classical philology,
orientalism and European new imperialism.[2] Starting in the 1930s, however, this definition of Western was replaced by one that was much more
contemporary and American centric.[3] America became the last bastion of

---

1   Hermann Broch, undated draft manuscript, Hermann Broch Archive. Yale Collection
     of German Literature, Beinecke Rare Book and Manuscript Library.
2   Suzanne L. Marchand, *Down from Olympus: Archaeology and Philhellenism in
     Germany, 1750–1970* (Princeton, NJ: Princeton University Press, 1996).
3   In *The City of Man Declaration* (authored by a committee of fifteen intellectuals,
     who were primarily European and included Broch), the idea of American leadership
     for western civilization is clearly articulated: 'The New World, if any, is the United
     States – now faced with an isolation of which no isolationist ever dreamed. With

democracy and the last safe harbour for European intellectuals to continue their intellectual or artistic critiques of modernity. This is not to imply that European intellectuals embraced US culture or foreign policy in positive or uncritical ways. Thinkers such as Theodor Adorno, Erich Fromm, Hannah Arendt and indeed Hermann Broch saw their role in the United States as a critical guide to democracy and freedom.[4]

In that intellectual moment, the West merged as closely as it ever would into a shared American and European identity. Hermann Broch brought to America a European value system, but applied it to political and economic issues in a much more globalized fashion. He understood that if European values were going to survive the self-destructive events of the early twentieth century, they would have to do so by expanding the definition of Western from a European one to a transatlantic democratic one.[5] The Atlantic Charter, the United Nations Proclamation and the Bretton Woods Agreement were all pragmatic expressions of a revamped Western ideal. For Broch, the American contribution to a reimagined West came in the form of Wilsonian idealism. The Cold War would soon change the dynamics of the political formula as the ideas of rational cooperation under the rules of international agreement gave way to a more ideological conflict. Broch's death in 1951, however, precluded him from seeing the full impact of Cold War political aims on the notion of a Western democratic ideal.

The idea of the West under the leadership of the free market-centred United States was easiest for England, where an Anglo-American cultural connection already existed and where socialism had a weaker foundation.

---

its natural allies in the Old World stricken or dead, with scattered elements of the European empires gravitating around it for protection, and with the Latin-American republics more in need of succor than likely to provide any as long as progressive leadership among them is threatened by totalitarian conspiracy, it is this country virtually alone that carries man's burden – the heir to all civilization if England falls, the leader and healer if England endures and bleeds' (13–14).

4 For example see Theodor Adorno *et al.*, *The Authoritarian Personality: Studies in Prejudice* (New York: Harper and Brothers, 1950).

5 This did not result in strictly positive views of American culture or political leadership, as I will argue in terms of Broch in Chapter 5, this volume.

It was a much more difficult for continental and central European intellectuals, who for centuries struggled with the competing ideas of Western
European values versus Central European values (as seen in the *Zivilization*
vs *Kultur* debates of the eighteenth and nineteenth centuries). Fascism had
violently ended the parochialism of such debates and pushed émigré intellectuals to conceive of the political theorizing in terms of democracy and
internationalism. For a brief decade and a half, this redirecting of European
views on Western politics and economics took place in an atmosphere of
frantic cooperation and compelled unity. It allowed intellectuals like Broch
to believe that European and American ideas could be merged and could
help build new avenues for democratic governance and citizen rights. Yet,
when examined in detail, Broch's Viennese notion of liberalism (too often
understood as dependent on Anglo-Saxon ideas such as those of Mill)
would challenge the centrality of classical liberal ideas like equality, independence and success in defining citizenship. He argued that American
democracy, in fact, represented an outdated form of liberalism – that is,
American liberalism emphasized rights over duties. With its economic
and military power, however, America could help establish a new form
of democracy, where individualism equated not simply to freedom from
interference or freedom for action, but to demands for obligation and
accountability.

    With the escalation of the Cold War and the new hegemonic position
for the United States in the global battle against communism, the period of
intellectual cooperation in the fight against fascism ended quickly. Many
émigré intellectuals returned home to focus on political issues within their
own states and in some cases abandoned the redefinition of the West as
a transatlantic entity. Broch died before he ever returned to Europe. His
work remained defined by the fifteen years from the mid-1930s to his death.
It was characterized by an attempt to merge central European values into
a new definition of Western leadership, whose goal was the creation of
international structures for the protection of life, wealth and opportunity.
Throughout this period, his focus was politics and it represented a new
brand of politics – American politics. What Broch referred to as the 'here
and now' pragmatism of American culture. The death of his aesthetic focus

brought forth his political activism. The story, however, was more complicated in that he carried forth his cognitive theory and his weak nationalism
into the new political agenda. In the end, he mixed American pragmatism
with European intellectualism. He produced a new theory of democracy
that focused on the protection of freedom within America as a necessity
for defeating fascism, but ultimately conceived of democratic reform on an
international basis. In this chapter, I analyse the broad outlines of Broch's
political theory from his psychological defence of individualism to his
internationalism and to his educational reform.

The Search for an Audience

The constant need for financial support contributed to the fragmentary
character of his political theory during his exile. The need to pursue other
projects – projects that paid – thwarted his efforts to complete his major
political work, *The Theory of Mass Delusion*. Even fellowships such as the
Guggenheim and the Rockefeller, which were essential for Broch's liveli-
hood, proved distractions in terms of the need to apply and reapply for
funding on a regular basis. These obligations forced Broch to present his
ideas on mass delusion in generalizations. In fact, the inherent nature of
fellowship application required that projects be prematurely offered in a
complete form and that their importance be tied to events or theories that
in a deeper sense were only tangential.

The second result of Broch's dependence on institutional funding was
the fact that many institutions, such as the Bollinger Foundation and Press,
were more attracted to his literary work than his political. His essay *Hugo
von Hofmannsthal and his Time* and his last novel *The Guiltless* became
good funding sources, but Broch himself complained often about the
distracting nature and irritating monetary necessity that underlay their
existence. Distraction, illness and financial insecurity combined to limit
the productivity of his new political mission. Furthermore, his theoretical

focus and intellectual development also promoted a piecemeal structure to his political work. Because all of his thought was concerned with the destruction of values, it was difficult for him to present his works in hermetically separate categories, such as literary, philosophical, psychological or cultural critical. It was in many ways easier for him to identify the centrality of politics than to locate the fundamental ideas of political theory in a single coherent account.

The problem is only heightened today because of the nature of his papers. Following his death in 1951, his manuscripts, letters and *Nachlass* were given to the special collections at the Beinecke Library, Yale University. The task of collecting and assembling his papers fell to his wife Anne Marie Meier-Graefe Broch, as well as Hannah Arendt, Robert Pick and Erich von Kahler. Broch's entire corpus consists of thousands of book-length pages, much of which was not published in his lifetime and a great deal of which is extant only in fragmentary form with heavy notation and handwritten corrections. The unfinished character of his papers contributed to the slow process of publication and its access to a wider readership. From 1951 to 1959, the Rhein Verlag, Zürich published his collected works in ten volumes.[6] In the 1970s and 1980s, an updated edition of his work by Paul Michael Lützeler provided a more thorough and systematic, as well as highly annotated collection of Broch's writings. These volumes have helped to close the gap between his theories and the reading public, allowing for a more accurate picture of his political and cultural criticism. Though the redaction of his *Theory on Mass Delusion* suggests a more complete and intellectually focused work than appears in the archives, it has made the

---

6   Hermann Broch, *Gesammelte Werke*, edited by Erich Kahler [*et al.*] (Zürich: Rhein Verlag, 1932–1961): vol. 1, *Gedichte*; vol. 2, *Die Schlafwandler, eine Romantrilogie. Der Erste Roman: '1888 – Pasenow oder die Romantik.' Der Zweite Roman: '1903 – 1918 – Huguenavu oder die Sachlichkeit'*; vol. 3, *Der Tod des Vergil*; vol. 4, *Der Versucher, Roman*; vol. 5, *Die Schuldlosen, Roman in elf Erzählungen*; vol. 6, *Dichten und Erkennen; Essays* (1); vol. 7, *Erkennen und Handeln; Essays* (2); vol. 8, *Briefe von 1929 bis 1951*; vol. 9, *Massenpsychologie; Schriften aus dem Nachlass*; vol. 10, *Die unbekannte Grösse und frühe Schriften mit den Briefen an Willa Muir*.

job of Broch scholars much easier and corrected false assumption that his exile period was primarily defined by his literary work on the Virgil novel.[7]

The greatest obstacle to increased recognition of his political theory, however, was Broch's failure to publish more during the 1940s and early 1950s. While others, like Arendt, Adorno and Marcuse, made significant contributions to the ideas such as democracy, totalitarianism and individualism, his voice was absent throughout the 1940s and silenced after 1951. If one wishes to understand Broch's relationship to this historical moment and its debate on political freedom, one must look to the posthumous editions of his notebooks and his letters. In this sense, Broch *als Politiker* is only understandable historically.[8]

Politics as Psychology

Until the mid-1930s, Broch assumed that freedom equated to cognitive empowerment, not legal protection.[9] After 1938, his understanding of value systems took on both a more pragmatic political angle and a more psychologically based defence of the individual. His *Theory on Mass Delusion* was at its base a system for freeing the individual from the distortions of crowd psychology, whose irrational impulses blocked individual value construction. It does not appear that he saw the period of world war and totalitarianism as a time for the creation of a new central value. The cognitive and aesthetic source of new ethics would have to wait; the no longer, not yet moment of his exile and the post-war period required a pragmatic and psychologically based political agenda.

---

7   Lützeler provides a detailed discussion of the redaction process and the incomplete
     nature of the work as found in the archive. See *KW* 12, 501–566.
8   Broch's correspondence with Hannah Arendt is a central piece in this process.
9   As I argued in Chapter 2, scholars have unfairly read this idea of the unbound intel-
     lectual back into Broch's political worldview of the 1920s.

His democratic theory was driven by the basic assumption that open societies were founded on the freedom and the sanctity of the individual as a source for value production. Yet, his political theory centred on the 'Law for the Protection of Human Dignity', which ran through all of Broch's political activities from the mid-1930s until his death in 1951. The concept involved, on the one hand, a detailed theory of knowledge and, on the other, a formal law for the inviolability of life. Broch felt that the solution to the political, social and ethical problems of the modern world required scientific understanding of epistemology and ethics on the individual level. Ethics operated in society through value systems, which can be organized and manipulated by governments and political parties; yet, these values systems were established and grounded in the mind and activities of the individual. It was with the individual that Broch started, and from there he hoped to establish laws for value systems that would withstand the hypertrophic forces of historical changes and, thus, withstand the onset of mass hysterical events.

Art by itself could not build a new civic humanism, which Broch now saw as the task of politics. He realized that being political was the fundamental human characteristic: 'The source of all politics is man; politics are operated by, for, and often against man. In order to be able to speak about politics, one must have a conception of humans; otherwise one speaks about empty mechanics'.[10] His critical humanist goal of ethical creativity morphed into a political goal. Nonetheless, it was still based on the Platonic notion of ideal types. As Ernestine Schlant writes in regards to his formula for the reintegration of values, 'A "central value" [...] should infuse each individual endeavour with directives and a goal, and contribute to a reintegration of values. Instead of pursuing the "laws of the I" for their own sake, exploration should occur in the service of a common, humanistic goal: the preservation of human dignity and human life, anchored in a constitutional framework and protected by law'.[11] Broch made this

10 *KW* 12, 458.
11 Schlant, 24–25. Schlant directs her discussion here at the pre-exilic thought of Broch and thus suggests the basis for viewing his thought as politically consistent. As I am

humanistic goal the central objective of his political theory. He retained the creative importance of the individual by approaching politics through cognition. It was no longer the artist who revealed the style of the age; it was the political theorist, who acted as an 'unbound intellectual,' the individual thinker who pursued ethical goals without regard to nation, party or ideology. In exile, he tied the opening of cognition to the protection of human life through legal empowerment.

Broch reformulated his value system theory so as to envision politics as psychology: the conflict between rationality and irrationality in the individual ego. He strove to understand the epistemological and psychological barriers to a secure human society. His conclusion was that human life must be protected and secured. Death played the central role in the psychology of fear underlying mass hysteria. In the last years of his life, he believed the key to creating open value systems (value systems that are capable of sustaining paradigm shifts in knowledge or historical changes, as well as avoiding mass hysterical events) was the scientific demonstration of the 'earthly absolute'. It was a theory of knowledge dependent on Kant and Husserl for its basic understanding of the ego as a space for cognitive activity.[12] Thus, Broch could talk about the 'expansion of the ego' and the 'diminution of the ego' as activities of the individual that linked the cognitive space of the ego to the external world of the non-ego.

It was in the activities of the ego as it interacted with the world of the non-ego that moments of mass hysteria arose (through ecstasy or panic). He argued for both a rational human structure to mental activity and an animalistic drive characterized by irrationality and biology. What separated humans from animals was the presence of a rational human structure to mental activity – the existence of an 'ego'. He saw value construction as based

---

arguing, his humanism was clearly consistent across his European and American contexts, but I do not think it was a politically engaged humanism until the late 1930s.

12   For a detailed discussion of Broch's 'Theory of Knowledge' see Hannah Arendt's introduction to *Hermann Broch Gesammelte Werk: Erkennen und Handeln*, vol. 2 (Zürich: Rhein Verlag, 1955) and her collection of essays in *Men in Dark Times* (New York: Harcourt, Brace, and World, 1968), 111–152.

in the ego, which meant it was based in the part of human consciousness directed at living (*Lebenstrieb*). Values came to life as a set of actions or ideas that promoted vitality (the ego) and redirected energy away from death or the fear of death (since death was inevitable). Death was the non-ego. The ego reacted to its fear of death by an expansion of what represented life, that is, the ego. Broch called this ego-expansion. He conceived of ego expansion as a vehicle for immortality, if it could expand the entire world into one's ego.[13] The ego, however, could also contract. Contraction became dangerous because it drove the ego towards death and panic.

If one could cognitively isolate the ego, the individual could separate itself from death. As Broch stated, the ego was 'completely incapable of imagining its own death'.[14] Death, fear, starvation and desire reflected relative evaluations of the material world of the non-ego. If the ego could separate its cognitive activities from such influences, it could separate itself from death. Broch referred to the process of negating death as the abrogation of time, by which he meant the individual could make value judgments from the 'Loneliness of the I', a place out of time and excluded from the secular concerns of avoiding death (for the cognitive ego was unaware of mortality). Hannah Arendt described the earthly absolute as 'abolishing in life the consciousness of death, liberating life, as long as it lives, from death, so that life goes on as if it were eternal'.[15]

The advantage of value production in the deathless sphere of the individual was that it removed the psychological basis for mass hysterical actions. From Broch's perspective, there was no external, worldly source of value that was not tainted by the fear of death and thus open to hypertrophical action. Proceeding from the belief that the ego was a source for open value systems, his political writings of the late 1930s until his death in 1951 equated the protection of individual human life with the protection of open value systems and ethical judgments devoid of the fear of death.

---

13   See *KW* 12, 492–495.
14   Hermann Broch's *'Werttheoretische Bemerkungen'*, as quoted by Hannah Arendt in *Men in Dark Times*, 132.
15   Ibid, 141.

Much of what he argued in this convoluted discussion of rationality and irrationality lacked any particularly original claim. As Arendt suggested, Broch worked within the intellectual tradition of social contract theory: he argued for balancing of natural rights within the bounds of civil society.[16] But, his originality, as he saw it, came in his ego modelling and his psychological explanation of the twilight consciousness. Whereas, earlier theories on natural rights justified civil society and popular sovereignty through claims of rationality and private property, Broch set the individual in civil society, with its protections and duties, both by reference to rational capability of the human animal and by reference to historical laws and necessity. He hoped to accomplish in his political theory: first, an explanation of how one can best access rationality and second, why we should be optimistic about the endeavour based on the cyclical nature of value construction. Again, as Arendt points out, his optimism was a bit utopian in that he assumed that mass aberrations were a momentary stage in the collapse of a closed system and the opening of a new era of human knowledge and creativity – what he called the 'new human type'.

His democratic theory was thus not universal in the natural law tradition; it was universal in the sense of supplying a centripetal value for a particular historical moment. This historicist aspect of his value theory made his idea less universalist than Arendt in the sense that she supported an Aristotelian view of the 'human condition'.[17] Even in her pre-political notions of human rights ('humans have the right to rights'), she suggested a universal value for human society.[18] Broch's universalism was more Kantian in its foundations, and thus rationality as *a priori* was universal, but the action of value construction was temporal and individual. Arendt

16   See Arendt–Broch correspondence from first half of 1949: *Hannah Arendt-Hermann Broch Briefwechsel, 1946 bis 1951*, edited by Paul Michael Lützeler (Frankfurt am Main: Jüdischer Verlag, 1996), 90–125.

17   Hannah Arendt, *The Human Condition* (Chicago: University of Chicago Press, 1958), see especially 22–91.

18   Hannah Arendt, *The Origins of Totalitarianism* (New York: Harcourt, 1994), see Part II, 'Imperialism'.

and Broch shared the political agenda of protecting human rights; they seemed to differ on the source of their endangerment. Arendt suggested a pragmatic problem linked to the use of force and the total reduction of public space (by which she meant voice or ability to dialogue – *logos*). With such totalitarian control entire groups of people could be silenced and made expendable. Broch, on the other hand, saw the issue as an extension of cognitive crisis traceable to the individual and the stability of his or her ego centre. Political outbreaks of mass hysteria developed out of the individual experience of 'twilight consciousness', as the individual searched for an outlet for ego-expansion or a halt to ego-diminution.[19]

Broch, Human Rights and Internationalism

The First World War played a central role in Broch's human rights work, especially his discussion of the League of Nations. Woodrow Wilson's Fourteen Points plan served in some sense as a model for his internationalism; it was, however, more a point of departure than a source of imitation. Broch took away from the peace negotiations at Versailles the historical lessons of Wilson's failure, and from there he attempted to construct a more thorough system of internationalism.[20] In face of French and English desires to return to a pre-war political system based on the notion of a concert or a balance of power maintained through pacts and alliances, Wilson pushed through a plan for internationalism based on the idea of freedom. Though Wilson's cult of personality seemed to the win the day

19 In his writings on human rights, Broch's position of exclusion is much closer to Arendt's loss of '*logos*'.
20 It is not a coincidence that both Wilson and Broch were in terms of their ethics Kantian. Where Broch believed Wilson had failed was not in his idealism or Kantian goals of a categorical imperative, but in his political understanding of how idealistic politics and *Realpolitik* coexisted in the 1919.

in Paris, it eventually lost the struggle for refashioning the European (and global) political system. Wilson's failure was a limited theory of freedom in the face of aggressive European *Realpolitik*. Broch's solutions expanded Wilson's idealism in terms of its theory of freedom. By doing so, he believed an international system for the maintenance of human rights could be victorious. He described this process as the turning of utopia into reality.

The limits of Wilson's plan were that he argued for the protection of only certain freedoms. What Broch called 'freedoms of', that is, freedom of speech and religion. Wilson trusted in an almost spiritual spread of democracy through the inherent human desire for freedom.

> Woodrow Wilson's concept of peace was based on his confidence in the common man. Although he saw the danger of war which lies in perpetuating the diversity of existing, independent states, and while, furthermore, he had to consent to an increase in their number on the principle of self determination, he thought he would succeed in banishing the possibility of wars, by entrusting all political responsibility everywhere to the common man and to his love of peace and freedom. [...] [H]uman freedom was the source from which the security of the world, the security of man was to flow.[21]

Wilson's theory of freedom had no mechanism for addressing the problem of security. In a world marked not only by insecurity in terms of destroyed infrastructure, ruined economies and open civil wars on the streets of Germany, Austria and Hungary, but also in terms of religious and intellectual traditions, appeals to the spiritual and magical allure of democracy and freedom rang hollow. Wilson's panacea of world democracy and national self-determination failed even to find an audience in the heart of democratic constitutionalism, the United States.[22]

In place of Wilson's spiritual democracy, Broch turned to Franklin Roosevelt's more balanced approach of four freedoms: 'freedoms of' and

---

21   *KW* 11, 249. The balance of security with freedom is even today an open debate in terms of internationalism and the US foreign policy.

22   The United States refused to sign the treaty of Versailles and to accept the Wilson's Fourteen Points Plan and the League of Nations. The United States ended its negotiations for a post-war peace through joint congressional resolution in July 1921.

'freedoms from'.[23] Freedom of speech and religion remained central to any notion of democracy, but in terms of internationalism, the freedoms from, that is, 'freedom from fear' and 'freedom from want' were equally as important.[24] Broch saw these freedoms as the source for security and as a counter option to Clemenceau's policy of security through a 'balance of power' (*Machtausbalancierung*).[25] 'The actual Freedoms "from" have in essence little to do with "freedom" albeit a good deal with security':

> Freedom from Want is nothing else than economic security, while Freedom from Fear is simply the security procured by peace. [...] The addition of Freedom from Want was particularly characteristic of the change that has taken place since 1918: the masses of the people want economic security, above all, and to them Freedom from Want is undoubtedly the most important. In other words, today, instead of the one-sided dependence of security on freedom, the interdependence of both is stipulated.[26]

Broch saw clearly that insecurity, especially economic want, would override any desire for democratic reform.[27] It was on this point that Broch's theory of individual value production and his internationalism most clearly coincided.

---

23   President Roosevelt announced the idea of the Four Freedoms in a congressional address on 6 January 1941. In response to the idea of Roosevelt's Four Freedoms, Broch stated, 'Although the Four Freedoms are not so precise as Wilson's Fourteen Points they have nevertheless evoked strong hopes among the peoples of the world and therefore the idealistic promises given in the declaration cannot be bypassed completely by the coming Peace Conference.' Broch, undated draft manuscript, Hermann Broch Archive. Yale Collection of German Literature, Beinecke Rare Book and Manuscript Library.

24   *KW* 11, 249. Broch uses English throughout his text when referring to these freedoms.

25   Ibid, 249.

26   Broch, undated draft manuscript, Hermann Broch Archive. Yale Collection of German Literature, Beinecke Rare Book and Manuscript Library , see also *KW* 11, 249–250.

27   'The masses always prefer the yoke of slavery to that of uncertainty.' Broch, undated draft manuscript, Hermann Broch Archive. Yale Collection of German Literature, Beinecke Rare Book and Manuscript Library.

From the time of his League of Nation Resolutions (1937) to his work
on an international law for the protection of human rights (post-1945),
Broch argued for restructuring the League of Nations from an idealistic
organ of internationalism to a pragmatic one. In his arguments for the 'Four
Freedoms,' Broch thought he had found the path to do so. 'Freedoms of'
served as the sign of a nation's or a people's 'recognition of human dignity
and its inviolability',[28] they received concrete expression in documents like
the Declaration of Independence and the Charter of the League of Nations.
Such expressions were a first step in the protection of human rights. On
their own, however, they provided no practical means for ending violations
of human rights. Even tying them to pure expression of military power did
not guarantee protection; it simply guaranteed war. As Broch stated in his
1937 resolution, the danger of blatant use of power in internationalism
contradicted the peace mission of any international organization, and thus
left internationalism in a position where it chose peace over human rights.
To correct this either/or situation, he wanted to create a legal system that
addressed the idealism of human dignity, expressed in the 'Freedoms of',
while at the same time addressing the practical issue of security, expressed
in the 'Freedoms from'.

As opposed to 'freedoms of', which were contained in the Declaration
of Independence and The Bill of Rights, 'freedoms from' found their expression in political treaties or bills of responsibilities. Broch wanted an international body that did more than promote peace and democracy; it also had
to have its hand in areas of material interest: 'agreements about territorial
frontiers, spheres of influence, trusteeships, armament limitations, raw
material distribution, [and] joint currencies'.[29] Such an organization would
need to serve as arbitrator and guarantor of these material agreements.
Thus, they would have to set up diplomatic and military wings in order to
enforce such freedoms. Broch felt that the 'freedoms from' more deeply
linked nations in international relationships. Material relationships implied
a two-way relationship, and in the case of a violation of such a relationship

28   *KW* ii, 250.
29   Ibid, 250–251.

it would entail damage on both sides. In this way, it would guarantee that all nations connected to any agreement would be motivated to take up its preservation. Material interest would be a greater motivation than moral interest. Broch hoped that the addition of freedoms based around the idea of material security (a bill of duties) would back up freedoms concerned with human dignity (a bill of rights).

Expansion of freedoms, however, did not on its own guarantee the protection of human rights or human life. Clearly, situations where nations honour their international treaties and ignore internal questions of human rights would arise; situations where questions of national sovereignty trump international obligations would arise, and almost certainly intervention would lead to war. Broch's expansion of the idea of freedom allowed for greater global linkage and leverage in international relations, but it did not fundamentally change the equation stated earlier: internationalism was a choice of either peace or human rights. For many, the question stopped right there, it was a clear indictment of the impotency of internationalism in a nationalistic world.[30] For Broch, however, such a moral position was untenable. He formulated a political solution to this conflict by pursuing a psychological solution to the attack on democracy. His psychological solution would encompass several areas: legal foundations for protections of human rights, active democratic propaganda and an international university system. Through a combination of these institutions and activities he hoped to redress the 'psychological dilemma of democracy'.[31] The problem and solution was at the level of mass psychology. If internationalism was to work it would have to be dependent on the 'good faith' of nations, which to Broch came only from a strong democratic tradition that honoured human dignity as a natural right. He, however, no longer had full confidence in the efficacy of democratic traditions of natural rights, certainly not in Europe and perhaps not even in the United States.[32]

30 Hannah Arendt can be counted as among this group.
31 *KW* ii, 253.
32 See my conclusion.

Broch developed his ideas on human rights around a growing notion
of a Bill of Duties or Responsibilities to augment the American constitutional notion of a Bill of Rights and the United Nations International Bill
of Rights.[33] His development of a Bill of Duties was presented as the solution to the enforcement of a Bill of Rights. In the context of international
politics, the League of Nations and from 1945 onward the United Nations
could proclaim the existence of a bill of human rights; they could not,
however, effectively enforce such a legal stance. The United Nations' policy
of non-intervention in domestic affairs assured the lack of enforcement.

> A country which fails to carry out the provisions of the Bill of Rights within its own
> borders will be able to do so with impunity, except where such actions and attitudes
> conflict with the interests of other countries: for example when its intolerance and
> persecution force masses of refugees across the borders, or when the disdain of human
> dignity lead to armament and acts of aggression against other countries. Then and
> then only will it have to reckon with counter-aggression by the union of nations.[34]

Broch's touchstone for the problem of international versus national autonomy was the Europe of the 1930s and 1940s. His sketch of refugee or rogue
government militarization was also Europe, yet his concerns for the limits
of an International Bill of Rights and the potential geo-political fallout
echoed the central problems of internationalism today, especially in regard
to the Third World.

His formulations of these problems and his solutions to these problems matured over the middle and late 1940s, as he took an active role in
the movement toward a United Nations (highlighted by San Francisco
Conference on International Organization).[35] Following the conclusion of
the war and the formation of the United Nations, he turned his attention

---

33   'Bill of Rights and Bill of Duties', Broch, undated draft manuscript, Beinecke Rare
     Book and Manuscript Library MSS; see also *KW* 11, 243–277.
34   Broch, undated draft manuscript, Hermann Broch Archive. Yale Collection of
     German Literature, Beinecke Rare Book and Manuscript Library; see also *KW* 11,
     243–244.
35   Broch's commitment to direct action comes in the context of increasing policies for
     international cooperation – including the Atlantic Charter, the declaration of the

directly to the problem of international enforcement for a 'Law for the Protection of Human Dignity'. The issue turned on the notion of resolving what he described as an 'antinomy' in the post-war internationalist movement: a contradiction between declaration of human freedom and the policy of non-invention. Because any declaration of human rights would be vacuous without the power to secure them, and because the security of human rights relied on the political and military decisions of individual nations within their borders, the policy of non-invention in order to avoid war guaranteed that violation of human rights would go unchecked. The idea of protecting human dignity as a source for ethical reinvention of Western values would remain a utopian goal as long as this antimony was not resolved.

Broch set forth three fundamental areas for consideration: 1) Can the concept of human rights be universally accepted as an international goal? And could a universal legal statement be created that would withstand the domestic reinterpretation? 2) Could any legal formula for the protection of human rights work in an atmosphere of separate states? 3) Could any 'Union of Nations' possess the necessity power to act against exceptional cases of the human rights abuses without impinging on actual or theoretical ideas of domestic sovereignty, and do so without the evoking war? If the antinomy between the 'dictates of humanity' and 'the recognition of sovereignty' could not be overcome, then any international bill of rights would remain impractical and utopian. Nevertheless, Broch saw the United Nations idea of a universal Bill of Rights as a necessary first step. In fact, he saw the internationalist movement as one that had to proceed with small steps; a radical call for World Democracy or the end of political ideologies would be unrealistic in the global environment of the early Cold War. Victory in war had heightened the role of ideology in the West. This situation only increased his belief in advancing democratic reform through the individual.

United Nations, Bretton Woods Agreement, the opening of the United Nations and the UN's issuance of the Universal Declaration of Human Rights.

In 1945, Broch drafted his treatise 'Remarks on the Utopia of an "International Bill of Rights and Responsibilities"'; it was sent to Eleanor Roosevelt and the UN Commission for Human Rights in the middle of 1946.[36] He envisioned this treatise as a second step in the process of resolving the antimony between the protection of human rights and the maintenance of national sovereignty. Broch presented a program that would change the 'Utopias of yesterday' into 'tomorrow's realities'.[37] The solution was the establishment of a universal criminal code for the prosecution of any individual who violates human rights, including individual serving as national officials. 'Mankind has always solved its apparent antinomies by discovering or inventing a unifying third principle, and in the present case it can be maintained that this third principle can be perceived in the criminal code, in criminal law as an institution. ... Today, the morality of the world demands that trial and punishment of war criminals at the hands of an international tribunal, and from this demand to the desire for an international criminal code, in which the new world-morality is codified, the road is short'.[38] Broch did not simply want post-facto tribunals; he wanted the establishment of a clear-cut criminal code backed by juridical system, both on the national and international level. In fact, his wanted issues of criminal actions against human rights to be adjudicated on the domestic level, only to reach the international level in exceptional cases. The creation of a criminal code for human rights would function not only as a means for policing the international arena, but would in a psychological and legal fashion function as a means for controlling the development of mass hysterical events within national borders.

The preceding outline of Broch's political platform of internationalism and democratic reform demonstrates a shift from the utopian and undefined internationalism of his 'League of Nations' pamphlet to his more directed and legally focused works, such as the 'Law for the Protection of

---

36   Broch, 'Bemerkungen zur Utopie einer "International Bill of Rights and of Responsibilities"', *KW* 11, 243–277. See especially fn 3, *KW* 11, 276–277.

37   Ibid, 245.

38   Ibid, 247.

Human Rights' and his 'Bill of Rights and Duties'.[39] This shift represented in the most obvious way my claim of discontinuity in narrative of Broch *as Politiker*. It was clearly a move towards pragmatism and the shift occurred not simply because he found himself exiled. It represented a more direct engagement with national culture. In his central European context, his cosmopolitan and imperial worldviews limited his desire or perhaps even his ability to see national culture as a mode of politics. In his American context, as he evaluated the potential for US leadership in the battle against fascism, he came to understand better the interaction between national culture and political action. It was very much as an American that he promoted a series of realistic legal changes in the foundation of citizenship in modern democracy. He came to embrace a more down to earth democratic activism, which he connected to the American frontier character (a sense of confrontation and resolve) and to a new world entrepreneurialism that produced a politics of the 'here and now'.[40]

Broch sought through his theory on mass hysteria first to understand the source of mass psychosis (this was an epistemological and psychological study), and then to apply that knowledge to the conflict between democracy and totalitarianism in modern world. This was the second half of Broch's work on the *Theory of Mass Delusion*. The 'indecency' (*schlechte Gesinnung*) of an individual nation had to be corrected and directed towards democracy and human rights.

> It follows that since no adequate protection for the International Bill of Rights can be expected of the union of nations, its arbitration procedure and its armed forces, the fulfilment is left entirely to the 'decency' (*guten Willen*) of the individual government or rather its population. Everything depends on a whether such a proper disposition (*guter Wille*) can be aroused and strengthened sufficiently to maintain itself against the evil of fascist power, and to help bring about their downfall. It is a task for mass psychology, more concretely one for mass pedagogy.[41]

39   See '22nd and 23rd Amendments', Broch, undated draft manuscript, Hermann Broch
        Archive. Yale Collection of German Literature, Beinecke Rare Book and Manuscript
        Library. See also Chapter 5, this volume.
40   See Broch '*Der Intellektuelle im Ost-West Konflikt*', KW 11, 460–492.
41   *KW* 11, 255–256.

After establishing the scope of the freedoms involved and basis of internationalism through both a bill of rights and a bill of duties, the crucial
step in taking Wilson's idealism and turning it into reality depended on
changing the individual minds of the people. Broch's first pragmatic step
towards changing minds was a legal one. The legal system served both a
purely formal function (defining legal or illegal behaviour) and an education
function. Social justice transmitted social morality. 'The criminal code is
the rational expression of the irrational trends which form the moral tradition of the nation. And the continual development of its laws safeguards
the continuity of this tradition, becoming the pedagogical instrument by
means of which generation after generation is brought up under the same
moral code'.[42] Written law and a public judiciary packaged the unconscious
and inherited fashions of communal tradition into a rational system of
proper behaviour.[43]

What Broch proposed was to add to the formal law code of a democratic society a law that protected the legal system itself. It was a defence
against the misappropriation of a central organ for social education: the
law.[44] The necessary definition of legal responsibility of individuals toward
human rights took the issue out of the political realm. If the question
of addressing human rights is political, it becomes bogged down by the
various forces operating within the political power system, forces often
unconnected to the issues at hand. As a question of judiciary violation, the
political issues are offset by the legal clarity of right and wrong, as opposed
to the ideologically messy notions of right and wrong in politics.

For Broch, since the overthrow of Imperial rule and Old Regime, all
states are abstractions, defined by their legal code. A bill of rights in the
legal code would theoretically protect an individual person from the abuse
of the state. In Fascist governments, as the National Socialist demonstrated,

42   Ibid, 256.
43   One sees here in the combination of religion, tradition and order the conservative
     nature of Broch's mind.
44   Almud Greiter and Anton Pelinka describe this aspect of Broch's human rights theory
     as expression of its taboo-phase: 'Democracy enters its Taboo-Phase, its central values
     are protected by Prohibitions.' See 'Hermann Broch als Demokratietheoretiker', 31.

however, the idea of the state and of citizenship can be redefined. The result is that people who were once citizens are now aliens or enemies of the state. The state could grant itself immunity vis-à-vis civil liberties as long as that immunity related to the protection of the citizenry. To offset the fluid nature of citizenship Broch proposed a law that trumped any action of the abstract state. It was a law aimed directly at individuals. One person, and a person was always a person regardless of whether he or she is an official of the state, could not violate the rights of another person. 'Full personal responsibility in all walks of life is a vital demand of democracy, one that calls for fulfilment to the letter, since otherwise the body politic becomes corrupt, thus nullifying everything democracy has achieved, and finally democracy itself'.[45] Any person in a democratic state has a bill of rights that cannot be violated, but they also have a bill of duties that they must maintain.[46] The fundamental duty was a duty to protect the sanctity of all lives within the state – to not uphold that duty was to make oneself liable to the penal code.[47]

Broch conceived of this law in terms of the domestic situation of European countries – countries with some democratic traditions. He

---

45 *KW* ii, 261.
46 'The proposed wording of the law, which provided only for the purpose of fixer les idees: Article 1: Whoever by spoken or written word, or by actions or other means assaults the moral equality of human persons (citizens and non-citizens), thus holding up to contempt or defamation a group of persons either collectively or individually, not for legal, but for biological or religious or other ideologically defined reasons; or whoever excludes such groups from exercising their legal rights as citizens (especially the right to the pursuit of happiness); or whoever prevents such a group from performing their civic duties; or exposes them to the hatred of their fellow citizens or incites the latter against them, commits a "crime against human dignity" – regardless of whether such an attempt was successful or not – and is liable to punishment. Article 2: Immunity of office, whether legislative, executive or judicial, shall not exempt from the consequences of any violations of this Law' (*KW* ii, 262).
47 Michael Lützeler points out in his book, *Hermann Brochs Kosmopolitismus: Europa, Menschenrechte, Universität* (Vienna: Picus Verlag, 2002), that Mary Robinson, chairperson for the UN Commission on Human Rights, employs today the same ideas that Broch put forth on rights and duties, 46.

thought, however, that the law must be applied universally across the globe. In order to make this possible, especially within countries where democratic or secular judiciaries were not present, he proposed the establishment of an international law court. The international court would be responsible for the hearing the case, but execution of the court's ruling would revert to the nation where the violation occurred. Thus, he has returned to his fundamental dilemma: to sustain international cooperation in the maintenance of human rights, he was reliant on the forcible cooperation of the nation in violation. If the nation refused, force or intervention would be necessary, again risking peace in pursuit of human rights. He could not rely on the 'decency' of nations with strong commitment to national sovereignty and with little established tradition in the area of natural rights. Before the 'Law for the Protection of Human Dignity' could be applied internationally it had to foster the roots of democracy on a national level.

For this reason, Broch pursued at the same time as his theories on an international law code efforts for the promotion (or propagandization) of democracy. Towards this end, he formulated a theory on the importance of international education. In a pamphlet from 1946, he described the threefold purpose of a series of new educational institutions in the United States: 1) to secure employment for European scientists and thinkers, 2) to bring European scientific methods into the American academy, 3) to establish an intellectual foundation for the fight against fascism.[48] By the end of the war, the first two issues had been become superfluous – the American scientific community had integrated both European methods and European scientists to a large degree, and those scientists who did not integrate would be returning to Europe very soon. It was the third, an intellectual foundation for the fight for fascism, that continued to need attention. The pressing issue in Broch's mind was the rebuilding of the scientific community in central Europe. To do so, he argued that the exile

---

48   See *KW* 11, 414 ff. In the accompanying footnotes, Lützeler summarizes the specific institutions Broch had in mind at the time of composition: The New School for Social Research in New York, in particular its new Graduate Faculty made up of exile thinkers. The graduate program became known as 'The University in Exile.'

institutions, established through American universities such as New School
for Social Research and Princeton University, needed to break free from a
purely American point of view. The rebuilding of Europe needed to be on
a democratic basis, and the rebuilding of the central European university
system would be a key aspect of the re-education of Europe.

Broch wanted to bring science to the service of any new international
organization for peace. He felt education, especially an educational system
that instilled democratic ideals and applied its knowledge to humane projects, was as necessary to the maintenance of peace as military force or
economic institutions. 'For any future peace organization an international
university is barely less important as an international bank'.[49] The university, however, had to be directed at the same internationalist issues (peace,
human rights and democracy) as were any legal, military or economic
activities. To understand Broch's position here, one must understand his
view on knowledge or science (*Wissenschaft*).

Science was the modern expression of what he called *Weltgeist* or
world spirit. By this he meant the collective mental efforts of humanity
applied to the construction of social values and interactions. His definition
of science was quite wide; it included medicine and technical sciences, but
also humanistic sciences from anthropology to philosophy, with psychology and history being especially importance.[50] Such a 'complete university
system' (*Voll-Universität*) would differ from the 'research institute model'
of the exile organizations. He found the university model more conducive
to cooperative work. 'On the one hand, university work is generally more
alive than a pure research institute, and on the other hand it better geared
to train a new generation for cooperation in establishing world peace'.[51] The
university setting would lessen the impact of an ideologically driven core.

Furthermore, the international university would represent something novel – a new foundation for the practice and teaching of science

49 *KW* 11, 416.
50 Though Broch acknowledged that medicine and technological science might find
institutional homes outside of his 'International University'.
51 *KW* 11, 416.

(a *Neuaufbau* or a new scientific Organon).[52] Science was to be directed toward a general theory of humanity: 'Humanity has become a task for exact science'.[53] Science must unite around the goal of understanding the cause of human motivation. The present condition of modernity was one in which man could not guarantee human freedom through the liberal notion of natural law, because the religious basis of that law had been removed. It was a situation where man without the guidance of an absolute force in education and politics turned to social institutions to mitigate the irrational forces like panic.

Broch felt that values conceived absolutely played a very small role in the life of most individuals, in their place concrete institutional forces shaped their existence:[54]

> Man had to create institutions to safeguard his concrete interests on earth and to make group life possible. These institutions, once created, having absorbed the values and ideals, began to use these for themselves, so that in the end, the institutions established absolute authority over their creators. While man wants peace, the political institutions he made want war. Man seeks truth, but the spiritual institutions he made chain the truth with dogmas to maintain themselves.[55]

In short, humans had since the Enlightenment put themselves between a rock and a hard place. Democracy and freedom was based on the ideas of natural rights, that is, on the idea that humans were created in the image of God. Broch referred to this concept as being a 'wholly humane person'. With the secularization of the Western mind in the nineteenth century the basis for human rights, humans as the image of God, was removed. But as the early twentieth century had shown, modern society was not

---

52   Ibid, 418–419.
53   Broch, undated draft manuscript, Hermann Broch Archive. Yale Collection of German Literature, Beinecke Rare Book and Manuscript Library.
54   This admission showed again that Broch had shifted his intellectual focus from the cognitive and aesthetic concerns of the artist to a more mundane sphere of daily political life.
55   Broch, undated draft manuscript, Hermann Broch Archive. Yale Collection of German Literature, Beinecke Rare Book and Manuscript Library.

able to replace the 'wholly humane person' with the 'perfect citizen'.[56] The foundational principles of freedom and equality had given way under the pressure of *Realpolitik*, interest politics and economic security. He offered the 'Law for the Protection of Human Dignity' as bulwark to the tendency of democracy to set freedom in front the inviolability of humanness – a blatant example of Broch's continued commitment to humanism and the Enlightenment.

His proposal for an 'International Academy' was another step in the process of re-establishing an absolute source for human motivation. Mass hysteria, which resulted from 'rational causes which the individual mis-interprets or entirely ignores' could be corrected, if science could explain the process of human motivation and rational choice. He envisioned an academy in which science worked toward an established humanist goal as opposed to specialized fields of knowledge operating independent of each other. 'Science itself is constantly bound to fight the curbing of truth by every institutionalism, and also, if not primarily, its own institutionality. By liberating mankind from this institutional prison, science frees itself'.[57] He proposed three essential categories of investigation: '1) knowledge of the basic qualities of human nature, 2) knowledge of human development, and 3) knowledge of the present condition of man and his social institu-tions'.[58] The fields of 'biology, physiology, medical psychology and psychia-try, especially primitive psychology and psychological anthropology, and ethnology, as well as religion', could be applied to the first category. For the second category, the historical study of 'human institutions' was needed. In the third category, psychology and social scientific fields would be applied.

The irony in his conception of a more democratic and open exchange of ideas through the university structure was that Broch, in fact, saw the purpose of the university to be clearly ideological. Structurally, he wanted

56   Broch, undated draft manuscript, Hermann Broch Archive. Yale Collection of
     German Literature, Beinecke Rare Book and Manuscript Library.
57   Broch, undated draft manuscript, Hermann Broch Archive. Yale Collection of
     German Literature, Beinecke Rare Book and Manuscript Library.
58   Broch, undated draft manuscript, Hermann Broch Archive. Yale Collection of
     German Literature, Beinecke Rare Book and Manuscript Library.

the university open, that is, he wanted students to have access to a wide variety of academic subjects (*Fächer*), and he wanted those subjects to be approached in a unified way. Science needed to be studied 'in its entirety and not only through individual branches'.[59] The openness and the breadth of study, however, had an obvious political aim: to place psychological and historical knowledge at the disposal of democratic governments. His university plan mirrored his ideas on human rights; the key force against the violation of human rights and for the destruction of fascism was the understanding and use of mass psychology.[60] As with his critique of American Democracy, the key concept here was the idea of totality: total democracy and total science.[61]

Broch felt that democracy was something that needed to be learned and to be reinforced through culture.

> If, then, it can be shown that what is true of mathematics is also true, must also be true, of methods of extra-mathematical disciplines, such all-pervading methodological homogeneity would not only disclose the starting point of a coming [...] unification of all science, all knowledge of science and its branches, but it would also furnish the strongest possible evidence supporting the assumption of a homogeneous structure of all that may be called human thought. With that, the whole complex reverts into the ethical. For if the homogeneity of human thought can thus be manifested in performance of a strict and sober analysis of science, it becomes not only permissible but an undeniable, and logical, duty to draw the further conclusions from this given fact. And these conclusions doubtlessly would amount to a secularization of the divinely borne natural law. Truly none could be too wicked to remain potentially a bearer of

59   *KW* 11, 416.
60   'The rapid rise of Fascism and Dictatorships demonstrates that in policy management psychological events are of decisive importance – events, which Fascism without exception have ingeniously used, but which democracies have almost completely ignored' (*KW* 11, 416).
61   Patrick Eiden points out the problematic nature of Broch's use of the idea of totality here in terms of its claims to positivism. Eiden refers to the idea of the 'scientification (Verwissenschaftlichung) of politics' in Broch (146). Patrick Eiden, 'Anstand und Abstand: Hermann Broch und die Frage der Demokratie' in Ulrich Kinzel, ed., *An den Rändern der Moral: Studien zur literarischen Ethik Ulrich Wergin gewidmet* (Würzburg: Königshausen and Neumann, 2008) 133–149.

the human spirit, and none too exalted to have to remember such human dignity of
the other's. But this, nothing else, is humanity – of science as well as democracy.[62]

Conclusion

Although Broch's theories on human rights and internationalism never
prompted any direct government action, his ideas on the importance of
internationalism as combination cultural (educational) and legal institutionalism provide still today a model for workable change on a global
scale. Much of what defines the United Nations today mirrors his ideas;
but they remain, however, undermined by the various forces of nationalism and government/citizenship rejection of the duties Broch formulated.
His political program for total democracy remains an intellectual system
in need of a spiritual or psychological commitment. In this sense, his criticism of American democracy was itself an intellectual activity that longed
for spiritual engagement. In examining Broch's critique on democracy in
the United States and his effort for international protection of human
rights, one uncovers an important European contribution to the theory
of democracy: critical humanism. By tracing Broch's connections and promotion of a critical humanist view, we expand the genealogy of humanism
and internationalism in the expansion of democracy. The results help to
disentangle the biases surrounding humanism and the Enlightenment –
biases that treat rationality, individual autonomy and belief in progress
as conservative or reactionary values. These ideas were in the late 1980s
co-opted by neo-Conservative thought in the United States to promote
the spread of liberal democracy. In Broch, however, we observed that a
sustained commitment to nineteenth-century ideas like humanism and
the Enlightenment provide a more complex view of how democracy can

---

62   Broch, undated draft manuscript, Hermann Broch Archive. Yale Collection of
     German Literature, Beinecke Rare Book and Manuscript Library.

or should function, and not simply a rubber stamp for idealistic visions of freedom and US-led democracy.

The sense of discontinuity in Broch's view of politics and public involvement was still tempered by his focus on cognition and the individual. The theoretical basis for historical change and the justification of individual human worth were not outgrowths of his new pragmatism; they were, in fact, continuations of his pre-exilic idealism. The paradox of Broch's American democratic theory was the merger of a sustained tradition of psychological and epistemological theories of value construction applied to an activist agenda of political and legal state building. His 'Bill of Human Responsibilities' united psychology, education and law as a bulwark to political activities of fascist governments, whose propaganda was just as much psychological and pedagogical in nature. He recognized that international organizations lacked political will to supplant their national interest to international one – world democracy was for the time being a utopian idea and very much otherworldly in its character. His discussion of human rights was itself heavily laden with religious terminology: 'Oppression is an integral part of political and economic life. Thus, one cannot hope to achieve the ideal *Civita Dei* simply by abolishing the present causes of oppression as it manifests itself in modern society [...]. The complete body of Human Rights is not a codified entity and never can be completely codified. Rather is it to be defined as an ethical attitude which draws its strongest support from the traditions of great religions of the World'.[63] He realized as well that legal barriers against human rights violations were easily overturned or reinterpreted to facilitate murder and torture.[64] What could be accomplished was the psychological redirection of the public toward what he called in religious terms 'good faith'.

---

63   Broch, undated draft manuscript, Hermann Broch Archive. Yale Collection of German Literature, Beinecke Rare Book and Manuscript Library.

64   'Whether a Bill of Rights is of international or merely of national scope, a government acting in bad faith can easily turn it into a meaningless scrap of paper by various devices, or by ignoring it completely. Laws are easily circumvented and such violations pass virtually unnoticed since they are not officially decreed by the government but

This process was very similar to the role the Federal Civil Rights laws played in the America South in the 1950s and 1960s. The parallels were not coincidental: when Broch arrived in the United States, the fundamental historical event in the American memory was not the rising tide of fascism; it was not even the First World War. It was the Civil War and the process of Reconstruction. In this milieu, a European provided a much different point of reference and pursued a much different focus. On 7 December 1941 these differences were overcome (at least temporally) as the United States started down the road to being the dominant world power.

In the context of forced exile and the movement of United States towards war, Hermann Broch focused his energies on politics. He saw this as a time when the death of the 'Old World' must be reported, but not mourned; it was a time for prophecy and teaching. This would mean educating the 'New World' about its new duties: first, to rescue the world from totalitarianism and secondly to redefine the goals and moral basis of democracy. The course for the United States was clear: it must break away from the isolationism and nationalism that had allowed it to forsake its part in building a modern democratic global system in the interwar years. What was required was first war and then peace based on a new paradigm for internationalism. For both war and peace, he advocated an aggressive form of internationalism guided by a commitment to a new definition of democracy – 'total democracy'. Total democracy would replace the vacuous and nationalistic democracy that had proven its weaknesses (moral, economic and political) in the face of the powerful and committed ideology of totalitarianism (communist and fascist). Total democracy would be backed by force but defined by peace; it would focus on the individual as the source of creativity, the people as the source power and international law as the source of justice and the enforcer of individual

---

happen incidentally, so to speak, with the sanction of regional or local authorities. In Germany with the blessing of petty officials, this brand of Fascism went on virtually under the eyes of the still functioning Reichstag and the still more or less democratic government and none of the liberal parties was strong enough to fight against this diffuse state of affairs' (*KW* 11, 255).

human dignity. In the next chapter, I examine more directly Broch's critique of the United States, both in terms of its racism and its notions of freedom and success. In doing so, I will reiterate Broch's basic claims for a more humane democracy.

CHAPTER 5

America and Democracy

Only little is achieved by proving the inoffensiveness of the Jew, however uninteresting he might be, but a lot can be gained by making uninteresting anti-Semitism per se.[1]

On 27 January 1944, Hermann Broch became a citizen of the United States.[2] It was a direct acknowledgement of the trust he put in the United States as the last defence against the spread of fascism. Throughout his exile, Broch examined the ideology of American democracy and found its ideological goals both admirable and flawed. They were admirable in their fundamental principles of human equality and freedom; they were flawed in their one-sided approach to regulating democratic life, that is, American democracy focused on the power of individual freedom and not on the duty of individuals towards society and fellow citizens. From his perspective, American democracy rested on the commitment of its citizens to curtail governmental abuse. It did not, however, have any mechanism to curtail the abuse of individuals by other individuals. American democracy was not total. Both his embrace of and criticism of the United States' democratic tradition reverberate in the current debates on the role the United States as a force for spreading democracy and freedom. Furthermore, the religious and humanist impulses in his call for democracies to protect human life foreshadowed the claims and goals of the movements for social change in

1   Hermann Broch, undated draft manuscript, Hermann Broch Archive. Yale Collection of German Literature, Beinecke Rare Book and Manuscript Library.
2   Lützeler, *A Biography*, 302.

the 1950s and 1960s. To date, the connection between Broch and these later political debates has been obscured by his marginalization within the historiography. The study of his political theory, however, suggests that even as a dilettante political theorist and a novelist he presaged an important intellectual development of the American mind. It was a development that took place in churches and in the counter-culture worlds of American youth, not in the universities or in the halls of government. In this chapter, I set out Broch's theory of 'total democracy' as an important critique on the United States as the standard-bearer for liberal democracy.

As in the previous chapter, I examine Broch's idea of total democracy as a means for understanding his shift towards engaged politics. Unlike Chapter 4, however, the pragmatic nature of his embrace of total democracy is much more evident and forceful. The *Theory on Mass Delusion* exhibited greater awareness for the stakes of mass politics, but it nonetheless forced pragmatic politics through a cognitive lens. In his statements on American democracy, Broch presented a more active political agenda. I highlight his activism by chronicling his specific discussion on totalitarianism and fascism vis-à-vis American leadership through various political essays and unpublished works, including again his work on mass delusion. In these articles, we find a political activism that called for immediate and aggressive reaction to the violence of fascism.

Debating American Democracy

Although Broch was, like the members of the Frankfurt School, highly critical of US culture, especially in terms of its race relations, he was at the same time much more assimilationist. He embraced the United States and its fundamental principles of freedom and equality as the starting point for re-educating Europe on how to build and maintain a free society. The challenge from his perspective was not to survive a period of separation and await his return to European society, but to engage the battle against fascism from an American vantage point. In terms of political theory this equated to his grafting a Viennese notion of social humanism onto an American tradition of negative rights. Broch, however, also offered a stern warning about the viability of US democracy. He warned of an uneasy similarity between the United States' myth of the American Dream and National Socialism's promotion of victory and superiority in terms of nation and race. Overall, he fashioned his exile as both an opportunity to clarify his understanding of democracy and as a duty to educate the United States about its potential to follow European democracy down the path of mass hysteria.

The exploration of his theories on fascism and democracy also helps expand the debate on mass society and modernity within the US exile community. H. Stuart Hughes and Martin Jay have exposed the important role of thinkers like Franz Neumann, Theodor Adorno and Max Horkheimer, as well as the influence of institutions like the Frankfurt School and the University of Chicago.[3] Broch's theories suggest a separate European approach to the questions of totalitarianism and fascism; it was an approach that rejected both Marxism and capitalism as holistic solutions to the value vacuum of the modern world. Broch, in fact, rejected socio-economic factors as the primary means for understanding mass hysteria.[4] As Almund Greiter and Anton Pelinka point out, this fact differentiated him from thinkers like Adorno and Horkheimer; for 'Broch's approach (to the question of mass hysteria) is the individual. All mass phenomena are explainable through processes, which take place in the individual. Moments of socialization, both primary and secondary, are to a large extent excluded from his analysis.'[5] His democratic theory was driven by the basic assumption that free, open societies were founded on the freedom and the sanctity

3   See Martin Jay, *The Dialectical Imagination A History of the Frankfurt School and the Institute of Social Research, 1923–1950* (Boston: Little, Brown, 1973) and *Permanent Exiles: Essays on the Intellectual Migration from Germany to America* (New York: Columbia University Press, 1985).
4   Greiter and Pelinka, 'Hermann Broch als Demokratietheoretiker', 25.
5   Ibid, 25.

of the individual as a source for value production.[6] He saw the breakdown of individual value production as direct cause for the breakdown of the larger social value system.[7]

As discussed in the last chapter, Broch saw his *Theory of Mass Delusion* as a moral duty and as his contribution to defending democracy.[8] He thought he could epistemologically diagnose and cure the breakdown of values and the resulting outbreaks of mass hysteria. He linked this project to his ideas on democracy by arguing that American democracy could only defeat fascism, if it avoided its own descent into political irrationality. He wanted to prevent the metamorphosis of 'community' into 'the mass', what he referred to a hypertrophy of values. Such a metamorphosis occurred through both the loss of rationality (commitment to universal values of equality and humane conduct) and the loss of positive irrationality (aspects of humanity like friendship, camaraderie, etc.).

The starting point for understanding his critique of American democracy is to understand his ideas on culture itself. Culture for Broch was the awakening of human initiative in the face of death.[9] He saw death as the ultimate non-value, yet it nonetheless played an important role in civilization, for it created the cultural goal of the universal, as seen in the mythological importance of words like infinity and eternity. In the face of that absolute non-value, human creativity opened the possibility for challenging death with an earthly absolute, a willed absolute created by man – in a sense, humankind's will to value. The earthly absolute was not in reality an *a priori* universal, but it did allow for the foundation of value. It represented humankind's rational ability to relate openly to irrational fears. Rationality thus became for Broch the shedding of light onto the darkness of the irrational.

6   This was the basic assumption behind Broch's theory on human rights as well.
7   Since the problem existed in the ego, he formulated his solution in the realm of cognition.
8   'The fight against Mass Hysteria, the enlistment of man into an open system of humanity is the task of democracy', *KW* 12, 63.
9   For a discussion of Broch's idea on value creation, see Broch, 'Das Böse im Wertsystem der Kunst', *KW* 9/2, 119–157.

In terms of his political theory, humankind's will to value was important because it was out of the ethical process of value construction that social value systems built universal values. Aesthetics was the effect of ethical action in the cultural arena; politics was the regulation of these aesthetic effects. In a sense, Broch saw politics as the superstructural reflection of an ethical substructure. He argued, however, that the relationship between ethical action and value systems was not a one-way process. Humankind's will to value initiated the creation of value. Society, however, when it embraced a value as complete and unchanging (the closing of the value system), endangered value production. For, at such a time, individuals shifted their creative impulse from value production to the pursuit of a goal. In a psychological sense, Broch saw such teleological activity as moving closer to death not creatively challenging it. Modern mass politics continually pressured the individual with closed value systems (business for business, nationalism, *l'art pour l'art*).[10] The result was a closing off of the creative mind and psychological insecurity. Modern politics, in this way, created the possibility for mass hysteria and opened up many groups in society to physical, economic and political oppression.

His 'Law for the Protection of Human Dignity' involved, on the one hand, the detailed theory of knowledge discussed above and on the other formal legislation for regulating citizen to citizen relationship. The goal of the law was to secure the physical environment of the individual, so that he/she could pursue his/her will to value from a psychologically secure space as citizen. Broch conceived of economic and political security as an extension of this law, but did not believe that healthy (open) social value systems could be created or sustained simply by economic action. It was only unhealthy, fascist (closed) value systems that tried to buy individual freedom through material security.

Open value systems were systems that pursued (but never fully defined) absolute values through constant activity of creative citizens, as opposed to closed value systems that defined an absolute value in simple national,

10   For a discussion of closed value systems, see Broch, 'The Disintegration of Values', *The Sleepwalkers*, 343–648.

economic or racist forms. Concretely defined absolute values only existed in 'hypertrophic' systems, and they set the stage for the onset of mass aberration. A value system became closed at the point when a crisis exposed its failure to secure an acceptable level of material and psychic security. A healthy society required the presence of a central value system that promoted the pursuit of maximum levels of material and emotional security. This was the democratic regulative principle of the 'pursuit of happiness'. The complete autonomy of the central value system, however, could initiate a stage of crisis or the closing of the system. In a state of complete autonomy the logic lost contact with the actual functioning of reality and began to promote values that were not applicable to the material world surrounding the system. Broch used the historical example of witch trials to demonstrate such hypertrophia. When a dominant value system, such as Christianity, promoted the truth that witches exist, the application of that truth to reality resulted in the development of a mass aberration: witch trials.

As Broch diagnosed the European phenomenon of fascism, he began to question the situation in the United States. He felt that there were signs of hypertrophia and argued that America must recognize and overcome two traditions in its democracy that tended toward the fascist value system. The two traditions that he addressed were both connected to the modern phenomenon of mass politics. The first was connected to the myth of the American Dream and the industrialization of the United States. He believed that too great an emphasis on material success led to the devaluation of psychological security. In essence, the United States had a tendency to rank material success above the inviolability of human life. The second tradition arose from the racial tensions within American society.

Broch associated American racial conflict with his notion of fascist demonology or the singling out of a communal enemy. Fascist demonology entailed the creation of a devil whose activities and mere existence in a society were viewed as a threat to the values of the majority. For Broch, both the Jew in European society and the African-American in the United States offered a minority identity that played the role of devil. In a period of crisis this devil fell victim to the need for exorcism, as the majority value system attempted to stabilize its feeling of panic. These two traditions, materialism and racism, threatened American democracy by fostering psychological insecurity in a historical context of war and economic crisis.

In his critique of the American Dream, he revealed a less than optimistic view about the United States' ability to address these weaknesses in its democratic traditions. He stated in an untitled manuscript from the late 1930s:

> The unemployed were approached with slogans denouncing the existing 'plutocracy', for the middle class a picture of a future anti-Communist order was envisaged, an order promising an increased volume of business; Pacificists were won over with slogans about 'Europe's internal affairs' which do not concern America; Communists were trapped with semi-Socialist slogans. In any event, the attempt was made, whenever possible, to denounce World Jewry as plutocratic, Communistic, war-mongering, reactionary, revolutionary – in short as World Enemy Number One. This propaganda, operating on a large scale, is very successful, and every convert means one step toward the complete subjugation of humanity and human liberty. This is how it worked in Europe, and there is no reason to believe that the American people will react differently. Man protests against barbarism only until he has become used to it.[11]

Broch questioned whether US democratic traditions would value human dignity over material security in the context of indifference. He even saw such indifference present in the exile community of Europeans – even European Jews.

> The [Europeans] whose physical, psychic, and, above all, economic existence has not been directly affected and, then, victimized [...] they are helpless; the right moment for defence is gone. But let us complete the gloomy picture by adding the undeniable fact that even those who, suffering bodily themselves, went through the apocalyptic horrors of today's Europe, as soon as they have reached [...] apparently safe shores, immediately join again the bulk of *indifferents* and do not belong any more to the class of the directly 'injured'.[12]

---

11   Broch, undated draft manuscript, Hermann Broch Archive. Yale Collection of German Literature, Beinecke Rare Book and Manuscript Library.
12   Broch, undated draft manuscript, Hermann Broch Archive. Yale Collection of German Literature, Beinecke Rare Book and Manuscript Library.

For the United States to serve as defender of Western civilization, it had to see beyond the prospects of 'accepting a victorious Germany as a financially sound buyer'.[13]

Policies of isolation and appeasement within Europe and the United States brought such a prospect into question. The policies reflected a greater concern for territorial integrity than for human suffering. The war was a 'logical inconsequence'; it only took place when Hitler's seizures of territories became too egregious. The obligation to defend territory 'proved strong enough to achieve what no act of barbarism, no provocation, no breach of treaties, no abuse of ideological values had been able to achieve'.[14] The object lesson of earlier European appeasement was not for Broch a simple call to arms, but a more fundamental call to reconsider the foundations of democracy. 'Whether the American people will be able to lift themselves out of the morass of such fatal conservatism depends on their ability to find their way back to the spiritual values inherent in their traditions'.[15] The only way fascism would be turned back would be by a spirited effort that came from a defence of humanity and a not a defence of territory.[16]

In considering the traditions of democracy in the United States, he concluded that classical American notions of liberalism, negative rights and governmental checks were an insufficient basis for sustainable democracy. American democracy's ultimate goal was complete individualism vis-à-vis the government. He regarded such unchecked individualism as a source of instability. For no matter how much the individual strove for complete separation from others, the nature of the world is that humans need other

13   Broch, undated draft manuscript, Hermann Broch Archive. Yale Collection of German Literature, Beinecke Rare Book and Manuscript Library.
14   Broch, undated draft manuscript, Hermann Broch Archive. Yale Collection of German Literature, Beinecke Rare Book and Manuscript Library.
15   In this context, Broch refers to traditions in American culture such as the religious communalism and pragmatism, not the democratic traditions discussed above. Broch, undated draft manuscript, Hermann Broch Archive. Yale Collection of German Literature, Beinecke Rare Book and Manuscript Library.
16   This was especially the case for the United States, whose territorial isolation distanced them from the menace of Hitler. In point of fact, one can argue that the United States did not see the Second World War as an ethical war until after Pearl Harbor.

humans.[17] In the modern world, if individual success were held out as ultimate goal of society, slavery would become a social necessity.[18] For in industrial, capitalist society, individual effort was insufficient for profit production. It required a community of labourers, managers and even government officials. Broch claimed that the idea of the American Dream ignored the necessity of community and the impact of industrialization on community in the modern age. For these reasons, any democratic system that defined individual success as its ultimate goal also carried the seeds for psychological insecurity of the masses. Democratic citizenship could not be 'totally' enacted, if it was defined only from the point of view of individual success. Another way of looking at this is that social values directed at individual material success drive the majority of the people closer to an awareness of death (psychological insecurity). Material success thus impeded the individual's will to value. Without value production in the form of creative individual will, citizens would turn to the immediate security of political, national or racial ideologies.

Starting with his work on a joint American and European project *The City of Man*, Broch began to focus on the process of enslavement (*Versklavung*) in modern society. The discussion of slavery and enslavement through ideology or economics received a great of deal of attention throughout the 1940s and 1950s. The idea played a prominent role in National Security Council Paper 68 (NSC-68), which became the policy blueprint for US Cold War policy. In the report, the authors make the claim that 'The idea of slavery can only be overcome by the timely and persistent demonstration of the superiority of the idea of freedom.'[19] Broch's discussion of freedom, responsibility and slavery, shared much of the same rhetoric as NSC-68. For Broch, however, the solution was not increased ideological commitment to unchecked freedom. It was a rational and legal

17 Arendt, *Men in Dark Times*, 135–136.
18 Broch repeatedly uses the term slavery in his work, by which he meant not just chattel slavery but basic economic and political oppression.
19 National Security Council Paper NSC-68, 'United States Objectives and Programs for National Security' Federation of American Scientists, <http://www.fas.org/irp/offdocs/nsc-hst/nsc-68-4.htm> accessed 10 June 2013.

structure that embodied the fundamental similarity of all humans. He suggested that materialism and economic capitalism needed regulation. *The City of Man* can thus be seen as his most public statement of his policy of totalizing democracy through scientific rationalization of society.

The City of Man, which was published in 1941 under the leadership of G. A. Borgese, represented the collaboration of American and European intellectuals on the issue of 'World Democracy' and the proposal for new political and economic policies in the United States. Ironically, whereas this represented his growing utilitarianism in politics, the project had no significant impact on the US policy makers or the general public, even the project's financial backer, William Benton, described the committee as elitist and detached. As Lewis Mumford observed, 'Benton intervened to express his opposition to Borgese's half outlined proposal. He told us flatly that we were all insignificant (read *'unpublicized'*) people: he even suggested – in the presence of Thomas Mann! – that none of us was as capable of composing an effective statement as were the advertising writers he hired. This unexpected assault, in the middle of our deliberations, was as Nielson later characterized it to me, exactly like a Nazi dive bomber breaking up a gathering of civilians going about their business.'[20]

G. A. Borgese as secretary was the driving force behind the composition and publication of the declaration, but Broch composed large sections of the document, including the economic discussion found in the third part of the 'proposal' section. He was also a confidant of the Borgese/Mann household.[21] Though it is difficult to separate the direction of influence in terms of political theory among Broch's own essays, his *Theory on Mass Delusion* and the political proposals created by the committee of fifteen,

20   Lewis Mumford, *My Works and Days: A Personal Chronicle* (Boston: Houghton Mifflin Harcourt, 1979), 391. See my discussion in Chapter 4, as well as Lützeler's fn 2, *KW* 13/2 243–244; for an extensive chronology of the *City of Man* project and Broch's contribution, see Lützeler, 'Visionaries in Exile: Broch's Cooperation with G. A. Borgese and Hannah Arendt', in Paul Michael Lützeler, ed., *Hermann Broch, Visionary in Exile* (Rochester, NY: Camden House: 2003), 67–88.
21   Borgese was Mann's son-in-law and Broch spent many days and evenings at the Mann house with Borgese.

there were key ideas in the *City of Man* that resembled the core of Broch's political activism in the 1940s. There were, in particular, the Brochian ideas of total democracy, citizen 'duties', internationalism and the dangers of materialism implied in the American attraction to victory. Mumford's description of Broch (a 'Austrian Sherlock Holmes') asserts convincingly that in terms of the characterization of democracy as 'total', which occupies a prominent position in the declaration, Broch was the key source.

> He (Thomas Mann) had, as a sort of shadow, brought to the conference at his suggestion a tall, stoop-shouldered, pipe-smoking intellectual named Hermann Broch: outwardly an Austrian Sherlock Holmes, a brilliant mind, but given to manic-depressive changes; now full of noble hopes and indignation, now saying that the dynamic Nazis were better than the isolationist democracies. At one point Broch asked me, in German, to convey to our colleagues his belief that the United States must itself become a 'totalitarian democracy' in order to defeat Nazi totalitarianism – a proposal I buried in silence.[22] (391)

Cleary Broch's close relationship to Borgese and his role as a primary writer resulted in the inclusion of total democracy as major pillar in the group's political agenda.[23]

His most direct contribution to the project was his treatise on free market economies and slavery.[24] It was an economic merger of socialist communalism – a form of humanism described in my second chapter, which developed out of the progressive liberal tradition of turn of century Vienna and early twentieth-century Austro-Marxism. In both the essays and his letters from 1939 to 1940, he concentrated on economic insecurity and what he termed modern slavery. The use of the term slavery obviously had a double meaning in an American context and could not have helped in terms of appealing to the US public. Nonetheless, he continued in much of his political writing to highlight the dangerous nature of America's racist past. Slavery in the modern context, however, was economic. Slavery manifested

---

22   Mumford, 391.
23   See *The City of Man: A Declaration on World Democracy* (New York: The Viking Press, 1941), 28–31.
24   See *The City of Man*, 85–93.

itself in Soviet communist control of freedom through smothering of private property, as well as through capitalism by disproportionate concern for profits over human suffering. Yet, Broch focused the economic idea of slavery in the battle against fascism. As he states, 'The world is moved by *Realpolitik* [...] everybody has to look after his own interests, and the man who doesn't want to become enslaved himself must try to enslave others; eat so as not be eaten. We must admit that enslavement will be or is already the genuine form of our modern industrial society'. He continues in the same document, 'All this is only sound and logical, it is sound *Realpolitik*, and Hitler is [its] most honest, most clever exponent'.[25] In so doing, he set up the fundamental comparison examined in this chapter between failed and successful democratic governance through extended comparison of the American attraction to victory with National Socialist racial exclusion.

As in his appeals to internationalism where he was highly supportive of the US presidential leadership of Wilson, he embraced the New Deal policies of President Roosevelt as a positive step towards reining in the power of pure capitalist profitability. His economic theory, which he wanted to present as anti-socialist because of the context of American anti-Marxism and anti-dogmatism in general, argued for regulation of industrial production and labour without an intrusion on the individual freedom.[26] His discussion retained a large amount of his socialist tinged liberalism from Vienna, in particular his rejection of profit as the central economic motivator and his desire to link some aspects of industrial production to a communal utility (*Benützungsrentabilität*) and not simple profit calculation (*Finanzrentabilität*).[27] He argued that public works needed to be given more 'room' in the economy and that return or interest (*Verzinsung*) in the economy needed to be controlled. While these programmatic claims were

25   Broch, undated draft manuscript, Hermann Broch Archive. Yale Collection of German Literature, Beinecke Rare Book and Manuscript Library. See also Broch's discussion of enslavement, 'Democracy in an Age of Enslavement' (*Die Demokratie im Zeitalter der Versklavung*), in *KW* 11, 110–191.
26   *KW* 13/2 176–177.
27   *KW* 11, 86–87 and *KW* 13/2 176–177 and 239.

direct in their economic applicability, much of what he argued was about value systems and the valuation of the individual in the democratic process.

In his work on mass psychology, he attempted to justify the balance between a planned economy and individual freedom through the concept of man being created in God's image (*Ebenbildhaftig*).[28] His planned economy was rational in its use of technology and productive power to end the issue of scarcity, which was in turn the source of insecurity, and ultimately the psychological impetus for implementing and accepting modern enslavement. 'The central components of the democratic mentality are first unsentimental, businesslike rationality and secondly a belief in the innermost similarity of all who are human'.[29] Democratic freedom only truly operated in an amiable environment, what Broch referred to as democratic 'decorum' (*Anständigkeit*).[30] Competition as justified by classical liberalism jeopardized social decorum, when it reached the level of forgetting that we share a basic human similarity, which prevented us from placing material gain in front of human dignity, that is, prevented us from accepting slavery.[31]

His modified free market economy offered a criticism of American freedom through his suggestion that unregulated individualism might increase the choice of some, but only at the cost of the enslavement of many. It was a mathematic formula that ultimately ended in the destruction of democracy as it pushed more and more citizens into the twilight consciousness of mass delusion. The mythology that American democracy created greater access for individual activity and individual success failed in its exclusive connection to profitability. The American Dream 'required the community to release the individual from all ethical obligations. [...]

28 See *KW* 12, 527–533.
29 *KW* 12, 531.
30 *KW* 12, 532.
31 This idea shows signs of continuity from Broch's early mentality of aristocratic disengagement and conservative fear of change, which I addressed in ch 2. Patrick Eiden provides an insightful analysis of the ways in which these ideas created a flawed understanding of 'conflict' in Broch's political theory. Eiden, 'Anstand und Abstand', see especially 145–149.

[T]he radical economic liberalism [...] meant nothing but the undisturbed pursuit of business'.[32] Broch took American politics at its word: The business of America was business. Democracy was here characterized by a commitment to isolationism and to strict capitalistic profit motives. He states:

> The country's miraculous security, its inexhaustible natural resources, the unlimited opportunities for work for its sky-rocketing population – all these facilitated the growth of a purely commercial political attitude able to do without any political content to such an extent that the two major parties today can hardly be distinguished from each other in their ideas and program.[33]

Within this tradition, American democracy constructed a rigid system of empty (or purely rhetorical) watchwords like pacifism, anti-imperialism and protection of civil liberties and of commercial pursuits. Broch asserted that a 'democracy that has become rigid has lost its power of resistance'. The American 'self-made man' has created the non-political herd. Both fascist ideology and the American Dream contained the same underlying value, that is, 'the idea of victory'.[34] Thus, Broch's political theory was a call for overcoming American moral ambiguity, the call for a 'victory over the idea of victory'.[35]

32   Broch, undated draft manuscript, Hermann Broch Archive. Yale Collection of German Literature, Beinecke Rare Book and Manuscript Library.
33   Broch, undated draft manuscript, Hermann Broch Archive. Yale Collection of German Literature, Beinecke Rare Book and Manuscript Library.
34   Broch, undated draft manuscript, Hermann Broch Archive. Yale Collection of German Literature, Beinecke Rare Book and Manuscript Library.
35   Broch, undated draft manuscript, Hermann Broch Archive. Yale Collection of German Literature, Beinecke Rare Book and Manuscript Library.

Total Democracy

In contrast to the material interpretation of the pursuit of happiness, Broch
offered his concept of total democracy, which protected the individual as a
value-creating citizen. He argued that the right of the pursuit of happiness
equated to the guarantee of a secure space in which each individual could
develop intellectually and spiritually. He saw all political action and all
social action (including religion) as locked in 'the world's commotion and
bustle' and unable to transcend earthly limitation of time, that is, they were
actions infused with the inevitability of death.[36] He claimed that social
value systems needed to be regulated not by socio-economic factors, but
by cultural and psychological ones. In a paradoxical way, he supported the
classical liberal notion of individualism, but the criterion for productive
individualism was psychological, not material.

As a defence against the irrational impulse to view the world as a man
eat man affair (this meant placing political man outside the realm of humanity), he put forth his concept of 'total democracy'. The term 'total' used to
modify democracy, as well as his references to a democratic 'dictatorship',
struck many observers at the time as problematic and even authoritarian.[37]
Broch, however, consciously contrasted a humane democratic totality to
an inhumane fascist totality. In his American exile, he repeatedly stressed
the thin line that divided most democracies from fascism. Democracy differentiated itself by its spirituality and its moral outlook, that is, democracy
preferred what he called open value systems. In an open value system there
was no attempt to impose community defined absolutes. Values defined
by a communal set of standards were merely attempts at securing a goal.
They were an attempt at conquest or victory. In a democracy, the value
system was designed to foster individual awareness of an absolute human

36   Hermann Broch, '*Die mythische Erbschaft*', quoted in Hannah Arendt, *Men in Dark
     Times*, 136.
37   Broch, undated draft manuscript, Hermann Broch Archive. Yale Collection of
     German Literature, Beinecke Rare Book and Manuscript Library.

value, not a particularist one.[38] 'Fascisms are caricatures of the true totality of values – exactly as their dynamics are nothing but a cartoon of the
genuine functional process. [...] If a total democracy were content with a
simple aping of the super-gratifications of the fascist methods, it would not
last, indeed'. The difference between fascist totality and total democracy
was that total democracy was built on the idea of creating communities
for the promotion of ethical values and the avoidance of human suffering.
Total democracy would pursue the moral goal of the victory of good over
evil. Fascism was different because it based its formation of community
on the idea and the reality of human suffering. It entailed the creation of
an outsider, who deserved and required punishment, and the creation of
a value system that was strictly external and material. Since humans are
not strictly external, material beings, fascism could not create a truly total
community or absolute ethical system.[39] His point in the end was to prove
that fascism lacked totality.

Democracy was not exempt from mass hysteria; it was, however, a
form of social organization historically conditioned to promote ideas
of freedom and equality. In terms of regulative principles of democratic
societies, Broch supported, as Almund Greiter and Anton Pelinka state,
the principles of 'freedom, equality, justice, and humanity. Principles established in the idea of human rights. [...] Human rights, which are developing
pacifically, are in the first instance the human rights of liberal democracies
– human rights that guaranteed the freedom of the individual from the
state. Broch postulated, however, an expansion of the tradition of liberal
Natural Law'.[40] The expansion to which Greiter and Pelinka refer was his

---

38   An idea that distances Broch's thought from both the French Revolutionaries and
     Jean Jacques Rousseau. Broch, undated draft manuscript, Hermann Broch Archive.
     Yale Collection of German Literature, Beinecke Rare Book and Manuscript Library.
39   Broch's anti-Marxist stance can be easily detected here. Broch, though educated in
     Vienna, the heart of logical positivism and scientific materialism, was strongly influ-
     enced by German Idealism and the Classical Humanism tradition. His Philosophy of
     History is very much nineteenth century, Hegelian and thus Marxist. But he rejects
     both the materialism and the exterminationist rhetoric of Marxism.
40   Greiter and Pelinka, 'Hermann Broch als Demokratietheoretiker', 31.

belief that the idea of natural rights should be expanded to the concrete relationship of individual humans. In the American context, these rights were limited to an abstract relationship of citizen and state. He used the example of Germany to demonstrate the weakness of natural rights based only on the regulation of citizen and state.

The rise of Hitler clearly validated Germany's failure to balance democratic regulative principles with the abstract power of the state. He used the example of the Weimar Republic's 'Law for the Protection of the Republic' to demonstrate the weakness of democracies that focus too much on regulating governmental and citizen exchange and not enough on creating individual security.[41] 'Democracy [...] cannot safeguard its own existence by means of an abstract "Law for the Protection of the Republic" [...] If there is a concrete danger for democracy, it must be encountered by concrete means'.[42] His point was that in regard to democracy legal protection must depend on the legal regulation of 'concrete partners'.

In addressing the issue of regulative principles, he was highly influenced by nineteenth-century historicism, and he argued that questions of democracy in the contemporary world were understandable only as a continuum of the democratic tradition in the West since the eighteenth century. Through the crucible of revolution, American and French, the foundational theories of state and citizenship had been forged. The operation of democracy was based on a tension between the regulative principles (created through a revolution and the throwing off of oppression) and the government as the organ by which democracy is administered and protected. In his historical philosophy, democracy in the West remained fragile because of its novelty.[43]

41 Passed by Reichstag in 1922 in response to the murder of Walter Rathenau.
42 Broch, undated draft manuscript, Hermann Broch Archive. Yale Collection of German Literature, Beinecke Rare Book and Manuscript Library.
43 England has 'almost forgotten her revolutionary origins, [...] every governmental spokesman, conservative or liberal, with his election becomes the object of real confidence. For every Englishman knows that the governmental power will be used in defence of the regulative principles on which the British way of life is based'. Broch, undated draft manuscript, Hermann Broch Archive. Yale Collection of German Literature, Beinecke Rare Book and Manuscript Library.

Both the American and the French Revolutions occurred during a period of historical transition from the hypertrophy of the Late Middle Ages (the breakdown of the stable and absolute system of values under the Universal Church) to a period of secular stability. Whereas the late Middle Ages and the Renaissance were periods of hypertrophy marked by mass hysteria in the form of witch trials and internecine struggles within Christianity, the nineteenth century was a period of general political stability and rising democracy. This meant in his system that European and American foundations for democracy, forged in the transitional period of the eighteenth century, were at once revolutionary and stabilizing. Much of the strength of democracy in the United States was in fact its continued revolutionary distrust of the government as a force for oppression. Such democratic awareness or defensiveness exposed, however, a democratic fatalism – a lack of awareness of any other dangers to democracy outside of governmental abuse, such as racial conflict, economic disparity or xenophobia.

Broch traced such democratic fatalism back to the founding of the United States. The founding fathers had set out the relationship between citizen and state; they did not, however, set out the relationship between citizen and citizen – in the context of the eighteenth century, they felt it unnecessary.

> The Founding Fathers of the United States had such a fear of tyranny that they felt obliged to embody their anti-tyrannical principles into the Declaration of Independence and the Bill of Rights, laws whose sole purpose is to protect the citizens against encroachment of the government; the basic principles of every-day civic life were so natural and self-evident to them – they felt them to be the very substance of life and democracy – that no one conceived their incorporation into a written law might be necessary, in order to protect state against encroachment on the part of the citizen or the citizen himself against evil conduct of his fellow citizen. It sufficed them if the regulative principles were effective as a negative source of law.[44]

After his experiences with National Socialism and his witnessing the racial tensions within the United States, he questioned whether the basic

---

44   Broch, undated draft manuscript, Hermann Broch Archive. Yale Collection of German Literature, Beinecke Rare Book and Manuscript Library.

principles governing citizen interaction in daily life were self-evident any longer.[45] His concerns were manifested in his investigations of fascist tendencies in American democracy and in his push to expand the regulative principles of democracy to include duty as well as freedom.

It was through his discussion of regulative principles that he linked his critique of the American Dream to the other problem in its democratic tradition, the issue of demonology. He observed in Europe that the National Socialists bet their political triumph on the idea that the German people, panicked by the insecurity of economic depression and national defeat, no longer saw freedom as a social value. They promoted, instead, materially measured values such as security and glory. The protection of such values became connected to abstract conceptions such as nation or blood, leaving some members of the society, both citizen and non-citizen, exposed to attack. The central value for fascism became 'victory', and the ritual of victory depended not only on the creation of success, but also on the creation of an opponent. Broch referred to the opponent in religious terms as the devil in the system.[46] Fascism also relied upon a system of magical justice, which corresponded to the irrational fears of the dominant society. The identification of demonology and the return to magical justice were crucial to a significant portion of his definition of fascism, and he openly identified such an ideology in the tradition of the American Dream and American racism.[47]

45 Even today the battles over the interpretation of the Fourteenth Amendment amongst various members of the Supreme Court and between constitutional scholars demonstrate that issue is still far from self-evident.

46 Broch, who worked very closely with Hannah Arendt during his American exile, developed a theory on the use and necessity of an opponent for the fascist system. The theory was very close to Arendt's notion of 'the other'.

47 Broch maintained a keen interest in the question of race in the United States throughout his exile. He even took active steps to support the protection of rights for African-Americans. Broch's banking record reveals that he made regular contributions to NAACP throughout his exile. Broch, undated draft manuscript, Hermann Broch Archive. Yale Collection of German Literature, Beinecke Rare Book and Manuscript Library.

His concerns about American race relations took a more central position in his fascist theory as the tensions turned into outright instances
of mass hysteria, such as the Detroit Riots of 1943. From the early 1940s
onward, the racial make-up of Detroit changed rapidly as the war industry
ramped up and turned the city into the 'arsenal of American democracy'.
African-Americans in large numbers migrated from the south to work in
the defence factories. The demographic shift was part of a larger migration
('The Great Migration') of African-Americans from the South to the North
between the First World War and the end of the Second World War.[48] In
June 1943 the growing tensions between white and blacks, competing for
housing in the rapid migration of workers to the city, led to clashes in the
streets. Fuelled by rumours of black mothers and babies being thrown from
bridges and white women being raped and murdered, groups of whites
and black attacked bystanders and polices for almost two days. In the
end, President Roosevelt had to send in federal troops to restore order. All
told, thirty-four people were killed and almost 2,000 arrested. The event
exposed for Broch the depth of the racial divide, as well as the danger of
mass hysteria, within American society.[49]

Broch used the event as a moment for considering the future of
American democracy.[50] As blood and hatred swept across Detroit, he
weighed these events against the claims of equality and freedom in the
United States. He suggested two polemical readings of the events: 'There
are many people, who contend that America always had her lynchings, her
assaults on labour and other unpleasant events, full of violence and corruption, and that, nevertheless, America remained the best democracy on
earth. Don't worry, they say, therefore, about the happenings in Detroit'. In

48   See Robert T. Ernst and Lawrence Hugg, *Black America: Geographic perspectives*
      (New York: Anchor, 1976), 271–372, 329–351.
49   See Dominic and Wilkerson, *Layered Violence: The Detroit Rioters of 1943* (Jackson,
      MS: University of Mississippi Press), 1991.
50   The discussion of the Detroit Riots is found in an unpublished manuscript (in English)
      attached to a pamphlet on 'The Law for the Protection of Human Dignity'. Broch,
      undated draft manuscript, Hermann Broch Archive. Yale Collection of German
      Literature, Beinecke Rare Book and Manuscript Library.

contradiction, 'there are others, who say that ... America will now have to pay for century-old sins against her basic democratic principles: to them, the happenings in Detroit are a symptom for an American repetition of the European development leading to fascism, are symptoms for the crumbling of democratic liberty, equality and fraternity, symptoms for the uprising of fascist intolerance and race hatred and the [victory] of the primitive right of the stronger'.[51] Broch rejected the complacency of the first attitude, and he engaged the second attitude not as a reality but as a more than possible future for the United States.

The attack on minority groups was the most dangerous political manifestation of fascist ideology. Its violent tendencies not only endangered the immediate lives of local minorities, but they also undercut the essential dignity of human life and reinforced a value system based on victory and violence. Broch portrayed the magical justice of fascism as a re-paganization of the modern world. Throughout history, civilizations had taken up the cause of humanity and fought to replace magical justice with humane justice.[52] In its encounter with modernity, however, Europe turned its back on humane justice. The 'enlightened' invention of the guillotine highlighted the corruption of humanity with the false security of the technology and its ability to minimize suffering. Celerity and cleanliness in murder did not

---

51 Broch, undated draft manuscript, Hermann Broch Archive. Yale Collection of German Literature, Beinecke Rare Book and Manuscript Library.

52 Broch claimed that the earliest notions of such a humane goal can be seen in the story of Abraham's substitution of a ram for Isaac. In terms of politics, democracy amounted to a similar re-humanizing and de-paganizing of the world, i.e., respecting God's separation between paganism and humaneness. For this reason, Broch called upon democracy to end capital punishment. The modern world's attempts at compromise with savagery in the form of new methods of execution and its removal from the public eye had not ended the anti-humanity implied in the antinomian notion of justice that calls for an eye for an eye. Democracy must embrace humanness without compromise, and, even though Broch conceded that, during a time of war, such measures could not be taken, he called for a resolution that would ensure the abolition of the death penalty in the future. Such a resolution would become the centrepiece of the democratic propaganda and tied directly to the peace aims of the democratic nations.

change the ultimate outcome, death. 'Democracy must embrace humanness without compromise, and the state can prove its humaneness only by
overcoming the negativism of death-warrants and by convincing the masses
of the inviolability of all human life. It must be made clear that no human
soul, however vile, shall be excluded from that right, and none placed so
high – not even in representing the state commonwealth – as to arrogate the
power of breaking this supreme democratic principle of human dignity'.[53]

For the German nation, any claim to a humane, democratic tradition
was made illegitimate by the economic depressions and national humiliation
following the First World War. The volkish religion of National Socialism
and its creation of the devil in the form of the Jew marked the ultimate
realization of such a violently hypertrophied system. In the United States,
the hypertrophy of the democratic tradition began with the defeat of the
Confederate states and the reconstruction of the South; the economic and
social insecurity produced a hypertrophy seen in the passing of the Black
Codes and the expansion of lynching and Ku Klux Klan activity. In both
cases, demonology and an irrational impulse to victory were sparked by
social panic.

> The national-socialist propaganda [...] is geared for stirring up anti-Semitism.
> Together with its extensions (as, for example, negrophobia), anti-Semitism is the
> very 'carrier' of contagion, the very contagion itself of the fascist lunacy – and this
> is the datum that has to direct the democratic fight against mass delusion and its
> propaganda. Certainly, as soon as the belief in the god of victory is smashed, the
> belief in his counterpart, the devil, is bound to collapse, too.[54]

Broch implies here that opposition to fascism in the United States must
be seen as something more than a confrontation between political and
nationalist ideologies. It must also become manifest in the protection of
minority rights and the universal value of human equality. His political,

---

53   Broch, undated draft manuscript, Hermann Broch Archive. Yale Collection of
      German Literature, Beinecke Rare Book and Manuscript Library.
54   Broch, undated draft manuscript, Hermann Broch Archive. Yale Collection of
      German Literature, Beinecke Rare Book and Manuscript Library.

and even his literary, works called for pragmatic solutions to mass delusions, such as the development of institutions for the protection of human life from individual murders, from state-sponsored murder (including the death penalty), from mob violence (such as lynchings and pogroms) and eventually from economic and nutritional deprivation.

Though Broch found historical examples of the hypertrophy of the American democratic tradition in its racism, especially in the political and cultural institutions of the southern United States, he saw the greater danger in the expansion of the fascist demonology to the arena of national politics and foreign policy. In this arena, the figure of the African-American slave would not serve as an effective devil. As the hypertrophy of American values moved beyond the regional issues of blood purity, issues of political and economic relationships would rise to the fore (godless Communism, the freedom hating economic authoritarianism, anti-modernization and religious terrorism). In this process, the centrality of success in the American democratic tradition took on more importance, as did nationalist rhetoric with the development of Cold War. The expansion of the demonology of the African-American would, in the historical context of fascism versus democracy (or communism versus democracy), be moved to the sidelines. In other historical contexts, such as the relationship of American democracy to the Third World, such demonology would still play a significant role.

The parallels between the United States and Germany were not exact for Broch. He saw the moral superiority of democracy over fascism as a 'given fact'. The difference between the 'god of victory' in National Socialism and the success of the American Dream was one of hypertrophy. In contrast to the continual evolution of the open system there was the dogma of the closed system. The closed system made claims to the infinite and the absolute through dogmatic 'theologies', whose force became the basis for the claims to justice and normal behaviour within a social group. An open system lacked absolute values: it 'endeavor[ed] to attain the desired absolute validity through the unrestricted development and expansion of the system. The 'open system' was aware of the infinity of the world; it, therefore, knew that absolute validity is an infinitely distant goal, and not a final state concretely to attain'.[55] Broch saw this as the intention behind the pursuit of happiness. It was an intention that had been lost as the material definition of 'happiness' gained ground in the late nineteenth and early twentieth centuries.

It was his belief that we must understand the difference between open and closed value systems on the individual level, what he called in Freudian terms normal and abnormal systems, because the psychosis or neurosis of the individual when reflected into the group value system resulted in periods of mass delusion (ritual killings, world wars and genocide). Such aberrations were generally directed at one group, who became the 'enemy' or the bringer of death and insecurity. From the development of these models of personal and group value systems, Broch applied a historical perspective. The combination of value system modelling and history allowed him to predicate the cycles of aberrations and to construct historical models of value disintegration and hypertrophy (the two instances where mass delusions develop).

He saw modernity as a period of disintegration that was open to mass delusion. The solution, thus, was historical. The examination of periods of conversion from a closed central value system (or from a period lacking a central value system) to open central value system could provide a model for the conversion process. In this vein, Broch chose the historical example of Christian conversion, and from that example set up a model for modern democratic conversion, that is, a method by which mass hysteria could be contained within an open value system that allowed for the release of sadistic impulses through sublimated release mechanisms. Through this process minority groups, who were often subject to persecutions as 'the enemy' of the dominant value system, would be protected. In truth, the American political system did allow for such an open process of creative sublimation. It can be seen in the marginalized cultures, such as Jazz and the Beat generation. These counter-cultures represented what Broch described as the frontier mentality in early American democracy.

---

55   Broch, undated draft manuscript, Hermann Broch Archive. Yale Collection of German Literature, Beinecke Rare Book and Manuscript Library.

The ultimate danger of the closed system was the point at which the closed system's absolute theology no longer explained or ordered the world of reality. At this point, the closed system had only two choices: die or carry through its dogma by force. Conceiving of fascism as a modern paganism, he called for a conversion to democracy.

> The fight against this aberration [Fascism], the return of man into the open system of humanitarianism, is the task of democracy. It is a fight against the magic ideology of victory, a fight for the idea of 'human justice'; and this is why the democratic mission must be regarded as the continuation of the Christian one, though on a secular, scientific, and especially psychological, basis. And the pattern that can be applied to all religious conversions may, obviously, well be applied to their secular continuation, too.[56]

The ultimate goal was the establishment of constitutions and laws that were based on an open value system whose underlying central value was protecting the dignity of human life.

Broch also strove to convince individuals that values other than materialistic ones should be the basis for democracy. In Europe, he saw no solution; fascism was too deeply entrenched, and the Nazis had been very effective in alienating any prophets of a 'counter-crusade' by identifying them as alien in race and character: Jewish and highbrow. In the United States, the effects of modernization also presented a roadblock to such a counter-crusade. The United States had exchanged its ethical or religious foundation for democracy for the foundational principle of business. Business, however, was simply material and thus could not produce an open value system.[57] Paradoxically, however, he found the solution in early American democracy,

---

56   Broch, undated draft manuscript, Hermann Broch Archive. Yale Collection of German Literature, Beinecke Rare Book and Manuscript Library.

57   Broch developed his political theory by expanding his aesthetic value theory to the world of politics. In his aesthetic system, art is judged on the basis of whether it can provoke an ethical response in the viewer. Art that cannot provoke such a response is empty of value or is kitsch. Fascism was, for Broch, the political kitsch of twentieth century. In the United States, and after the rise of the Third Reich, Broch recognized that his theory on the disintegration of values could be applied not only to art, but also to the political context of his time.

because he saw its origins as deeply connected to the issues of spirituality, morality and human dignity. He saw the basis of a humane democracy in the preindustrial United States, where it developed out of the religious communalism of the early settlers.[58] These communities contained a spiritual and social communion that 'stood godfather to modern democracy';[59] it was a tradition that 'by virtue of its ethical and religious tinge, demanded an attitude of obligation to the community which was truly political'.[60]

Democracy, like any other institution of civilization, had to be supported by a fundamental value. In the case of democracy that value was originally freedom. By the early 1930s, however, it was obvious to Broch that democratic freedom had lost its redemptive power. He claimed that value systems became visible in society through ritual, but the modern world had seen a fundamental change in the expression and location of ritual. Since the Reformation and the Enlightenment, ritual had become steadily more private or less institutional. The modern world preached a religion without God; but, the secularization of the modern world had not ended the basic human need for ritual – it had only killed its major symbols. In this atmosphere of value disintegration, both capitalism and fascism had erected a new god. It was the god of success: 'a Machiavellianism of success that entered, without exception, all the other spheres of value as well. In the end the old chivalrousness of the military ritual was displaced by the wretched ritualization of success'.[61] His discussion of fascism questioned

58 Paradoxically, Broch also argued that American individualism and its political independence (what he termed anarchism) developed out its early religious communities.
59 Broch, undated draft manuscript, Hermann Broch Archive. Yale Collection of German Literature, Beinecke Rare Book and Manuscript Library.
60 Broch, undated draft manuscript, Hermann Broch Archive. Yale Collection of German Literature, Beinecke Rare Book and Manuscript Library.
61 Broch, undated draft manuscript, Hermann Broch Archive. Yale Collection of German Literature, Beinecke Rare Book and Manuscript Library. See also the letter of Esch to Frau Huguenau in the final section of Broch's novel, *The Sleepwalkers*, which vividly portrays this value vacuum as an example of the capitalistic Machiavellianism. Esch, rapist and murder, calmly asserts his right to an equitable settlement of his affairs with the Huguenau family, a right seemingly undeniably protected by value of commerce and legal contracts.

how long American democratic tradition can remain open and free under the central value of materialism.

He appealed to the American populace to recognize that fascism was already attempting to turn the United States away from its position as leader of a free, democratic world. He did not see National Socialism as the culmination of a German tradition, but rather as the turning away from a civilised German tradition. The destruction of people and cities clearly signified that culture had lost its redemptive value.[62] What was needed was a means by which the individual could reconnect with these ethical sources. It was a matter of individual responsibility: 'democratic conviction means democratic responsibility, and only in such personal responsibility can one find the will to defend democratic freedom'.[63] In a sense, he was arguing for a crisis of democracy in Europe, similar to a crisis of liberalism, but the root of this crisis was not liberalism's inability to come to terms with politicization of the masses, its restrictive franchise and its concern for class preservation; it was the loss of democratic personal responsibility stemming from the disintegration of values. Democracy had become a matter of fact, there was no engaged relationship to its functioning. Citizens no longer asked where their personal responsibilities began or where the government's ended.

He viewed European democracy as a failure, and he saw little hope in the democratic tradition that developed in the US during the nineteenth century. However, he found hope in the notion of a new American Dream, conceived around the ancient notions of reason and truth and constructed by a new generation of Americans, what Broch terms the American youth.

62   Broch offered this idea in the form of a question hinting at some degree of pessimism and ambiguity towards the ultimate good in humanity: 'Do the intrinsic human values – provided that they still exist – offer sufficient justification for the appeal to defend these values against the assault of the dictators?' Broch, undated draft manuscript, Hermann Broch Archive. Yale Collection of German Literature, Beinecke Rare Book and Manuscript Library.
63   Broch, undated draft manuscript, Hermann Broch Archive. Yale Collection of German Literature, Beinecke Rare Book and Manuscript Library.

The great hope here is directed toward [...] overcoming of Pragmatism which can be
regarded as the perfect expression of the non-political manner of thought in the last
few decades. [...] It becomes the unbound duty of anyone concerned with the future
of humanity to address his own efforts to this youth among which the will to believe
in truth, to believe in political sacrifice and responsibility is again taking shape. What
youth wants, what it needs and strives for, is the restoration of the democratic idea,
in its platonic reasoning as well as realistic program.[64]

What Broch foreshadowed here is the counter-culture movement of 1960s.
The importance of the youth and the separation of a younger generation
from the material values of their parents were his solution to the growing
threat of fascist thought in America.

Even though Broch died before the Beat Generation created a truly
visible culture and well before the rise of the counter-culture movement
of the 1960s, the intellectual similarities between these movements and
his critique on American democracy in the 1930s and 1940s demonstrate
that the intellectual emigration of the interwar years brought more to the
United States than simply a positivistic science and a theoretical basis for
new social science. They brought the possibility of conceiving of a society
where religious thought and the idea of love (here Platonic in its truest
sense) formed the fundamental social value.[65] Broch was not alone in this
development. Herbert Marcuse and Karl Popper also promoted similar
notions of conceptualizing Western society outside of a strict democratic/
communist dichotomy or a strict democratic/totalitarian one.

His solutions, however, were not simple calls for 'love thy neighbour'.
His theory of mass hysteria was based on the epistemological notion that
a transcendent and universal value was accessible – an earthly absolute,
around which the conversion process would turn. Since access to such an
earthly absolute was through a cognitive process, the central position of the

64   Broch, undated draft manuscript, Hermann Broch Archive. Yale Collection of
      German Literature, Beinecke Rare Book and Manuscript Library.
65   Paul Michael Lützeler makes a similar argument for the importance of Broch's politi-
      cal thought and its relationship to later movements, such as Amnesty International.
      See Lützeler, 'Introduction' and 'Visionaries in Exile', in *Hermann Broch Visionary
      in Exile*, 1–10 and 67–88.

individual in Broch's democratic theory is a sine qua non. This translated in pragmatic terms to the creation of a new regulative principle based not just on the negative rights tradition of the United States, but also on the notion of an enforceable duty, in which all citizens would be forced to ensure their access to full development (ego-expansion) by enforcement of a law for the protection of human life and dignity. The enforcement would by necessity be backed up by force.[66] This was total democracy.

From the discussion of slavery to the embrace of religious communalism in the American colonial period to the spiritual elements of Broch's Platonic/Christian rhetoric of political 'conversion', what he built in his political and psychological theories of total democracy was a road map for overthrowing capitalist values without a material revolution. Even his discussion of free love (found in his letters to various lovers during the 1940s) invoked a radical rejection of cultural norms through a shift in cognition not an ecstatic and irrational mass movement. He argued in his letters that individual cognitive freedom needed to be valued more than physical freedom, imagined here as material in the sense of physical/emotional jealousy and monogamy.[67] The conservative position he held in Vienna, which lacked a pragmatic understanding of having to address activism and change in the material world, became in the US context a means for ameliorating the sources of modern enslavement through individual freedom and agency. It was a plan that did not require a revolutionary process, but a conversion process. Unlike Huguenau in *The Sleepwalkers*, who resorted to violence and conflict, citizens in a total democracy would resort to ethical creativity. His political theory of the 1940s was a harbinger of the religious communalism of the freedom riders and the individual pursuit of spiritual fulfilment through vitality and ego expansion found in the poetry and music of the Beat movement and popularization of American folk music. The countercultural shifts of the 1950s and 1960s reflected many of the

---

66 Greiter and Pelinka, 'Hermann Broch als Demokratietheoretiker', 25.
67 Unpublished letters to Jean Untermeyer Starr and Marion Canby, Hermann Broch Archive. Yale Collection of German Literature, Beinecke Rare Book and Manuscript Library.

values connected to Broch's re-imagining of democratic citizenship: anti-materialism, utilitarian economics, unbound intellectual creativity and a humanist sense of responsibility for the protection of life, all of which fostered a vitalism suggestive of religious conversion. The cultural changes of the 1950s and 1960s, however, did not actually manifest themselves in ways Broch would have expected or appreciated, because they developed in a new historical context of the American global dominance, greater control in reproductive choices, and the merger of drugs and popular culture that even *fin-de-siècle* Vienna lacked.

Broch conceived of his reforms within a context of continued commitment to the Enlightenment, rationality, science and constitutionalism that ordered progress. In his approach to the issue of capitalist enslavement, Broch rejected a Marxist (especially Soviet) solution of revolution and proletarian re-education. He presented what may remain today a pathway to capitalist reform in the United States, a country that clearly possesses, as Broch pointed out, the values for such a reform. The major political obstacles to reform were for Broch the danger that reform would become revolution; by 1938, he came to realize that avoiding violent revolution through the abdication of political involvement was equally as dangerous to modern democracies. The indictment of present day reform in areas such as health care, banking and minimum wage as socialist or communist (read un-American) reinforce this fundamental conservativism in the American middle class. Broch maintained his earlier middle class fear of revolution during the 1940s, but he nonetheless engaged the necessity to actively pursue reforms in the materialist tradition of American individualism and economics. Clearly, his approach to democratic reform through cognitive change backed by education and legal protection still has value in the current American political discourse.

Throughout this chapter, I have discussed how Broch's political theory, based on the notion of a totalizing value system, confronted problems of racism and anti-Semitism in a democratic polity. He argued that only in a democracy would the totalizing value system be open and designed to promote individual freedom. Totalitarianism, on the other hand, used its value system to close off individual freedom. The central method of such a closing off, or as Broch stated a hypertrophy of the logic of the social value system, was the identification of a demonic force within society – a force against which all political and cultural energy could be turned. Such demonology was historically expressed through the lynching of African Americans and the systematic murder of European Jews.

Broch's political writings from his exile allow us a European view of American democracy. Since the time of de Tocqueville, American democracy has been an object of both admiration and criticism for European intellectuals. The sharpness of such criticism has reached its greatest degree over the last few decades of the 'American Century' and the first years of the twenty-first century. Hermann Broch, who came to America as an exile in 1938, provided another opportunity to examine the European perspective on democracy. His observations on American democracy formed only a part of his political theory, which on a separate front would strive for the construction of an international, democratic structure that could serve as the bulwark against the expansion of fascism. His political theory, which was both utopian and practical, promoted a notion of cosmopolitan democracy based on the protection of human life. It was a theory that looked beyond national borders and obviously reflected his experience of Jewish assimilation in turn-of-the-century Vienna. He provided a critique and a plan for the future of democracy in the United States that suggested ties between the German speaking émigré and later manifestations of American political resistance. For these reason, the re-evaluation of both his work and his position in the intellectual migration of the interwar years are important.

The earliest interpretations of Broch and his exile saw both as marginal. It was an evaluation that was based on a sense of failure and tragedy. Recently, however, his exile in the United States has undergone substantial re-evaluations by scholars, who have come to see his thought as a window into the intellectual tenor of 1930s and 1940s United States.[68] They have come to see the pertinent nature of his social and aesthetic thought to contemporary American culture. I have addressed in a similar vein the 'visionary' nature of Broch's political theory of fascism. The result, in terms

---

68   In particular the edited volume from the 2001 Yale Symposium, *Hermann Broch: Visionary in Exile.*

of intellectual history, is that we gain a fuller view of intellectual confrontation with fascism in the United States. In so doing, we find that the role of religious and creative thought provided an alternate perspective for the functioning of the United States in a liberal democratic West. It demonstrates that this alternative view had European connections, if not roots. It suggests a connection between the intellectual worlds of 1940s Jewish immigration with both the counterculture movement and the religious-based civil rights movement of the 1960s. The dismissal of such alternative views of democracy was a direct result of political shifts that followed 1945 and the development of the Cold War. In the last chapter, I question the historical reliability of Broch's own memory of his exile experience in terms of political engagement, and then use that analysis as a jumping off point for arguing that his relevance to American intellectual history is more significant than the veil of tragedy surrounding his exile allows.

CONCLUSION

Reconsidering Failure in Hermann Broch's Exile Narrative

A simple, human happiness is almost unknown to me.[1]

Early on the morning of 30 May 1951, a milkman discovered Hermann Broch's dead body. Broch had been diagnosed with *angina pectoris* in November of 1950 and had not fully recovered from his first heart attack (1 April 1951), when he suffered a fatal attack that morning. His body was found on the floor of his apartment. Not far from where he lay was a half-packed suitcase, preparation for a pending trip to Europe. His death, like his life, reflected a pattern of incompleteness – the half-packed suitcase and the aborted return home symbolized neatly his final years: his exile, his itinerant life, his frenzied matter of work and his inability to bring projects to a close.

The tragic nature of this scene and its symbolism fit well with Broch's own hyperbolic rhetoric about death, impotence and failure, as well as much of the literature on him. My book began as an investigation to the reality behind this sense of failure and tragedy. In 2001 at the Hermann Broch Yale Symposium, scholars gathered to consider his exile experience. The symposium produced new momentum in understanding his intellectual importance beyond the assumptions of marginality or failure. I have attempted to clarify that experience in this book through an historical account of his political thought. In this chapter I address the historiography

---

1   Hermann Broch, 'Psychische Selbstbiographie,' in Paul Michael Lützeler, ed., *Psychische Selbstbiographie* (Frankfurt am Main: Suhrkamp Verlag, 1999), 82.

around Broch as exile in order to illuminate the influences and the assumptions that have crafted the historical narrative of his intellectual biography.

My research into his political theory started with its theoretical groundings in Vienna. As I examined the shift from epistemology to aesthetics to politics in his thought, I realized that the historiographical narrative, which depicted him as a long time committed liberal democrat, contained some misperceptions. In particular, I found that his relationship to politics was weak until well into the 1930s. In this chapter, I delve deeper into the idea of historical misperception: first, by analysing Broch's autobiographical contributions to the misperception of both political engagement and failure. Secondly, I analyse the larger historiographical paradigm of Broch as a tortured and defeated exile. As a setup to my analysis, I present upfront the biographical aspects of his immigration to the United States. Then, I analyse his reflections on the process of intellectual transformation during his exile. In his self-portrait of political conversion, we find a story of intellectual consistency and political astuteness, which was peppered with a tone of moral superiority. Through a detailed reading of his autobiographical notes from the early 1940s, I question the historical reliability of Broch's words in assessing his intellectual evolution to an engagé intellectual. In the final section of the chapter, I argue that the problematic nature of Broch's autobiography aided in the creation of a historiography of failure and tragedy around his exile experience.

Exile Biography

The inherent danger of being an intellectual and a Jew in post-*Anschluss* Austria became immediately clear to Hermann Broch on 13 March 1938. One day after Hitler invaded Austria he was arrested by the members of the local National Socialist party and imprisoned in a provincial jail.[2]

---

2   Broch was arrested on suspicions of being a political radical and not for being a Jew.

Due to the efforts of friends in Vienna and to sickness, he was released and allowed to return to Vienna, though his movements were restricted. In Vienna, he felt the 'noose tightening'[3] and over the next several months he worked to secure papers for emigration.[4] He left Vienna on 20 July 1938; he would not return.[5] Thus, Hermann Broch joined the growing number of European Jews, socialists, artists and intellectuals, who in fleeing fascist terror, came to the United States in what H. Stuart Hughes described as a 'sea change' in Western intellectual history.[6]

Following his escape from Vienna, he spent several months in Scotland with Willa and Edwin Muir,[7] the translators of his first novel, *The Sleepwalkers*. He eventually obtained an America visa and arrived in New York City on 9 October 1938. He had 600 dollars in his pocket.[8] Like most of the intellectual refugees from Europe, Broch viewed his arrival in America both as deliverance and misfortune. Although he escaped almost certain death, he felt a deep sense of survivor guilt, tremendous financial insecurity and the absence of leisure (the time and space to think and write). He found himself in a new and challenging situation for an upper-middle class, European male – the need for 'five hundred pounds and a room of one's own'.

There were several factors that mitigated the feelings of loss and hopelessness that accompany the refugee. Foremost for Broch was a sense of

---

3   'I felt only the noose/around my neck', quoted in Lützeler, *A Biography*, 166.
4   See Broch's letter to Emmy Ferand (Scotland, 17.8.38) for Broch's own discussion of the events surrounding his emigration, *KW* 13/2, 17–20.
5   See Michael Lützeler's biography of Hermann Broch for a detailed account of these months and Broch's desperate attempts to leave Austria. Owing to age and her fear of financial uncertainty, Broch's mother hesitated to emigrate with him. In 1942, Nazi officials arrested her, and she died later that year in Theresienstadt concentration camp. Lützeler, *A Biography*, 155–166.
6   H. Stuart Hughes, *The Sea Change*, reprinted in *Between Commitment and Disillusion* (Middletown, CT: Wesleyan University Press, 1987), 1–34.
7   20 Queens Garden, St. Andrews, Fife, Scotland. For a description of Broch's life during his stay in England and Scotland, see his letters to Ruth Norden, Anne Marie Meier-Graefe and Emmy Ferand. *KW* 13/2, 14–36.
8   Lützeler, *A Biography*, 173–174.

duty. Duty to the love ones and friends left behind in Europe, but also the duty to protect the notions of civilization and humanity, which he connected to his life in Europe. Like all of his endeavours, however, his attempt to find a political solution reflected a sense of duty tempered by despair. He states at the beginning of his 'Self-psychoanalysis', 'The extension of my responsibility, which is no longer limited to the family, but applies to nearly all my human relations, and in the end has been extended to a general responsibility to humanity and truth, so that my powers, even though they are at times productive, are easily outstripped.' The internal battle between Broch's sense of duty and the limitations of his mental and emotional existence in exile was mirrored by the external conflict between the strains of everyday life (finances, work, housing and health) and the mitigating effects of community and fellowship. The exploration of these factors in the development of his theories on fascism and democracy establish the groundwork for greater insight into the general formulation and history of the mass society debates within the exile community of 1940s America.[10]

During the first four years after his arrival in New York, he shuttled between residences. His first and most frequent residence during this period was in New York City, 420 West 121st Street, near Columbia University. He rented a small one-room apartment there for the first six months of his exile, and he returned to this boarding house in June 1940, remaining until February 1942.[11] For most of 1939, he moved about between rooms in New York City, Princeton and Cleveland. He stayed in rented rooms, with friends (many female companions whose relationship to Broch, though clearly sexual, remained undefined, overlapped with other relationships and often erupted into jealous conflict) or at various college dormitories on Princeton and Yale campuses. For four weeks, he stayed at Albert Einstein's home, while Einstein was away, and in June 1939, the Yaddo Artist Colony in Saratoga Springs, New York offered Broch a six-week residence. By the

9   Broch, *Psychische Selbstbiographie*, 9.
10   See also Christian Borch, 'Modern mass aberration: Hermann Broch and the problem of irrationality'.
11   For detailed discussion of his biography, see also Lützeler, *A Biography*, 175–206.

middle of the 1939, the pressures of emigration and his constant moving had taken a toll on him physically. Life-long stomach and intestinal problems resurfaced, he developed a high fever, and shortly thereafter pneumonia.[12] In order to recuperate and finish his novel *The Death of Virgil*, Henry Seidel Canby, a professor of English literature at Yale University, allowed him to stay at his country house in Killingworth, Connecticut.

Broch's frequent relocations were connected to his poor financial situation. He never obtained a permanent academic position in America, and his literary work, while receiving critical praise, had little financial success. His major sources of income were grants and fellowships. In 1939, he pieced together several small grants from the American Guild for German Cultural Freedom, the Oberlaender Trust and the Office of Public Opinion Research at Princeton University. In July 1940, the Guggenheim Foundation awarded him a 2,500-dollar fellowship. The fellowship, which lasted from July 1940 until June 1941, funded his efforts at finishing his *Virgil* novel. In June 1941, the fellowship was extended another six months, while he worked on his *Theory of Mass Delusion*. The Guggenheim allowed him to end his itinerant lifestyle, which marked his first year in America, and to recover physically.

The income from the Guggenheim and other small grants would have provided enough for Broch to live somewhat comfortably, if he had not had to cover the cost of obtaining visas for both his mother and son. After the start of the war, their situation, both still in Europe, grew increasingly dangerous. Broch had to spend a great deal of time and money during 1940 and 1941 to obtain travel documents for them. In April 1940, he secured a visa for his mother and had arranged for her departure. Unfortunately, Johanna Broch hesitated to leave Austria and the visa expired. In late 1942, he secured a second visa for his mother, this time a Cuban visa. Again, however, Johanna Broch was unable to emigrate, this time owing to factors beyond her control. On 11 December 1941, Germany declared war on the United States and travel from Austria to Cuba was halted. In May 1942,

---

12   Letter to Anne Marie Meier-Graefe, 6 April 1939, *KW* 13/2, 63–64 and to Stefan Zweig, 22 April 1939, *KW* 13/2, 72–73.

she was arrested and taken to Theresienstadt concentration camp. She died there on 28 October 1942. Broch did not learn of her deportation until September 1943 and of her death until May 1944. He was able to arrange safe passage for his son and his son's fiancée; in September 1941, Armand Broch de Rothermann left France for Portugal; from Lisbon he was able to arrange passage to New York.[13]

By 1941, his situation in America stabilized, though it was never comfortable. For the last ten years of his life, he had the opportunity to pursue both political and literary work and to engage in the intellectual community of New York/New England. Nevertheless, the financial and emotional costs of emigration were heavy for Broch. His letters from the early 1940s indicated a growing sense of despair. Such concerns and discomforts, however, were rarely central to his correspondence. He usually referred to the situation with his mother or son in only one or two brief lines within letters that were often many pages in length, such as, 'News about my mother, however, is not good; she has been detained; I do not know what is to be done'.[14] Yet, the concern was still omnipresence in his letters. Moments of dolour within a sea of political and intellectual debate demonstrated the poignant sense of duality in Broch's mind – the ever-present conflict of duty and despair. It was out of this conflict that the impulse for generating theoretical solutions to the political crisis arose. The difficulty for the historian is separating both the immediate and the lifelong emotional and intellectual conflicts in him from his political program in exile.

---

13   See Lützeler, *A Biography* and Durzak, *Dokumenten*.
14   Broch, undated draft manuscript, Beinecke Rare Book and Manuscript Library MSS.

Becoming Political, 1932–1940

The importance of Broch's correspondence and his autobiographical writings to his own historical characterization cannot be overstated. These are the most accessible sources for evaluating his exile experience. In the following discussion, I examine his letters and autobiography in order to challenge the reliability of these sources for understanding what I consider to be a fundamental realignment of Broch's intellectual worldview – his shift from disengaged to engaged political criticism. In particular, I examine three autobiographical passages from his *Nachlass*. Each passage represents a declaration about the timing and reasoning for a sudden and deliberative rejection of art in order to embrace political action. He composed all of the passages in early 1940s, and he signified three specific political moments (Hitler's appointment to Chancellor, Italy's leaving the League of Nations, German/Austrian *Anschluss*) as *the* turning point in his political awakening. The assertiveness of each claim is difficult to reconcile with a single, determinative intellectual epiphany. In examining the three passages, I point out the historical weakness of these sources owing to the dramatic hyperbole generated by his poetic nature, as well as a self-defensive flaw in his own memory. Of the three significant moments for political awakening that he set forth, only the final one correlates to any elemental changes in his intellectual activities and theories.

In the earliest passage, Broch asserted that Hitler's appointment as Chancellor clarified the moral landscape and demanded that intellectuals abandon their ivory towers. He writes,

> Whoever, in that moment, wanted to do something against barbarism, bloodthirst and war, was not allowed to deviate; he had to endeavour to serve immediately those forces that still were able to resist the evil to come. Whoever did not do it in those days, continued to commit the sin of the brain-workers and intellectuals, their sin of the ivory tower and its irresponsibility; Germany, in the year 1933, gave the best proof of the consequences that were to arise from the political indifference of the intellectual liberal: had Germany possessed more men with the political zeal of a Max

Weber, had the German intellectual not secluded himself for decades from political
life, German democracy would have been better off.[15]

This passage highlights the remembered or constructed image of his political awakening, which has came to obscure his earlier political complacency.
His use of phrasing such as 'irresponsibility', 'indifference', 'political zeal'
and 'seclusion', as well as 'ivory tower' produced an image of himself as
politically fervent.[16] The indictment of German intellectuals for their
indifference, however, rings somewhat hollow, when one notes that his
focus in 1933 was on literary activities. Likewise, he produced no directly
critical work about either the National Socialist state or the new corporatist
government in Austria. Both physically and creatively, he abandoned the
city for the countryside. He amplified the importance of the mystical in
his writing, even popularizing it in novel form and turned to more direct
and accessible aesthetic outlets such as film. In all of these activities, he
came increasing close to turning his art from an exercise in cognitive cultural criticism to what he himself characterized as kitsch, but what Walter
Benjamin more pragmatically called aestheticization of politics. This was
certainly a problematic approach to challenging fascist politics, which built
their platforms on such activities.

Letters from 1933 to 1934 demonstrate that Broch did recognize a
change in the political circumstances. He was aware that his work (novels,
film and drama pieces) were '*Brotarbeit*', whose value was primarily pecu-
niary.[17] Letters to his editor Daniel Brody and his wife Daisy exhibited
his questioning of art and his vocation as a writer. Such questioning was
also theoretically examined in essays on kitsch from this same period. As
he stated in a letter to Daniel Brody in October 1934, the inability of art

15   Broch', An Autobiography As Program for Future Work', 1941, Hermann Broch
      Archive. Yale Collection of German Literature, Beinecke Rare Book and Manuscript
      Library. See also *Psychische Selbstbiographie*, 83–131.
16   His criticism of German intellectuals of the early 1930s, however, comes very close to
      Dagmar Barnouw's pointed criticism of Broch and others from the Weimar period.
      See Chapter 2, this volume.
17   See letter to Edit Rènyi-Gyömroi (2 September 1934), *KW* 13/1 293–294.

to represent the world (*Undarstellbarkeit*) left him in a position of either having to find a new calling or to kill himself.[18] Yet, his letters to Stefan Zweig from the exact historical moment of fascist takeover in Austria nurtured ambivalence toward mass aberration and contained a clearly apolitical tone. What Broch did throughout the early 1930s was to continue to work on novels and plays and essays, searching for a new path to a usable '*logos*' and a modern form of myth.[19] He openly stated his continued identity as a writer and his sustained commitment to art as a vehicle for value reconstruction. In a letter to Angel Flores in July 1934, he stated that it was doubly and triply demanded of the artist (*Künstler*) to discover a new source of knowledge.[20] Taken as a whole, his work, which lacked any direct interface with the politics of the time, and his letters implied an indictment of art and a sense of dispiritedness. They did not, however, suggest a pragmatic solution through 'political zeal'. Broch certainly lacked the emotional and professional commitment to politics that he himself suggested was needed and could be exemplified in someone like Max Weber.

In a second passage from the autobiography, he claimed that 1935 was the key moment of re-evaluation of politics and the moral duty of the artist.

> Hitler's taking over had confronted the whole of Europe with an Either/Or. If there still should be any ethical effects at all, they could be attained only by immediate participation in politics; devious ways were not permitted any longer, they showed themselves more and more to be loopholes for those who did not want to leave their ivory towers. Therefore, in 1935, I discontinued my esoteric poetry, which was addressed to the public, in order to devote myself instead to practical politics. [...] [A]ll of the sudden death had come palpably near us all, who lived as it were on the edge of the concentration camp, that the metaphysical argument with him [death] could no longer be delayed.[21]

18   See letter to Daniel Brody (19 October 1934), *KW* 13/1 301–302.
19   See Broch's essays 'Das Böse im Wertsystem der Kunst', 'Mythos und Altersstil' and 'James Joyce und die Gegenwart' in Paul Michael Lützeler, ed., *Geist und Zeitgeist: Essays zur Kultur der Moderne* (Frankfurt: Suhrkampf, 1997).
20   See letter to Angel Flores (16 July 1934), *KW* 13/1 288–289.
21   Broch, undated draft manuscript, Hermann Broch Archive. Yale Collection of German Literature, Beinecke Rare Book and Manuscript Library.

One must acknowledge that his political studies on the League Nation, which was prompted by Italy's departure from the League in 1935, were the bases for his later political theory, especially his ideas on citizen rights, constitutionalism and questions of state sovereignty. The general ideas he would clarify and broaden from 1939 to his death were presaged in these studies. This was a period of intellectual re-examination and growing political concern. Furthermore, John and Anne White, in arguing that his novel *The Death of Virgil* refashioned the literary symbology of the ivory tower (from the guardianship of revealed knowledge to one that criticized the seclusion of the intellectual from the political world), lend support to Broch's own accounting.[22] Nonetheless, it is difficult to interpret this period as an essential political turn, when he devoted so much energy to a major modernist literary undertaking. He began the novel in 1936 and did not complete it until 1943. The novel was a prose/poetry exploration of the poet Vergil's last day of life. It explored the poet's fever induced, delirious journey into his own ego and his confrontation with death. Its major theme was the relationship between art and society and even the tensions between friendship and duty, but it lacked a clearly stated political aim.[23]

The Death of Virgil indicated a shift in Broch's earlier hope for the ethical efficacy of art and revealed his increasing belief in the ineffectiveness of the word to elaborate on the ethical demands of contemporary Europe. In a purposefully ironic manner, he reformulated his early aesthetic solutions as anti-aesthetic or as an overcoming of what he diagnosed as an ethically empty art. Paul Michael Lützeler argues that his disillusionment with the power of art and literature led Broch to craft the novel as homage to 'negative aesthetics'. 'His *Virgil* novel returns to the literary medium, but

22   'Questions about poetry's place and value in a world of politicized inhumanity, violence and nationalism, about its limitations in comparison with philosophy, politics and humanists values are here explored at the very time when Broch wanted to abandon literature in favour of political activity.' John White and Anne White, 'Other Ivory Towers and Literary Counterfactuals', *Publications of the English Goethe Society*, LXXIX No. 1, 2010, 23.

23   See Patrick Eiden, *Das Reich der Demokratie: Hermann Brochs Der Tod des Vergil*, for a political reading of the novel.

primarily in order to expose its helplessness, its limits and ethical faults.'[24] The thrust of the modernist movement lacked significant connection to the centre of ethical activity, which to Broch was the individual. 'If we want to have anything left to hope for, we have to scale down our hopes to the smallest proportion, and that is the rescue of the Individual from utter enslavement'.[25] The Kantian call to break out of our self-imposed imma-turity could not be articulated through aesthetics, which were trapped by pure expressionism or lost in a search for the mythic and the expansive.

The *Death of Virgil* was a poetic expression of the central focus of modern values – understanding death. The diminution of the ego, as well as the fear and neurosis connected with such diminution, were for Broch the greatest obstacle to the creation of an open value system in Western society. He would later use his work on mass delusion to fill the gap left by literature. And it was only in his political writings that one can discern the full force of his attempts at reanimating ethics as a legitimate force in modern society. It was clear from his letters that he no longer felt that crea-tive writing contained enough pragmatic influence in the modern Europe.

The mere fact that he spent nine years writing, translating and rewrit-ing a poem that would announce the death of poetry and continued to fret about the moral shame of such an undertaking makes one question whether Broch had the profound realization about the political dangers surround-ing him as early as he asserted. The ubiquity of street violence, growing anti-Semitism and anti-democratic political success made avoiding politics in terms of everyday life impossible. He could not and did not avoid the question of whether his art lacked the ability to affect social change. He did not, however, reorder his intellectual concerns in any noticeable way. He certainly did not act with the moral urgency and rectitude he demanded of German intellectuals in the early passage, or with the commitment he showed after 1938. As for example in a letter to Willa Muir from 1940, here

24 Paul Michael Lützeler, 'The Avant-Garde in Crisis: Hermann Broch's Negative Aesthetics in Exile', in Paul Michael Lützeler, ed., *Hermann Broch, Literature, Philosophy, Politics: The Yale Broch Symposium* (Columbia, SC: Camden Book, 1988), 26.

25 Letter from Broch to Hubertus Prinz zu Löwenstein (22 April 1940), *KW* 13/2, 202.

he represented the maturation of his social criticism from art to politics as a moral demand. He, like Adorno, saw the moral disconnect of writing poetry in the midst of social and political disintegration. He understood the moral failure of indulging in what he called 'esoteric' activities, while democracies collapsed into totalitarian states: 'But I leave it [*Virgil*] as it stands now, for, I feel, in these times you have no right to dwell forever on a work which – in spite of the truth it may contain – is much too far away from the actual misery of this world. It would be immoral, or at least not far from immoral'.[26] Nothing in his letters or activities from his pre-exile period suggested that his venture into negative aesthetics equated to such a moral recalculation.

'The League of Nations Resolution' (1936/7) deserves some detailed discussion as it suggested a growing awareness of the dangers of German fascism in the period of the mid-1930s – even if that awareness remained sidelined while Broch worked out his aesthetic theory.[27] In the resolution, he exposed his early undervaluation of the importance of mass violence and technological war, while also demonstrating that his political views had taken a large step forward in judging the danger of militarist foreign policies like those of Hitler and Mussolini.[28] 'The World War', he writes, 'already itself the fruit of the pseudo-absolutist phantom, a terrible fruit, but nevertheless, it was still a relatively harmless preparation stage. It is separate from the actual insanity which incites it. [...] Clearly the imperialistic foreign policy of individual states and their holy egoism has allowed this the Machiavellian justification to ignore treaties, to go back on one's word and to partake in any act of violence'.[29] The resolution presented a justification for the League of Nations as well as direct proposals for creating international institutions for the protection of human life and a specific office for propaganda. This office would serve as a bulwark to the spread

26   Letter from Broch to Willa Muir (17 March 1940), *KW* 13/2, 190.
27   The resolution was never published. *KW* 11, 195–232.
28   *KW* 12, 195–232.
29   *KW* 11, 214.

of fascist propaganda and provide a platform for spreading the ideas of peace and democracy.

The resolution also called for the strengthening of international law, especially in regard to the jurisdiction of the League of Nations. He wanted the League to claim final authority, regardless of national borders, in case of human rights violations. Structurally, the resolution consisted of a general description of the historical need for an international legal body, along with seven key principles that addressed ideas such as the relationship of domestic and international law, the problem of mass hysteria and the unchecked use of state power. Broch referred to the League of Nations in these writing, but he recognized that by 1937 that organization was moribund. His writing from the 1940s referred instead to a 'new' League of Nations.[30] In these later writing, he argued for an organization with much greater teeth, wanting this organization to have plenary authority vis-à-vis national borders.[31] Furthermore, his later political goals went well beyond the organizational or geo-political levels; he addressed the dynamics behind the insecurity of the individual and the development of mass delusion.

The 'resolution', however, did highlight his growing belief that the protection of human rights required a clear legal foundation and did diagnose the disintegration of European values through epistemology. He turned to legal protections as the first step in reinventing an absolute value system for Western civilization. The legal protection of human rights was an ethical calling, and its efficacy rested on the notions of religious interpretations of human value, or in the American context Natural Law theory. 'The penal law is the backbone of every society's morals. If the morals of a society would be coherently self evident for every society member, i.e. for every citizen, penal law would be become superfluous. On the other hand penal law was and is always able to create morals. As the Nazis decided to create their own specific morals (or rather non-morals) of racism, they invented

---

30 For Broch's works on internationalism, see Hermann Broch, *KW* 12, 195–277.
31 A power the United Nations lacked in 1948 and today.

the Nuremberg laws'.[32] For Western democracies, especially in Europe, key assumptions about freedom and equality had been set aside. These assumptions still existed outside the legal system in religious theologies, in historical documents like the Rights of Man and Citizen or the Declaration of the Independence. Their position outside of the constitutional and legal structure of Western society, however, meant that their ethical import went the way of religious moral import in the world of modern secularization.

In his 'resolution', Broch suggested a three-fold legal development. First, he sought to establish to a legitimate, non-national source of authority vis-à-vis the security of individual human life. He specifically rejected the autonomy of individual states as it pertained to human life. He felt that the authority (*Herrschaft*) of individual states too often in the modern world oppressed minority opinion as an expression of majority rights.[33] Even if the League of Nations was conceived at a fundamental level as a peace organization, that role extended by necessity into the domestic arena of human rights. 'The league of nations is of the opinion that, in questions pertaining to human dignity, it does not have to recognize internal state autonomy, because in those cases it concerns fundamental moral opinions, whose universality must also be expressed in internal state legislation: every disruption of such universality means the danger of war'.[34] Secondly, Broch sought to educate or indoctrinate the public about the inherent link between democracy and freedom.[35] He characterized this educational platform as democratic propaganda. Thirdly, he sought the introduction into the national legal codes universal statements concerning inviolability of human rights. From 1938 onward, it was the Declaration of Independence that strongly influenced Broch's formulations for integrity of the individual.

32   Broch, undated draft manuscript, Hermann Broch Archive. Yale Collection of German Literature, Beinecke Rare Book and Manuscript Library.

33   The German term implies a sense of dominance not found in the English word authority and more closely equivalent to the Latin term *potestas* – the power to rule.

34   Broch, '*Völkerbund-Resolution*', *KW* 11, 199.

35   In this context he meant the masses or the crowd in the same sense as Le Bon, Ortega y Gassett, or Freud did.

'The League of Nations Resolution' was a key moment in Broch's turn to pragmatic politics, though it had no impact on the political debate in Austria or Europe.[36] By 1936 it was clear to most that the League simply lacked any international influence. The United States had turned its back on the League directly following the First World War, and Japan and Germany had left the League in the early 1930s. Chamberlain's declaration of 'peace in our time' in 1938 was the final manifestation of the impotence of internationalism in the face of fascism and the rise of Nazi Germany. As Broch said of the resolution:

> During the years 1936/37, I was in correspondence with a number of important European personalities, in order to draw up a collective statement, which would have been brought before League of Nations. The political development of 1937 forced us to give up the project; it had become senseless. In opposition to the opinion of many of my friends, I did not publish the League of Nations work. Such enterprises are bound up in the moment of their conception; after that they lose their impact and sink to the level of utopian, wishful thinking.[37]

Broch's admission that this proposal was ill-timed reflects the general argument of my chapter. 1936 is a very late date for the pragmatic realization of the dangers of fascism. The 1934 civil war in Austrian and forceful destruction of social democracy two years earlier should have done more to shake his commitment to the cognitive/aesthetic program of creative ethical construction. It should have prompted him to leave the world of the Alpine village where mysticism and isolated strangers symbolized the dangers of twilight consciousness. But, instead, it drove him deeper into the mythical, pushing him back to the crowded streets of Brundisium and internality. Again, his discussion of national sovereignty lacked the recognition of national zeal and the power and importance of the nation as a modern political actor. Much like he failed to recognize the dangers of growing anti-Semitism as he parodied the plight of Hungarian Jews in

36   Broch pointed out in a letter to his future wife Anne Marie Meier Graefe on March 26, 1938, that his decision not to publish the resolution along with its insignificance could have saved him from further trouble with the Nazis. *KW* 13/1, 502.

37   See fn 3, *KW* 11, 237.

1921.[38] By 1936, internationalism became his pragmatic solution to what appeared to be a question of international law and individual cognition. He never wrestled with the question of how and why mass political organizations embraced and employed the vitalism of nationalistic violence.[39] His internationalism was throughout the 1930s and his exile an extension of the blindness to the power and importance of nationalism as the political driver of modern politics.

In 1932, Hermann Broch produced his first explicitly political article in well over a decade ('*Pamphlet gegen die Hochschätzung des Menschen*'), and in 1936/7 he directly engaged the political issues of fascism with his 'League of Nations Resolution'. His pamphlet from 1932, his letters from the period and his incomplete novel *Die Verzauberung* (1935–1936), all attest to his growing awareness of political change and its dangerous elements. Nevertheless, his attempt at negative aesthetics did not mark the key shift from novelist to political theorist. What was lacking in these subtle political shifts and the growing disillusionment with art was the conviction that political action, including legal and economic reform, would have utility. He had not yet made the mental and emotional realignment necessary for him to value terrestrial deeds as superior to intellectual deeds. His letters from the early 1930s affirm that he understood the need to do so. And his post facto descriptions of this revelation demonstrate that he saw the moral necessity of doing it.

It was only with his arrest and exile that the reality of Broch's intellectual drift from literature toward politics can be seen as fully activated. In an extended CV from the Beinecke archives, he himself acknowledged that fact and provided us with yet a third claim of true political awakening (The *Anschluss* in March 1938):

---

38   See ch. 2.

39   Walter Benjamin's work on aestheticism and politics with its realist approach to power and art contrasts deeply with Broch's individualist and mythical approach to value construction and kitsch. See Walter Benjamin's 'Art in the Age of Mechanical Reproduction', also written in 1936, in *Illuminations*, edited by Hannah Arendt and translated by Harry Zohn (New York: Schoken Books, 1968), 217–252.

I had already come to realize that the new era of world horror would soon prevent anyone from devoting himself to purely intellectual, philosophical and creative pursuits. My most recent experiences in Germany had given me the incontrovertible conviction that, for me, at the destruction of the dark forces which had arisen in the world. For these reasons, I felt compelled to concentrate more and more on the problems of politics, and especially on those of mass processes in order to find an approach to their theoretical foundation.[40]

Unlike the earlier passages, this claim's veracity was reinforced by the flurry of essays and resolutions written between 1939 and 1940. These works were all political and pragmatic in natural, though his essay, 'Proposal for the Foundation of a Research Institute for political psychology and the study of occurrences of mass delusion', focused heavily on the psychological, epistemological and historical aspects of democracy in a modern mass society.[41] This work remained unpublished, but he did circulate the 'proposal' as a practical step towards challenging fascism.[42] Three other works, which were more directly political, demonstrate in their tone a heightened sense of urgency and praxis: 'On the Dictatorhip of Humanity within a total democracy', 'the Political Function of the American Guild for German Cultural Freedom' and *The City of Man*.

By examining these three political projects, I weigh the sense of political engagement and urgency in these activities with the implied sense of engagement and moral righteousness from his autobiographical passages above. The record shows that it was in the period after his arrest that a transvaluation of aesthetics for politics took place. Much of the historical investigation of Broch's exile has understood his political turn in terms of a moral crossroads and an abandonment of aesthetics. In his article on Broch's intellectual oeuvre from exile, Daniel Wiedner framed his discussion around Broch's story of moral choice, that is, the ethical choice of writing on 'esoteric' or 'exoteric' themes. Wiedner examined whether exile

---

40 Broch, undated draft manuscript, Hermann Broch Archive. Yale Collection of German Literature, Beinecke Rare Book and Manuscript Library.

41 *KW* 12, 11–42.

42 The proposal was sent to the Advanced Studies Institute, Albert Einstein and Alvin Johnson (president of the New School), see *KW* 12, fn 1, 42.

demanded that Broch abandon literature for active politics. In the end, he concludes that exile did create a new political focus in his work. It did not, however, demand the abandonment of his 'esoteric' style and themes. Wiedner argues that his political theory was in many ways an extension of the esoteric sensibilities found in his novel *The Death of Virgil*. While, I agree that there was a strong degree of overlap in the political and psychological works, and that they fashion his political theory as metaphysical. I argue for a more forceful ethical shift in Broch's works owing to his arrest and exile, as well as a more definitive cultural awakening and shift in his intellectual priorities.[43] Wiedner's discussion and mine challenge the imagery of the moral crossroad and try to instil some historical clarity into the relationship between politics and literature in his thought. While the well established historiographical image of Broch as 'poet against his will', which assumes a failed attempt to turn towards politics, touched upon the process of intellectual conversion, it remained wedded to a tragic or metaphorical narrative of his intellectual biography.[44]

Exile did not mark the beginning of Broch's political theorizing, but it did signal an undeniable and purposeful transvaluation of politics and art. From 1932 to 1938, he struggled with his own understanding of the value of art, but nonetheless remained primarily occupied with literary business. After 1938, although he still worked on his Virgil novel, he transvalued literature for political theory. The transvaluation started in the crucible of appeasement, exile and war. One could argue that his political activism was nothing more than the reaction of an exile with no other choices. In a letter to James Franck in 1946, however, Broch confirmed that the shift to politics was not arbitrary or temporal, though it was undesired. He wrote to Franck that 'there is no longer any ivory tower for the so-called intellectual worker; whether one likes it or not, one is forced into politics'.[45]

43   Daniel Wiedner, 'Hermann Broch and the Ethics of Exile' in Eckart Goebel and Sigrid Weigel, eds, 'Escape to Life', *German Intellectuals in New York: A Compendium on Exile after 1933* (Berlin: De Gruyter, 2012), 162–181.
44   Erich von Kahler *et al.*, eds, *Dichter wider Willen* (Zürich: Rhein Verlag, 1958), see Kahler, 'Introduction'.
45   Letter to James Franck (27 February 1946), *KW* 13/3, 74–79.

He continued that he had planned to return to mathematical logic on his sixtieth birthday, but he now recognized that what he called 'the cognitive human' had a moral responsibility to produce ethical formulas through political means.

The visceral nature of this shift can be seen in three key political writings from 1939 to 1940. By analysing these works, we can articulate this transvaluation through the tone and actions their represent. The first was 'On the Dictatorship of Humanity within a Total Democracy' (1939). It was the first extended discussion of the centrepiece to his political theory – the concept of total democracy.[46] The claim was that democracy was losing to fascism in the battle for models of governance because it lacked the ability to enforce a basic humane law for the inviolability of human life. He posed the issues in legal terms, something he carried over from his study on internationalism in his early 'resolution'. Failed European democracies and even the United States lacked a fundamental regulative principle – a legal means of enforcing community peace. As with the proposal for a research institute mentioned above, this political essay was not published, only circulated to friends in second half of 1939.

Also written in 1939, was a political piece written to the American Guild for German Cultural Freedom, one in a series of memo correspondences among Broch and the officials of the guild (Volkmar von Zühlsdorff and Herbertus Prinz zu Löwenstein).[47] Here, Broch was both theorizing on total democracy and taking direct political action. In the memo a sense of urgency was most clearly stated as Broch outlined the need for the American Guild to become explicitly political. As he stated, 'However, politics is a practical matter, and it is a question of power. Power as such does not create ideology; it must first be brought to power. [...] Today, the task of the intellectual worker is to furnish the models for [an] ethical position [to political leadership] – and practical models for the most part – which will be necessary for the future reconstruction of humanity.'[48] The

---

46   *KW* 11, 24–71.
47   *KW* 11, 399–411; see especially fn 1, 410.
48   *KW* 11, 399–400.

goal of the memo was to encourage the publication of the Guild's goals as in line with the idea of an 'ethical political program'. Like the League of Nations resolution, an ethical political program equated to a new basis for international cooperation and the elimination of national interest in lieu of humanity's interest.

The City of Man (1940) exemplified most fully the urgency that political theory came to represent to Broch in his immediate exile period. Starting before his exile, he began to call for the establishment of international institutions to protect humans from the violence of both private individuals and the state. He applied his value theory to the task of ending totalitarianism. In preparing his contribution (on economics) to the project, Broch began to research more fully the economic implications of totalitarianism and to formulate his language for democratic reform (economic, anti-Marxist, anti-materialist blend of liberal socialism from Austro-Marxism with a strong defence of individual rights). His letters to G. A. Borgese and Ruth Norden throughout late 1939 and early 1940 highlighted the significance of the project to Broch, especially his belief that it was a real contribution to the fight against fascism, as opposed to his failed intellectualism and artistic work of the early 1930s.[49]

In the proposal appended to the declaration, there were four keys to the reform of democracy following the hoped-for victory of the Allies: 1) redefinition of individual freedom from simply 'citizen rights' to 'rights and duties', 2) the inclusion of church in the formation of social values of right and wrong, 3) the economic reform of capitalism in order to shift production from production for profit to production for use, and 4) the replacement of nationalist value construction with internationalist.[50] In the context of the proposal these ideas were generalized and underdeveloped, but there was clear support for individual freedom, regulation of the economy from a non-Marxist point of view and a rejection of nationalism. The language and assumptions in these generalizations were often Brochian in the wording, and it showed wide support for the basic reform

49   I discuss the *City of Man* project more fully in Chapter 5, this volume.
50   See *The City of Man*, 76–96.

of liberalism that all these intellectuals saw as having fallen into crisis since the Great War. In this context of perceived failures in liberalism and the danger of growing fascism, Broch expanded his political involvement. These four bases loosely marked the parameters of his political platform for democratic reform and anti-fascist activism of the 1940s.

The City of Man project, however, was not an isolated activity. Throughout the early period of his exile, Broch dove head first into the political activism. His agenda was two-fold in these initial political activities: first, he worked to secure immigration for European artists and writers through direct correspondence with individuals and through appeals to United States government, as well as his work for Emergency Rescue Committee.[51] This work included publicizing the democratic and anti-fascist nature of German culture through organizations such as the 'Immigrant Loyalty League' and American Guild for German Cultural Freedom.[52] On a daily basis, he interacted with American educational and business leaders (such as Alvin Johnson, Henry Seidel Canby, Oscar G. Villard and foundations such as the Guggenheim), with European émigrés (such as Thiess, Zweig, Einstein and Mann) and governmental officials (mostly in terms of visa requests, but he also mailed Eleanor Roosevelt his resolution on human rights in 1946). Though his work on *The Death of Virgil* occupied some of his time during the early 1940s, his *Nachlass* clearly shows that his primary efforts were 1) political activism in terms of securing immigration documents for friends and family, 2) his work on *The Theory of Mass Delusion*, which was epistemological and psychological in method, but political in goal, and 3) active publication of political declarations and opinion pieces in popular venues. In a letter to his son on 1 July 1939, he reiterated the theme of 'Brotarbeit' in regards to his literary efforts. He stressed the need for recognition and notoriety (*mir hier einen Namen zu machen*), which

---

51   See fn 1, *KW* 13/2, 246.
52   See *KW* 13/2, 240; letter to William Yandell Elliott, October 1940 and *KW* 11, 399–409, especially fn 1, 410.

the Virgil novel could bring him, was essential.[53] It was essential, however, because it provide him the means an émigré required to have influence.

Judging Broch

If winners get to write history, then Broch's concern for making a name for himself was a valid one. And his present obscurity in American intellectual culture would justify the tragic sense of failure expressed in my opening description of his death. The influence of many other interwar European émigrés on the intellectual history of the United States was broad and long lasting. They created new fields and new schools of thought through access to the commanding heights of the American academy, on both the left and the right. Broch, however, did not follow this path and his influence, while political in nature, was not felt in public opinion or theoretical arenas of policy debate. His early death may have had a lot to do with this, as intellectuals like Hannah Arendt only found their audience in the 1950s and 1960s. The similarity of focus on human rights and shared concern for totalitarianism at least suggest this possibility. Nonetheless, it is clear that his immediate impact fell well short of other thinkers, such as those connected with the Frankfurt School or major universities (Neumann, Adorno, Strauss) or more public intellectuals like Hannah Arendt. In the end, Broch's public legacy can only be viewed historically.

Furthermore, the dominance of science, social science and critical studies in the historical narrative of intellectual immigration has left little room for him. The narratives of both Martin Jay and H. S. Hughes found minimal space for thinkers like Broch, an academic subaltern. Jay and Hughes illuminated the development of social scientific method and Marxist/ Freudian critical studies, developments most noted for how deeply they imbued professional academic fields of the humanities and social sciences.

53   *KW* 13/2, 93–94.

These were by and large stories of success in terms of intellectual influence and notoriety. His lack of both influence and notoriety formulated its own story of failure in comparison. Because of his focus on known thinkers, Hughes's book has little to say on the contribution to American culture of artists, writers and creative minds, whose exile experience appeared to Hughes to be a failure. As he says of Broch, 'In this respect the creative writers and the social thinkers among the émigrés faced different problems. The former continued to use their own language and to depend on translators for their American public; the greater part of them, including men as eminent as the dramatist Carl Zuckmayer and the novelist Hermann Broch, passed their years in the United States in almost total obscurity'.[54] If, however, one looks beyond notoriety and fame, the question of failure is much more difficult to judge.

Broch's story was one of active participation in the intellectual community of New York and New England, as well as engagement with the intellectual tidal surge of problem solving in regard to fascism, modernism and the future of liberal democracy. And if one is to judge the success or failure of his influence on American culture, one must look beyond the context of his physical and emotional life, where the sense of failure was primarily the result of his own rhetoric. While he was in terms of institutional affiliation or in terms of popular readership alienated in America, and his political value system was not successful in terms of its influence or its ability to direct contemporary debates, his efforts should not be understood as tragic or insignificant. For twelve years, he established cultural and political roots in America. He worked to apply his studies on human psychology and value systems to his new historical context. He lived a life of engaged citizenship; he supported and challenged those around him to do the same. He offered new paths for freedom and security to his adopted home. On a personal level his political activism created a sense of collaborative defence. But, the sense of cooperation was followed by recognition of deep differences and mistrust, which ultimately failed to produce any useful public platform for advocating democratic reform. In

---

54   Ibid, 28.

place of unified reform, *The City of Man* project, for example, produced a
little read pamphlet for challenging totalitarianism through total democracy. The failed experience of political activism, however, did not discourage
Broch from continuing his theoretical work on mass psychology or lessen
his direct political engagement and the publication of articles about legal
and political reform.

By studying Broch's archival writings and his political essays, I do
not claim to place him alongside the likes of Strauss or Arendt in terms
of intellectual influence; but I do show that he was at the centre of these
discussions and activities. In the case of Broch and Arendt, for instance,
they read and discussed each other's views on fascism, human rights and
the future of democracy.[55] Arendt found many similarities in their basic
concerns and solutions, but ultimately she found Broch's theory flawed.
She questioned whether idealism and an *a priori* model for explaining
social interaction could produce real political engagement. Put another
way, whether Plato's Republic could ever prompt anything more than an
individual exploration of truth that would be forever locked in the problem of expressing the inexpressible. This quandary has until the recent
developments of cognitive science left the political discussion of idealism
trapped in the drinking games of intellectuals and their continual reinven-
tions of the symposium. In contradiction, the notion of the Aristotelian
logos and its active position in the political life (the idea of the man as a
political animal) postulated engagement as a sine qua non of human activity. Arendt's intellectual commitment to basic Aristotelian values such as
a public space and the contested dialogue helped explain the separation
between her and Broch in terms of their theories of human rights.[56]

Broch did recognize the importance of *logos* in his aesthetic essays
of the 1930s, suggesting like Arendt in her later political theory, that the

55   Hermann Broch and Hannah Arendt, *Briefwechsel 1946 bis 1951.*
56   See for discussions of the Arendt/Broch correspondence Csaba Olay, 'Hannah
     Arendt und Hermann Broch Roman und Moderne' and Karol Sauerland, 'Hermann
     Broch und Hannah Arendt: Massenwahn und Menschenrecht' in Endre Kiss *et al.*,
     eds, *Hermann Brochs literarische Freundschaften* (Tübingen: Stauffenburg, 2008)
     305–318 and 319–331.

modern world had silenced itself through the abandonment of *logos*. His discussion, however, remained centred on the issue of the mind and the *Zeitgeist*. His solutions focused on the creative activities of the individual as a guide to a universal truth. The solution to social value disintegration was the artist rearranging the shadows on the cave wall in order to quiet down the psychological rumbling of those tied in front it. As they faced the epistemological dead end caused by their ever-shrinking peripheral view, Broch hoped to ignite a brighter fire through aesthetic creativity and the reviving of the *Geist*. In his American context, however, he came to realize that the crisis of modern politics was not solvable by purely idealistic methods. He embraced the pragmatism of American frontier inventiveness and sought direct political solutions through legal and constitution change, especially the empowerment of the law to function in a total way and towards individual democratic activity. This shift in political engagement brought Broch and Arendt onto the same theoretical playing field; but, as Arendt understood, his pragmatism never lost its idealistic, pre-exile groundings. Ultimately these groundings in her opinion left him unable to perceive the real danger in modernity and modern politics.

Broch suggested in his political theory that relativism could be challenged by a universal ethical process, but only if the greatest liberal democratic power of the twentieth century recognized the weaknesses of parochialism, materialism and über-rationality in its democratic foundations. In the context of the Cold War, even he recognized that the retooling of democracy in the United States would be a secondary and perhaps utopian task for intellectuals and artists and the youth to pursue. But, he believed firmly that to not pursue the restructuring of American obsession with 'victory', nationalism and materialism would expose this last bastion of democracy to hypertrophic dangers of relativism disguised as universal support for a freedom that was an innate or god-given natural right. It is an open question, whether Broch's prediction of hypertrophy in American democracy, outside of the mythological guidelines of the Cold War, will come to fruition or not.

Contemporary intellectuals, such as Sartre and Adorno, shared a general concern for humanism and totality, while rejecting explicitly the intellectual legacy of both the Enlightenment and the early twentieth century.

Both thinkers turned in the end to some form of Marxism and sought their universal humanisms there. Broch recognized the religious appeal of Marxism and understood its humanist impulse: 'Marxism was the first post-religious system of thought which seriously and practically set out to resume that knowledge-unifying function of theology so indispensable to the human spirit. It secularized it, and so showed a way out of the discomfort'.[57] For Broch, however, the democratic impulse and Kantianism of his Austrian legacy made Marxist humanism unappealing. If one considers Karl Popper and Eric Voegelin, however, two thinkers who are from the same generation as Adorno and Sartre but like Broch rejected Marxism, one should not beg the question of whether national culture trumps generational culture.

In the midst of world war and early Cold War uncertainty, the fluidity and ad hoc nature of the émigré experience made the debates on democracy equally as fluid and uncertain. Broch's full commitment to these debates and his close friendships and professional associations made his story as central to the process as any other. Owing to the incomplete nature of his political theory, his ideas can only adequately be judged from an historical point of view. From an intellectual historical point of view his letters and essays provide fresh insight into the interchange between central European and American conceptions of liberalism. And since the 1970s his ideas have directly influenced contemporary theory on human rights.[58]

57   Broch, undated draft manuscript, Hermann Broch Archive. Yale Collection of German Literature, Beinecke Rare Book and Manuscript Library.
58   See Thomas Eicher, Michael Lützeler and Hartmut Steinecke, *Hermann Broch: Politik, Menschenrecht – und Literatur?*, especially Michael Kessler, 'Menschenrecht, Demokratie, Toleranz', 11–50.

Conclusion

Hermann Broch is buried in Union Cemetery, just off a narrow country road in Killingworth, Connecticut. He is buried in the far corner of the cemetery, cut off from the other graves by the jutting out of the tree line. His grave is the only gravestone in that part of the cemetery, and it stands out not simply because of its physical separation but because of the modern styled headstone and its well-preserved condition.[59] The remainder of the cemetery is primarily eighteenth-century plots with many headstones faded and bent. The physical separation and seclusion offer yet another opportunity to understand Broch's exile as tragedy; yet, the image holds just as much optimism as pessimism, when one recognizes that his separation (European from American) provided an opportunity to embrace difference and merge a long tradition of European civic humanism with both American individualism of the eighteenth century and American political idealism of the twentieth century. The growing necessity to comprehend democracy on a global scale was obvious by 1945. For Broch, this necessitated a transnational platform of legal, educational and economic cooperation. His distance from American nationalism along with his Central European, Jewish commitment to cosmopolitanism and the Enlightenment allowed him to envision a US-led reformation for humane democracy. His ideas suggested a path that could avoid the exceptionalism of American material dominance.

Broch's life from 1938 to 1951 was a world apart from his earlier existence. Exile, of course, defined this separation more than anything else. But, it was not simply physical separation from Austria or Europe; it was a world apart in terms of Broch's sense of self and in terms of Broch's mission in life. In Chapter 1, I examined his Viennese world to allow the reader to chart the changes in Broch's intellectual worldview. In 1927, Broch remade his Viennese world. He exchanged his position as businessman for one of writer. He entered psychoanalysis. He broke with the major emotional figures in

59   See book cover for image.

his life (divorce in 1921, end of a long term affair with Ea von Allesch in 1927 and collapse of his relationship to his family). He entered university in 1925, but by 1927 had abandoned the idea of pursing a degree in order to become a 'professionalized' intellectual. From 1927 until his exile, he spent more and more time outside Vienna, his financial situation was precarious and dependent on his literary efforts. His father died in 1931, at which point Broch was completely free from the emotional world of his youth.

Nevertheless, he remained European and Viennese in an intellectual and cultural sense. The interwar period was one of self re-fashioning, but it did not require Broch to become an outsider, to write or think in a new language or social idiom, or to understand the problems and dangers in his world as existential threats. Like Luft and Hacohen – though in condensed and more specifically directed manner – my first three chapters examined Broch's political activism and theory during the Austrian First Republic in order to better understand the possibilities of thought in Vienna. My conclusions were also similar to Luft and Hacohen in that I found in Broch a critically engaged thinker, who specifically attacked ideas of ahistoricality and aestheticism. And that politically, if Broch displayed any legacy from the nineteenth century it was a liberal, progressive one. At most, however, what all this suggests is that Schorske's thesis cannot be extended beyond the late nineteenth century.

On the other hand, I also found in Broch a psychological tendency towards internality and alienation, as well as a conservative repulsion in regard to mass culture. While this was not traced to the historical process of a failure of liberalism as in the Schorske case, it did suggest that the conservative, German culture of the late Habsburg empire provided fertile ground for disinterest or disengagement, a easy slippage into the world of the ego and the mind; thus it allowed the pragmatic world of politics and social action to be dismissed as untidy and bothersome. Allan Janik's model for Viennese intellectual development, critical modernism, provides a workable paradigm for thinkers such as Musil, Popper and Broch, as well as more direct social reformist activities such as social democracy.

By the early 1930s, Broch began to write more directly political essays and novels, such as *The Spell*, and to worry about the fascist developments in Germany and Austria. His pre-exilic world of the 1930s, however, remained aesthetically and intellectually focused on his self identity as a novelist. With his exile (1938 to 1951) he embraced a new identity: activist for a humane democratic world order. This was a role that consumed all of his energy – his direct work on émigré rescue, his massive correspondences with family, intellectuals and political figures, his work on mass delusion theory, his published articles on politics and cultural criticism, his novelistic work and his constant travel around the intellectual centres of New York and New England. Even in the carrying on of his sexual relationships and numerous affairs, democratic crusader framed his relationships and justified his actions – at least justified them to himself.

Broch's exile brought about political awareness and concerns that were absent from his European existence. In exile, he embraced democracy as a historical necessity and as a humane solution to the death of the civilization he knew for all of his life. The awakening of his political consciousness, however, did little to change the fundamentals of how he understand freedom, critical humanism, the cognitive and psychology structure of the human mind, the purpose and development of ethical creativity and its aesthetic expression in society. He formulated these ideas in the Vienna of his youth and they remained at the core of his thought. What changed was the historical urgency of translating these ideas into a pragmatic, political form.

What also changed was the national cultural in which such developments had to occur. His cosmopolitanism made the latter change easy for him. Although he was critical of the possible weakness of American democracy, he was not hostile to American culture or social organization. He openly praised the vitality, resources and ingenuity of American society, and he became an American citizen. He understood his democratic crusade as an American undertaking. The result was that his theories on total democracy and mass delusion were hybrid. He did not plant the seed of European thought on American soil in order to create an invasive challenger to American thought. He did not attempt to colonize America with European values. He addressed his political theory to the historical moment of America's emergence as democratic world power. His criticism of its weaknesses and his solutions to its conflicts in global politics were created specifically for the United States. In this sense, his exilic thought is incomparable to any of his European endeavours, for in Europe, Broch lacked the ability to think as an exile or an American, two of the basic points of view in his political theory. Furthermore, he could not have created his political theory in Europe, because he was not conscious of the need to do so.

Nonetheless, simply because he thought as both an exile and an American, and he desired to contribute to fashioning of a humane democracy in the United States, it does not mean that his ideas would find a receptive audience. His thought was tinged with the language of 'internationalism', 'obligation', 'subordination to the super-state' and 'propaganda', and it was critical of American definitions of success and libertarian individualism. Throughout the 1940s, the critical response to his theory ranged from 'utopian' to 'naïve' to 'elitist'; repeatedly his psychological and epistemological approaches were met with concerns about the lack of social scientific methodology. And by the time of his death in 1951, both the tolerance and the public stage for debating his open criticism of the American democracy was being closed down by Cold War ideologues. As I argue in Chapter 5, the Cold War sidelined Broch's critical humanism, but the shared values of his theory with the later youth and civil rights movements highlight for the historian the American context for the composition of his political theory.

While in American exile, Broch devoted much of his intellectual energy to conceiving anew democratic constitutions and basic laws in order to stabilize democratic states in the face of the fascist onslaught and to allow individual citizens the ability to think and act in ethically creative ways. His theory combined the liberal cosmopolitanism of his youth with a call for American leadership. In the immediate post-1945 period, American global leadership (from the Nuremburg trails to the founding of the United Nations to Bretton Woods) suggested that Broch's views on empowering international institutes aligned well with US political culture. American democracy, however, soon deviated from his internationalist position. By the middle of the 1950s, American democracy became more and more defined by the mass delusion of American exceptionalism and a growing distrust with internationalism. While Broch hoped that America could lead the world towards an internationalist policy that would create the legal basis for protecting citizens from governmental and private abuses. He failed to realize that nationalism and the Cold War would make such a solution impossible. His life and political theory were an attempt at saving a European (and strongly Jewish) idea – cosmopolitan, progressive democracy. The irony was that that idea was encapsulated in the auto-cratic image of Empire. When liberal democracy under the leadership of Anglo-American capitalism destroyed central European plans of Empire, it replaced them with a globalization process whose stability was based on neo-imperial economics and revitalized nationalism.

Broch's death in 1951 meant that he did not see the expansion of the American Dream ideology into an American exceptionalism linked to the idea of the American Century. It was in many ways the realization of his concerns about American democracy. For, the Cold War only heighted the embrace of materialism and the importance of victory in mainstream culture: from Nixon's kitchen debates to the existential craze for bomb shel-ters. Broch's political vision for greater community building, for responsible individualism and for international leadership would become the vision of the marginalized. His visions of creative ethics presaged developments in American social and intellectual history, such as the youth, civil rights and free love movements of the 1960s, as well as an increasing globalized concern among some elements of American society for the international protection of human life and dignity.

In some ways, his political ideas about the future of democracy were prescient. The United States did go to war, it did defeat fascism, it did take its position as a world leader in the globalization process. But, the basic definitions of US-led democracy, liberalism and global capitalism were quite different from the definition of his total democracy. He only saw the beginning of globalization, the Cold War, the nuclear age and post-colonialism. He clearly expressed some sense of hope that the death of civi-lization as defined by European culture would be followed by the rebirth of civilization defined by a global democracy. Much of what he hoped, however, failed to materialize as the moral and economic ideology of US democracy helped to craft a world that continued to promote what he saw as the moral and political weaknesses of capitalistic materialism, as well as promoting a continued conflict between globalization and nationalism.

His theory of total democracy suggested that there was an inherent conflict between global democracy on the one hand and the United States' particular commitment to success on the other. It is this fact more than any other that makes the investigation into his thought timely and important. For, in order to understand Broch's questions and examine some of his answers to the problems of modern society, we must go through a historical investigation that reconstructs a world in which such questions and answers were not as yet concretized. The solutions suggested in his work, however, have more to do with the development of the individual and the application of liberal politics through the exploration of metaphysics. He, like many other writers of the *fin-de-siècle* Europe, struggled with the role of the irrational in modern society. Both the dangers and the rewards of irrational impulses dominated the ethical, political and aesthetic conflicts within his work. Today, however, the irrational has become either tamed or illegitimate in the eyes of much of society. The legacy of fascism has been the exclusion of the metaphysical and subconscious from public political debate. The effects of both the Second World War and the Cold War have left the mainstream American mind alienated from and in fear of the powers of the irrational.[60] The linkage between politics and capitalism, on the individual and the communal level, is no longer a source for debate. Like the irrational, opposition to the modern Western societal teleology of the market system is almost a dead question. The American mainstream culture has reached the 'end of history'.[61]

Since 11 September 2001, American society has had to come to grips with the fact that beyond the limits of this imagined Western civilization questions about the linkage between materialism and happiness are far from dead. In an epoch with only one superpower there is always the danger of

60   This is a driving force in the present political climate of America and in its approach to the 'War on Terror'.

61   Francis Fukuyama, *The End of History and the Last Man* (New York: Free Press, 1992).

forgetting that ideas of democracy, human rights and individual autonomy are not exclusively the province of the United States. From the point of view that European values had failed, Hermann Broch acknowledged the merit of the American liberal democratic tradition. As an exile, however, he was situated far enough from American nationalism to question whether its assumptions about freedom were capable of promoting a universal social value system, that is, whether American democracy could spread freedom and promote internationalism and still maintain its 'pursuit of happiness'. Broch's relevance lies in answering this question.

Overall, I conclude that at its heart, Broch's political theory was humanist. His value theory focused on individual human participation in the maintenance of social values and institutions. It was through the individual that values were articulated into the world. His political theory developed out of his value theory centred on the legal protection of human life from all forms of violence (state and private). The foundation of his political system stretched back into his Viennese world and the political context of rising fascism. Broch did not abandon the earlier influences. He, in fact, furthered his involvement with Husserl and Kant in search of a scientific and earthly source of ethical duty – an absolute foundation for value production. He went in search of the source of a new power of conversion, a new god, a new categorical imperative. In that same milieu, he crafted his ideas about responsibility, freedom and the slide into the irrational ('twilight consciousness'). The depth of his commitment to a critical humanism, to the power of the individual and the danger of hypertrophy was demonstrated by the central role it played in Broch's self-conception.

The ego, the individual and the psychological basis for social structure from his exilic political theory were an extension of his social and intellectual development in Vienna. They were an extension of his emotional and sexual development. In the context of Vienna, they remained mainly apolitical. After his exile, they became explicitly political. His humanism, however, tempered his acceptance of American democracy. His unfinished work was meant to be an ethical demand, the scientific proof that humanity contained within itself the force of its own salvation. It had already proven its ability at its own destruction. As a historical figure, scholars have tended to see Broch as idiosyncratic and exceptional. I argue, however, that his life was not a source for exploring what was exceptional in *fin-de-siècle* Vienna or post-war United States; rather his life and his thought open to us a wider field of social, cultural and intellectual activity. With Broch, we see that intellectual life cannot be completely subsumed under titles such as Jewish, Austrian or democratic. Temporal and geographical location or dislocation is not fully determinative of intellectual outlook. His position as an outsider within Vienna and as an exile in the United States affected the development of his thought and the impact of his work; his position outside of academia infused his work with an eclecticism that still strikes many as naïve; yet, it also allowed him to develop an important critique on the dangers of specialization in the sciences.

His position as a textile engineer and a businessman locked him out of the university for the two thirds of his life and limited his active involvement in the cultural and political leadership of Vienna 1900; yet, his distance from that world allowed him to see Vienna from an historical perspective and to hold up Viennese values (aesthetic and social) to the light of moral criticism. His lack of academic credentials and his poor financial situation in the United States prevented him from fully integrating into the world of America intelligentsia and from finishing his work on mass hysteria; yet, from his position outside of the university, the government and research institutions Broch was able to continue his attempts at 'making utopias real'. As a perpetual outsider, his humanism was perhaps his only access to a universal experience. Hannah Arendt and Eric Voegelin thought Broch's idea fell short of a workable solution to the disintegration of value in the modern world. It remained too closely aligned to older notions of natural law. From a current perspective, however, Broch's views on total democracy, internationalism and human rights suggest a broader view for democracy in the twenty-first century than the Manichean simplicity behind the dichotomy of democratic freedom and tyrannical oppression.

Nevertheless, we must still approach Broch's humanism with caution for his humanism relies on the universal notion of human reason. His total democracy was a call for the forceful imposition of an epistemological conception of the human mind that is culturally constructed. The danger of hypertrophy in his own system looms large once you move outside of the confines of his Western worldview. Broch remained so fixated on the struggles of European ideologies that he never conceived of his theories in a context outside of the West. But, we might forgive Broch to some degree – he had already crossed more boundaries than most.

Bibliography

Archives

H. F. Broch de Rothermann Archive. Yale Collection of German Literature, Beinecke Rare Book and Manuscript Library.
Hermann Broch Archive. Yale Collection of German Literature, Beinecke Rare Book and Manuscript Library.
Hermann Broch Museum. Teesdorf, Austria.

Works by Hermann Broch

Broch, Hermann, *The Death of Virgil*, Random House edition, Jean Starr Untermeyer, tr. (New York: Vintage International, 1972).
——. *Geist und Zeitgeist: Essays zur Kultur der Moderne*, Paul Michael Lützeler, ed. (Frankfurt: Suhrkampf, 1997).
——. *Geist and Zeitgeist: The Spirit in an Unspiritual Age*, John Hargraves, tr. (New York: Counterpoint, 2002).
——. *Gesammelte Werke*, 10 vols, Erich Kahler *et al.*, eds (Zürich: Rhein Verlag, 1932–1961).
——. *The Guiltless*, Ralph Manheim, tr. (Evanston, IL: Northwestern University Press, 1974).
——. *Hugo von Hofmannsthal and his Time: European Imagination, 1866–1920*, Michael Steinberg, tr. (Chicago: University of Chicago Press, 1984).
——. *Kommentierte Werkausgabe*, 13 vols, Paul Michael Lützeler, ed. (Frankfurt am Main: Suhrkamp, 1974–1981).
——. *Psychische Selbstbiographie*, Paul Michael Lützeler, ed. (Frankfurt am Main: Suhrkamp Verlag, 1999).
——. *Short Stories*, E. W. Herd, ed. (London: Oxford University Press, 1966).

——. *The Sleepwalkers*, Willa and Edwin Muir, trs. (New York: Vintage Books, 1996).

——. *The Spell*, H. F. Broch de Rothermann, tr. (New York: Farrar, Straus and Giroux, 1987).

——. *Das Teesdorfer Tagebuch für Ea von Allesch*, Paul Michael Lützeler, ed. (Frankfurt am Main: Suhrkamp Verlag, 1995).

——. *The Unknown Quantity*, Marlboro Press edition, Willa and Edwin Muir, tr. (Evanston, IL: Northwestern University Press, 2000).

——. *Völkerbund-Resolution: Das vollständige politische Pamphlet von 1937 mit Kommentar, Entwurf und Korrespondenz*, Paul Michael Lützeler, ed. (Salzburg: Otto Müller Verlag, 1973).

——. '*Vom Geist der Massen*', *The American Journal of International Law* 41 (January, 1947), 359.

——. *Zur Universitätsreform*, Götz Wienold, ed. (Frankfurt am Main: Suhrkamp Verlag, 1969).

Broch, Hermann and Annemarie Meier-Graefe, *Der Tod im Exil: Hermann Broch, Annemarie Meier-Graefe Briefwechsel 1950/1*, Paul Michael Lützeler, ed. (Frankfurt am Main: Suhrkamp, 2001).

Broch, Hermann and Daniel Brody, *Briefwechsel 1930–1951*, Bertold Hack and Marietta Kleiß, eds (Frankfurt am Main: Buchhändler-Vereinigung GMBH, 1971).

Broch, Hermann and Hannah Arendt, *Briefwechsel 1946 bis 1951*, Paul Michael Lützeler, ed. (Frankfurt am Main: Jüdischer Verlag, 1996).

Broch, Hermann and Volkmar von Zühlsdorff, *Briefe über Deutschland, 1945–1949: die Korrespondenz mit Volkmar von Zühlsdorff and Hermann Broch*, Paul Michael Lützeler, ed. (Frankfurt am Main: Suhrkamp, 1986).

Broch, Hermann *et al.*, *The City of Man: A Declaration on World Democracy* (New York: The Viking Press, 1940).

General Works

Abouzid, Sayed A., *Hermann Brochs Romane als Epochenanalyse und Zeitkritik* (Frankfurt am Main: Peter Lang, 2001).

Adorno, Theodor *et al.*, *The Authoritarian Personality: Studies in Prejudice* (New York: Harper and Brothers, 1950).

Amann, Klaus and Helmut Grote, *Die 'Wiener Bibliothek' Hermann Brochs: Kommentiertes Verzeichnis des rekonstruierten Bestandes* (Vienna: Böhlau Verlag, 1990).

Ansbacher, Heinz and Rowena R. Ansbacher, eds, *The Individual Psychology of Alfred Adler: A Systematic Presentation in Selections from His Writings* (New York: Harper Torchbook, 1964).

Arendt, Hannah, 'The Achievement of Hermann Broch' in *Kenyon Review* 11 (1949), 476–483.

——, *The Human Condition* (Chicago: University of Chicago Press, 2013).

——, *Men in Dark Times* (New York: Harcourt, Brace, and World, 1968).

——, *The Origins of Totalitarianism* (New York: Harcourt Press, 1975).

Aschheim, Steven E., *Culture and Catastrophe: German and Jewish Confrontations with National Socialism and Other Crises* (New York: New York University Press, 1996).

——, *The Nietzsche Legacy in Germany, 1890–1990* (Berkeley, CA: University of California Press, 1992).

Barnouw, Dagmar, *Weimar Intellectuals and the Threat of Modernity* (Bloomington, IN: University of Indiana Press, 1988).

Beller, Steven, *Vienna and the Jews, 1867–1938: A Cultural History* (Cambridge: Cambridge University Press, 1989).

——, 'What is Austrian about Austrian Culture?' in *Weltanschauungen des Wiener Fin de Siècle 1900/2000: Festgabe für Kurt Rudolf Fischer zum achtzigen Geburtstag*, Gertraud Diem-Wille, Ludwig Nagl and Friedrich Stadler, eds (Frankfurt am Main: Peter Lang, 2002).

——, ed., *Rethinking Vienna 1900* (New York: Berghahn Books, 2001).

Benjamin, Walter. *Illuminations*, Hannah Arendt, ed. and Harry Zohn, tr. (New York: Schoken Books, 1968).

Berkley, George E. *Vienna and Its Jews: The Tragedy of Success, 1880s–1980s* (Cambridge, MA: Abt Books, 1988).

Bloom, Allan, *The Closing of the American Mind: How Higher Education has Failed Democracy and Impoverished the Souls of Today's Students* (New York: Simon and Schuster, 1987).

Borch, Christian, 'Modern mass aberration: Hermann Broch and the problem of irrationality' in *History of the Human Sciences* 21/2 (2008), 63–83.

Brinkmann, Richard, 'On Broch's Concept of Symbol', in *Hermann Broch: Literature, Philosophy, Politics*, Stephen D. Dowden, ed. (Columbia, SC: Camden Books, 1988), 193–206.

Broch de Rothermann, H. F. *Liebe Frau Strigl: A Memoir of Hermann Broch by his Son*, John Hargraves, tr. (New Haven, CT: The Beinecke Rare Book and Manuscript Library, 2001).

Bronner, Stephen Eric and F. Peter Wagner, *Vienna: The World of Yesterday, 1889–1914* (New Jersey: Humanities Press, 1997).

Brude-Firnau, Gisela, ed., *Materialien zu Hermann Brochs 'Die Schlafwandler'* (Frankfurt am Main: Suhrkamp Verlag, 1972).

Budi Hardiman, Fransisco, *Die Herrschaft der Gleichen. Masse und totalitäre Herrschaft. Eine kritische Überprüfung der Texte von Georg Simmel, Hermann Broch, Elias Canetti und Hannah Arendt* (Frankfurt am Main: Peter Lang, 2001).

Caesar, Claus, *Poetik der Wiederholung. Ethische Dichtung und ökonomisches 'Spiel' in Hermann Brochs Romanen Der Tod des Vergil und Die Schuldlosen* (Würzburg: Königshausen and Neumann, 2001).

Canetti, Elias, 'Hermann Broch: Rede zu seinem 50. Geburtstag' in *Welt im Kopf* (Graz: Stiyasny, 1962), 91–108.

Capeci, Dominic J., Jr. and Martha Wilkerson, *Layered Violence: The Detroit Riots of 1943* (Jackson, MS: The University Press of Mississippi, 1991).

Cassirer, Sidonie, 'Hermann Broch's Early Writings,' in *PMLAA* 75 (1960), 453–462.

Cohn, Dorrit Claire, *The Sleepwalkers: Elucidations of Hermann Broch's Trilogy* (The Hague: Mouton, 1966).

Diem-Wille, Gertraud, Ludwig Nagl, and Friedrich Stadler, eds, *Weltanschauungen des Wiener Fin de Siècle 1900/2000: Festgabe für Kurt Rudolf Fischer zum achtzigen Geburtstag* (Frankfurt am Main: Peter Lang, 2002).

Dörwald, Uwe, *Über das Ethische bei Hermann Broch: Kritische Historiographie zur ethischen Intention und ihrer Funktion bei Hermann Broch* (Frankfurt am Main: Peter Lang, 1994).

Dowden, Stephen D., ed., *Hermann Broch: Literature, Philosophy, Politics: The Yale Broch Symposium 1986* (Columbia, SC: Camden House, 1988).

Durzak, Manfred, 'Apokalypse oder Utopie? Bemerkungen zu Hermann Brochs Schlafwandlern', in *Etudes Germaniques* 24/1 (1969), 16–35.

——, 'Epitaph auf einen Industriellen. Zu einer Komödie Hermann Brochs', in *Literatur und Kritik* 1/7 (1966), 21–28.

——, 'Ein Frühwerk Hermann Brochs', in *Neue Deutsche Hefte* 13/2 (1966), 10–18.

——, *Hermann Broch.* (Stuttgart: Metzler, 1967).

——, 'Hermann Brochs Anfänge. Zum Einfluß Weiningers und Schopenhauers', in *Germanisch-romanische Monatsschrift* 17/3 (1967), 293–306.

——, *Hermann Brochs Demeter*, in *Neue Deutsche Hefte* 14 (1967), 177–180.

——, *Hermann Broch, der Dichter und seine Zeit* (Stuttgart: Kohlhammer, 1968).

——, *Hermann Broch. Dichtung und Erkenntnis. Studien zum dichterischen Werk* (Stuttgart: Kohlhammer, 1978).

——, *Hermann Broch: Perspektiven der Forschung* (Munich: Fink, 1972).

——, 'Hermann Broch und James Joyce. Zur Ästhetik des modernen Romans', in *DVfLG* 40/3 (1966), 391–433.

——, ed., *Hermann Broch in Selbstzeugnissen und Bilddokumenten* (Hamburg: Rowohlt, 1966).

Eicher, Thomas, Paul Michael Lützeler and Hartmut Steinecke, eds, *Hermann Broch: Politik, Menschenrechte – und Literatur?* (Oberhausen: Athena, 2005).

Eiden, Patrick, 'Anstand und Abstand: Hermann Broch und die Frage der Demokratie' in Ulrich Kinzel, ed., *An den Rändern der Moral: Studien zur literarischen Ethik Ulrich Wergin gewidmet* (Würzburg: Königshausen and Neumann, 2008), 133–149.

——, *Das Reich der Demokratie: Hermann Brochs Der Tod des Vergil* (Munich: Wilhelm Fink, 2011).

Ernst, Robert T. and Lawrence Hugg, *Black America: Geographic Perspective* (Garden City, NY: Anchor Press, 1976).

Fermi, Laura, *Illustrious Immigrants: The Intellectual Migration from Europe, 1930–1941*, 2nd edn (Chicago: University of Chicago Press, 1971).

Fetz, Bernhard. 'Zum Gutsein verurteilt: Der Kulturkritiker Hermann Broch oder die Moral der Literatur', *Literatur und Kritik 357–358 (September 2001)*, 54–62.

Freese, Wolfgang, '*Brochforschung im Lichte der Rezeptionstheorie*', *Modern Austrian Literature* 13 (1980), 159–188.

Freidenreich, Harriet Pass, *Jewish Politics in Vienna, 1918–1938* (Bloomington, IN: Indiana University Press, 1991).

Freud, Sigmund, *Civilization and its Discontents*, James Strachey ed. and tr. (New York: W. W. Norton, 1961).

——, *Group Psychology and The Analysis of the Ego*. James Strachey, tr. (New York: Bantam Books, 1971).

Frischmuth, Barbara. 'Brochs Spuren im Ausseerland' in *Literatur und Kritik 357–358 (September 2001)*, 46–54.

Fukuyama, Francis, *The End of History and the Last Man* (New York: Free Press, 1992).

Gasset y Ortega, José, *The Revolt of the Masses* (New York: Norton, 1994 reissued).

Goebel, Goebel and Sigrid Weigel, eds, *German Intellectuals in New York: A Compendium on Exile after 1933* (Berlin: De Gruyter, 2012).

Greenfeld, Liah, *Five Roads to Modernity* (Cambridge, MA: Harvard University Press, 1992).

Grabowsky-Hotamanidis, Anja, *Zur Bedeutung mystischer Denktraditionen im Werk von Hermann Broch* (Tübingen, Germany: Max Niemeyer, 1995).

Greiter, Almund and Anton Pelinka, 'Hermann Broch als Demokratietheoretiker', in Richard Thieberger, ed., *Hermann Broch und Seine Zeit* (Bern: Peter Lang, 1980, 24–36).

Gulick, Charles, *Austria from Habsburg to Hitler* (Berkeley: University of California Press, 1948).

Hacohen, Malachi H., *Karl Popper – The Formative Years, 1902–1945: Politics and Philosophy in Interwar Vienna* (Cambridge: Cambridge University Press, 2000).

Haller, Rudolf, *Questions on Wittgenstein* (London: Routledge, 1988).

Halliwell, Martin and Andy Mousley, *Critical Humanisms: Humanist, anti-Humanist Dialogues* (Edinburgh: Edinburgh University Press, 2003).

Halsall, Robert. 'The Individual and the Epoch: Herman Broch's *Die Schlafwandler* as a Historical Novel' in Osman Durrani and Julian Preece, eds, *Travellers in Time and Space: The German Historical Novel* (Amsterdam: Rodopi, 2001), 227–241.

——, *The Problem of Autonomy in the Works of Hermann Broch* (Oxford: Peter Lang, 2000).

Hamann, Brigitte, *Hitler's Vienna: A dictator's apprenticeship*, Thomas Thornton, tr. (New York: Oxford University Press, 1999).

Hargraves, John, *Music in the Works of Broch, Mann, and Kafka* (Rochester, NY: Camden House, 2001).

Hermanns, William, *Einstein and the Poet: In Search of the Cosmic Man* (Brookline, MA: Branden Press, 1983).

Horkheimer, Max and Theodor W. Adorno, *Dialectic of Enlightenment: Philosophical Fragments*, Edmund Jephcott, tr. (Stanford, CA: Stanford University Press, 2002).

Hughes, H. Stuart, *Consciousness and Society: The Reorientation of European Social Thought, 1890–1930* (New York: Vintage Books, 1958).

——, *The Sea Change*, reprinted in *Between Commitment and Disillusion* (Middletown, CT: Wesleyan University Press, 1987).

Huxley, Aldous, 'Hermann Broch', *Die Fähre* 1 (1946), 122.

——, 'Hermann Broch: *Der Tod des Vergil*', *Die Fähre* 1 (1946), 508.

——, 'Hermann Broch zum 60. Geburtstag', in *Das Silberboot* 2/8 (1946), 160.

Jäckel, Hartmut. 'Hermann Broch and Politics' in Stephen D. Dowden, ed., *Hermann Broch: Literature, Philosophy, Politics* (Columbia, SC: Camden House, 1988), 93–106.

—— and Stephen Toulmin, *Wittgenstein's Vienna* (New York: Simon and Schuster, 1973).

Janik, Allan, *Essays on Wittgenstein and Weininger* (Amsterdam: Rodopi B.V., 1985).

——, 'Vienna 1900 Revisited: Paradigms and Problems', in Steven Beller, ed., *Rethinking Vienna 1900* (New York: Berghahn Books, 2001), 27–56.

——, *Wittgenstein's Vienna Revisited* (New Brunswick, NJ: Transaction Publishers, 2001).

Jay, Martin, *The Dialectical Imagination: A History of the Frankfurt School and the Institute of Social Research, 1923–1950* (Boston: Little, Brown, 1973).

——, *Permanent Exiles: Essays on the Intellectual Migration from Germany to America* (New York: Columbia University Press, 1985).

Jelavich, Barbara, *Modern Austria: Empire and Republic, 1815–1986* (London: Cambridge University Press, 1987).

Johnston, William M., *The Austrian Mind: An Intellectual and Social History, 1848–1938* (Berkeley: University of California Press, 1972).

Jonas, Klaus W. and Lothar E. Zeidler, 'Hermann Broch. Eine bibliographische Studie', *Philobiblon* 6 (1962), 291–323.

Judson, Pieter, *Exclusive Revolutionaries: Liberal Politics, Social Experience, and National Identity in the Austrian Empire, 1848–1914* (Ann Arbor, MI: University of Michigan Press, 1996).

Kahler, Erich, 'The Epochal Innovations in Hermann Broch's Narrative', *Salmagundi* 100/11 (1969/70), 186–192.

——, *Die Philosophie von Hermann Broch* (Tübingen: J.C.B. Mohr, 1962).

——, *et al.*, eds, *Dichter wider Willen* (Zürich: Rhein Verlag, 1958).

Kampf, Louis, 'The Permanence of Modernism', *College English* 28/1 (Oct. 1966), 1–15.

Kann, Robert, *A History of the Habsburg Empire, 1526–1918* (Berkeley: University of California Press, 1974).

Kant, Immanuel, *Beantwortung der Frage: Was ist Aufklärung?* Gutenberg Project Ebook (2009), <http://www.gutenberg.org/files/30821/30821-h/30821-h.htm> accessed 13 November 2013.

——, *Groundwork for the Metaphysics of Morals*, Allen W. Wood, ed., and tr. (New Haven, CT: Yale University Press, 2002).

Kaye, Howard L. 'Hermann Broch's *Sleepwalkers*: Social Theory in Literary Form', *Mosaic* XV/4, 79–88.

Kessler, Michael, 'Contradictio in adiecto? Hermann Brochs Votum für eine 'totalitäre' Demokratie' in Michael Kessler *et al.*, eds, *Konfliktherd Toleranz? Analysen – Sondierungen – Klarstellungen* (Tübingen: Stauffenberg, 2002), 13–56.

——, 'Menschenrecht, Demokratie, Toleranz', *Hermann Broch: Politik, Menschenrecht – und Literatur*, Thomas Eicher, Paul Michael Lützeler and Hartmut Steinecke, eds (Oberhausen: Athena, 2005), 11–50.

——, ed., *Hermann Broch, Neue Studien: Festschrift für Paul Michael Lützeler zum 60. Geburtstag* (Tübingen: Stauffenburg Verlag, 2003).

Kiss, Endre, *Philosophie und Literatur des negativen Universalismus. Intellektuelle Monographie über Hermann Broch* (Cuxhaven-Dartford: Traude Junghans, 2001).

——, ed., *Hermann Broch. Werk und Wirkung* (Bonn: Bouvier, 1985).

——, Michael Paul Lützeler and Gabriella Rácz, eds, *Hermann Brochs literarische Freundenschaften* (Tübingen: Stauffenburg, 2008).

Kitchen, Martin, *The Coming of Austrian Fascism* (London: Croom Helm; Montreal: McGill-Queen's University Press, 1980).

Klinger, Monika, *Broch und Die Demokratie* (Berlin: Duncker und Humblot, 1994).

Koebner, Thomas, *Hermann Broch. Leben und Werk* (Bern: Francke, 1965).

Koelb, Clayton, *Legendary Figures: Ancient History in Modern Novels* (Lincoln, NE: University of Nebraska Press, 1998).

Koester, Rudolf, *Hermann Broch* (Berlin: Colliquium, 1987).

Könneker, Carsten, '*Auflösung der Natur Auflösung der Geschichte*', *Moderner Roman und NS-'Weltanschauung' im Zeichen der theoretischen Physik* (Stuttgart, Weimar: J. B. Metzler, 2001).

——, 'Moderne Wissenschaft und moderne Dichtung. Hermann Brochs Beitrag zur Beilegung der "Grundlagenkrise" der Mathematik', *DVjs* 73 (1999), 319–351.

Le Bon, Gustave, *The Crowd*, Robert A. Nye, tr. (New Brunswick, NJ: Transaction Pub., 1995).

Le Rider, Jacques, *Modernity and Crises of Identity: Culture and Society in fin-de-siècle Vienna*, Rosemary Morris, tr. (New York: Continuum Books, 1993).

Lehrer, Keith and Johann Christian Marek, eds, *Austrian Philosophy Past and Present* (Dordrecht: Kluwer Academic Publishers, 1997).

Lewis, Sinclair, *It Can't Happen Here* (New York: New American Library, 2005).

Luft, David S., *Eros and Inwardness in Vienna: Weininger, Musil, Doderer* (Chicago: University of Chicago Press, 2003).

——, *Robert Musil and the Crisis of European Culture* (Berkeley: University of California Press, 1980).

Lützeler, Paul Michael, 'The Avant-Garde in Crisis: Hermann Broch's Negative Aesthetics in Exile', in Stephen D. Dowden, ed., *Hermann Broch, Literature, Philosophy, Politics* (Columbia, SC: Camden House, 1988), 19–31.

——, *Die Entropie des Menschen. Studien zum Werk Hermann Brochs* (Würzburg: Königshausen & Neumann, 2000).

——, *Hermann Broch. 1886–1951. Eine Chronik.* (Marbach: Deutsche Schillergesellschaft, 2001).

——, *Hermann Broch: A Biography*, Janice Furness, tr. London: Quartet Books, 1987.

——, *Hermann Broch, Ethik und Politik: Studien zum Frühwerk und zur Romantrilogie Die Schlafwandler* (Munich: Winkler Verlag, 1973).

——, *Hermann Brochs Kosmopolitismus: Europa, Menschenrechte, Universität* (Vienna: Picus Verlag, 2002).

——. *Hermann Broch und die Moderne: Roman, Menschenrecht, Biografie* (Munich: Wilhelm Fink, 2011).

——. *Kulturbruch und Glaubenskrise. Brochs 'Schlafwandler' und Grünewalds 'Isenheimer Altar'* (Tübingen: A. Francke, 2001).

——, 'Raum, Ort, Gebäude: Hermann Brochs "1888. Pasenow oder die Romantik" als Berlin-Roman', Helmut Koopmann and Manfred Misch, eds, *Grenzgänge*.

Studien zur Literatur der Moderne. Festschrift für Hans-Jörg Knobloch (Paderborn: Mentis, 2002), 179–201.

——. 'Schlafwandler am Zauberberg. Die Europa-Diskussion in Hermann Brochs und Thomas Manns Zeitromanen' *Thomas Mann Jahrbuch* 14 (2001), 49–62.

——. 'Visionaries in Exile: Broch's Cooperation with G. A. Borgese and Hannah Arendt', in Paul Michael Lützeler, ed., *Hermann Broch, Visionary in Exile* (Rochester, NY: Camden House: 2003), 67–88.

——, ed., *Hermann Broch, Visionary in Exile: The 2001 Yale Symposium* (Rochester, NY: Camden House, 2003).

—— and Michael Kessler, eds, *Brochs theoretisches Werk* (Frankfurt am Main: Suhrkamp Verlag, 1988).

Macenka, Switlana. 'Das System der Leitmotive im Roman von H. Broch 'Die Schuldlosen', *Stylistyka XII, Multilingualism and Style* (2003), 237–250.

Mack, Karin and Wolfgang Hofer, *Spiegelungen: Denkbilder zur Biographie Brochs* (Vienna: Sonderzahl, 1984).

Mann, Thomas, 'Hermann Broch: Der Tod des Vergil', *Die Fähre* 1 (1946), 509.

Marchand, Suzanne L., *Down from Olympus: Archaeology and Philhellenism in Germany, 1750–1970* (Princeton: Princeton University Press, 1996).

McGarth, William, *Dionysian Art and Populist Politics in Austria* (New Haven, CT: Yale University Press, 1974).

Medina, P. 'Massa e respiro in Elias Canetti e Hermann Broch', *Nuova Corrente, 129 (2002),* 159–172.

Meinert, Dietrich, *Die Darstellung der Dimensionen menschlicher Existenz in Brochs 'Der Tod des Vergil'* (Bern: Francke, 1962).

Mendelsohn, Ezra, *The Jews of East Central Europe Between the World Wars* (Bloomington, IN: Indiana University Press, 1987).

Menges, Karl, 'Bemerkungen zum Problem der ästhetischen Zeitgenossenschaft in Hermann Brochs *Der Tod des Vergil', Modern Austrian Literature: Journal of the International Arthur Schnitzler Research Association*, 'Special Hermann Broch Issue', 13/ 4 (1980), 31–50.

——, *Kritische Studien zur Wertphilosophie Hermann Brochs* (Tübingen: Max Niemeyer, 1970).

Miller, Leslie Lewis. 'Hermann Broch's *Die Schlafwandler*: A Critical Study in the Light of his Letters, Exposés, and an Unpublished Manuscript Version of the Novel', Doctoral Dissertation, University of California, Berkeley, 1964.

Mitchell, Breon, *James Joyce and the German Novel, 1922–1933* (Athens, OH: Ohio University Press, 1976).

Mondon, Christine, 'Hermann Broch und die Psychoananlyse', in *Hermann Broch, Neue Studien: Festschrift für Paul Michael Lützeler zum 60. Geburtstag* (Tübingen: Stauffenburg Verlag, 2003), 510–523.

Mosse, George, *Masses and Man: Nationalist and Fascist Perceptions of Reality* (New York: H. Fertig, 1980).

——, *The Nationalization of the Masses* (New York: H. Fertig, 1975).

Mueller, William R., *Celebration of Life: Studies in Modern Fiction* (New York: Sheed and Ward, 1972).

Müller-Funk, Wolfgang, 'Die fürchterliche Pflicht zur Freiheit: Überlegungen zu Hermann Brochs Meta-Politik', in Ronald Speirs, ed., *The Writers' Morality/Die Moral der Schriftsteller* (Oxford: Peter Lang, 2000), 77–95.

Mumford, Lewis, *My Works and Days: A Personal Chronicle* (New York: Harcourt Brace Jovanovich, 1979).

Nietzsche, Friedrich. 'Schopenhauer as Educator', in Daniel Breazeale, ed., and R. J. Hollingdale, tr., *Nietzsche Untimely Meditations* (Cambridge: Cambridge University Press, 2013).

Olay, Csaba. 'Hannah Arendt und Hermann Broch Roman und Moderne' in Endre Kiss *et al.*, eds, *Hermann Brochs literarische Freundenschaften* (Tübingen: Stauffenburg, 2008), 305–318.

Osterle, Heinze D., 'Hermann Broch, *Die Schlafwandler*: Revolution and Apocalypse', *PMLA* 86/5 (1971), 946–958.

Österreichische Liga für Menschenrechte, ed., *Hermann Broch – ein Engagierter zwischen Literatur und Politik* (Innsbruck: Studienverlag, 2004).

Oxaal, Ivar, Michael Pollak and Gerhard Botz, eds, *Jews, Antisemitism and Culture in Vienna* (New York: Routledge and Kegan Paul, 1987).

Perez, Arvid H. 'The Disintegration of Values: A Social and Intellectual Study of the Austrian Philosopher-Novelist Hermann Broch, 1890–1930', Doctoral Dissertation, University of California, Los Angeles, 1971.

Posse, Abel. 'Hermann Broch: El esteta absoluto', *Suplemento Cultura La Nación* (June 30 2002), 1–2.

Rabinbach, Anson, *The Crisis of Austrian Socialism. From Red Vienna to Civil War 1927–1934* (Chicago: University of Chicago Press, 1983).

Rechter, David, *The Jews of Vienna and the First World War* (London: Littman Library of Jewish Civilization, 2001).

Ritzer, Monika, *Hermann Broch und die Kulturekrise im frühen 20. Jahrhundert* (Stuttgart: Metzler, 1988).

Rizzo, Roberto, 'Psychoanalyse eines pädagogischen Eros', in Michael Kessler, ed., *Hermann Broch, Neue Studien: Festschrift für Paul Michael Lützeler zum 60. Geburtstag* (Tübingen: Stauffenburg Verlag, 2003), 553–584.

Rothe, Wolfgang. '*Der junge Broch*', in *Neue Deutsche Hefte* 7 (1960), 780–797.

——, '*Hermann Broch als politische Denker*', *Zeitschrift für Politik* 5 (1958), 329–341.

Rozenbilt, Marsha, *The Jews of Vienna, 1867–1914: Assimilation and Identity* (Albany, NY: State University of New York Press, 1988).

Sachar, Howard M., *Dreamland: Europeans and Jews in the Aftermath of the Great War* (New York: Random House, 2007).

Saito, Shigeo, '*Die Schlafwandler*. Die moderne Dialektik', In *The Multi-faced World of the Faculty of the Humanities*. (Tokyo: Universität Morioka, 2003), 904–918.

Sandberg, Glenn Robert, *The Genealogy of the Massenführer: Hermann Broch's* Die Verzauberung *as a Religious Novel*. (Heidelberg: Unversitätverlag C. Winter, 1997).

Sartre, Jean-Paul, *What is Literature?*, Bernard Frechtman, tr. (New York: The Philosophical Library, 1949).

Sauerland, Karol, 'Hermann Broch und Hannah Arendt: Massenwahn und Menschenrecht' in Endre Kiss *et al.*, eds, *Hermann Brochs literarische Freundenschaften* (Tübingen: Stauffenburg, 2008), 319–331.

Scheichl, Sigurd Paul, '"Nebbich noch immer Princeton Hospital", Jüdische Selbststilisierung in Brochs Briefen an Daniel Brody', in Michael Kessler, ed., *Hermann Broch, Neue Studien: Festschrift für Paul Michael Lützeler zum 60. Geburtstag* (Tübingen: Stauffenburg Verlag, 2003), 362–378.

Schlant, Ernestine, *Hermann Broch* (Boston: Twayne Publishers, 1978).

——, 'Hermann Broch und die Demokratie: A Review', *The German Quarterly*, 70/1 (Winter 1997), 86–87.

Schmidt-Dengler, Wendlin, '"Kurzum die Hölle": Broch's Early Political Text "Die Straße"', in Paul Michael Lützeler, *Hermann Broch: Visionary in Exile: The 2001 Yale Symposium* (New York: Camden House, 2003), 55–66.

Segel, Harold B., ed., *Egon Erwin Kisch, The Raging Reporter – A Bio-Anthology* (West Lafayette, IN: Purdue University Press, 1997).

Schmid-Bortenschlager, Sigrid. *Hermann Broch. Éthique et estéthique* (Paris: Presses Universitaires de France, 2001).

Schorkse, Carl, *Fin de Siècle Vienna: Politics and Culture* (New York: Vintage Books, 1980).

Schuhmann, Rolf, *Die Massenwahntheorie im Spiegel der Autorenkrise. Gewalt, Anarchie und die Kunst der Sublimierung im Werk Hermann Brochs* (Frankfurt am Main: Peter Lang, 2000).

Sengoopta, Chandak, *Otto Weininger: Sex, Science, and Self in Imperial Vienna* (Chicago: University of Chicago Press, 2000).

Somm, Walter, *Hermann Broch. Geist, Prophetie und Mystik* (Freiburg: Universitätsverlag, 1965).

Southard, Robert, *Droysen and the Prussian School of History* (Lexington: University of Kentucky Press, 1995).

Spengler, Oswald, *The Decline of the West*, Charles Francis Atkinson, tr. (Oxford: Oxford University Press, 1991).

Spiel, Hilde, *Vienna's Golden Autumn: 1866–1938* (London: Weidenfeld and Nicolson, 1987).

Steinecke, Hartmut, *Hermann Broch und der polyhistorische Roman. Studien zur Theorie und Technik eines Romantyps der Moderne* (Bonn: Bouvier, 1968).

———, '"Unpersönlich bin ich ein Opfer," Jüdische Spuren im Spätwerk Hermann Brochs,' in Michael Kessler, ed., *Hermann Broch, Neue Studien: Festschrift für Paul Michael Lützeler zum 60. Geburtstag* (Tübingen: Stauffenburg Verlag, 2003), 379–394.

———, *Von Lenau bis Broch. Studien zur österreichischen Literatur – von aussen betrachtet* (Tübingen: Francke, 2002).

——— and Joseph Strelka, eds, *Romanstruktur und Menschenrecht bei Hermann Broch* (Bern: Peter Lang, 1990).

Stevens, Adrian, Fred Wagner and Sigurd Paul Scheichl, eds, *Hermann Broch: Modernismus, Kulturkrise und Hitlerzeit* (Innsbruck, Austria: Innsbrucker Beiträge zur Kulturwissenschaft, 1994).

Strelka, Joseph, 'Politics and the Human Condition: Broch's Model of a Mass Psychology,' in Stephen D. Dowden, ed., *Hermann Broch: Literature, Philosophy, Politics* (Columbia, SC: Camden House, 1988), 76–86.

———, *Poeta Doctus Hermann Broch* (Tübingen: Franke, 2001).

———, ed., *Broch heute* (Bern: Francke, 1978).

Swanson, John, *The Remnants of the Habsburg Monarchy: The Shaping of Modern Austria and Hungary, 1918–1922* (New York: Columbia University Press, 2001).

Thieberger, Richard, 'Hermann Brochs Novellenroman und seine Vorgeschichte,' *DVfLG* 36/4 (1962), 562–582.

———, 'Situation de la Broch-Forschung,' *Austriaca* 5 (Feb. 1979), 149–161.

Thieberger, Richard, ed., *Hermann Broch und seine Zeit* (Bern: Peter Lang, 1980).

———, *Hermann Broch und seine Zeit: Akten des Internationalen Broch-Symposiums, Nice 1979* (Bern: Peter Lang, 1980).

Treiber, Gerhard, *Philosophie der Existenz. Das Entscheidungsproblem bei Kierkegaard, Jaspers, Heidegger, Sartre, Camus. Literarische Erkundungen von Kundera, Céline, Broch, Musil* (Frankfurt am Main: Peter Lang, 2000).

Untermeyer, Jean Starr, 'Eine unbekannte Nachdichtung Hermann Brochs,' *Wort in der Zeit* 2 (1956), 32–33.

———, *Private Collection* (New York: Alfred A. Knopf, 1965).

Vollhardt, Friedrich, *Hermann Brochs geschichtliche Stellung: Studien zum philosophischen Frühwerk und zur Romantrilogie 'Die Schlafwandler', 1914–1932* (Tübingen: Max Niedermeyer, 1986).

Waldeck, Peter Bruce, *Die Kinderheitsproblematik bei Hermann Broch* (Munich: Wilhelm Fink Verlag, 1968).

Wiedner, Daniel, , 'Hermann Broch and the Ethics of Exile' in Eckart Goebel and Sigrid Weigel, eds, 'Escape to Life', *German Intellectuals in New York: A Compendium on Exile after 1933* (Berlin: De Gruyter, 2012), 162–181.

Weigand, Hermann, 'Hermann Broch's *Death of Vergil*. Program Notes,' in A. Leslie Willson ed., *Surveys and Soundings in European Literature* (Princeton, NJ: Princeton University Press, 1966), 308–343.

——, 'Hermann Broch's *Die Schuldlosen*. An Approach,' *PMLAA* 68 (1953), 323–334.

Weigel, Robert G., *Zur geistigen Einheit von Hermann Brochs Werk: Massenpsychologie. Politologie. Romane* (Tübingen: A. Francke Verlag, 1994).

Werfel, Franz, *Barbara oder die Frömmigkeit* (Frankfurt am Main: Fischer Verlag: 1996).

Wheeler, Brett R., 'Modernist Reenchantments I: Liberalism to Aestheticized Politics', *The German Quarterly*, 74/3 (Summer, 2001) 223–236.

White, John and Anne White, 'Other Ivory Towers and Literary Counterfactuals', *Publications of the English Goethe Society*, LXXIX No. 1, 2010, 18–27.

Wistrich, Robert S., *The Jews of Vienna in the Age of Franz Joseph* (Oxford: Oxford University Press, 1989).

Wittgenstein, Ludwig, 'A Lecture on Ethics', *The Philosophical Review*, vol. 74, no. 1 (January, 1965), 7.

——, *Schriften*, vol. 1 (Frankfurt am Main: Suhrkamp, 1960).

Young-Bruehl, Elisabeth, *Hannah Arendt: For Love of the World* (New Haven, CT: Yale University Press, 1983).

Ziolkowski, Theodore, *Hermann Broch* (New York: Columbia University Press, 1964).

Zweig, Stefan, *The World of Yesterday* (Lincoln, NE: University of Nebraska Press, 1964).

Index

composition of 154–155, 190,
217
Theresienstadt 218
Thiess, Frank 127, 233
total democracy, concept of 9, 16–18,
60–61, 176–182, 191, 195–209,
229–231, 236, 241–246

United Nations 4, 152, 166–167, 177,
242
United States
Bill of Rights 16, 164, 166
citizenship 161, 241
Civil War 179
Constitution 16, 162, 166
counter-culture 25, 182, 204, 208
foreign policy of 24–25, 152, 162 n,
203, 244
industrialization in 186–189
nationalism 177–180, 220, 232,
239–247
racism in 180, 187, 199, 203, 210
youth movements 102, 207–208, 237,
242–243

value systems
autonomy and relativity in 6, 14, 90,
108–109, 129–148, 208–210,
245
definition of 4–5, 11–15, 28–29
disintegration of values, theory
of 45, 58, 109, 130–148, 155,
183–186, 206–207, 225, 237,
246
open versus closed 4, 15–16, 29,
107–108, 158–159, 184–185, 195,
197–198, 203–206, 223

politics and 32–33, 43, 156–161,
163, 173–174, 178, 183–186, 189,
192–193, 195–196, 201–204
value vacuum *see* value systems, disintegration of values, theory of
Varnhagen, Rahel 87–88
Vergil
character 99, 114, 146
poet 13
Vienna
aestheticization in 3, 33, 60, 71, 79,
96–97, 101, 104, 111–112, 117, 122,
131, 222, 240
anti-Semitism in 10, 31, 35–36, 43,
62–64, 66–67, 71, 86–88, 118
Jewish culture in 10–11, 31–51,
60–71, 86–88
liberalism in 2–3, 32–33, 60–71, 75,
153, 240
progressivism in 11, 38, 43, 64–65,
69–70, 75, 94, 191
scientific materialism in 10–11, 32, 68
Villard, Oscar 233
vitalism 103, 109, 148, 210, 228
see also Lebensphilosophie
Voegelin, Eric 238, 246

Weber, Max 113, 146, 220–221
Weininger, Otto 49–51, 58, 86, 106
Werfel, Franz 90
Wilson, Woodrow 161–163, 190
see also idealism, Wilsonian
Wittgenstein, Ludwig 6, 11, 128

Zuckmayer, Carl 235
Zühlsdorff, Volkmar von 231–233
Zweig, Stefan 121, 217, 221, 233